SCENARIO PLANNING
FOR CITIES AND REGIONS

SCENARIO PLANNING FOR CITIES AND REGIONS

MANAGING AND ENVISIONING UNCERTAIN FUTURES

ROBERT GOODSPEED

LINCOLN INSTITUTE
OF LAND POLICY

Cambridge, Massachusetts

Library of Congress Cataloging-in-Publishing Data
Names: Goodspeed, Robert, author.
Title: Scenario planning for cities and regions : managing and envisioning
    uncertain futures / Robert Goodspeed.
Description: Cambridge : Lincoln Institute of Land Policy, 2020. | Includes
    bibliographical references and index. | Summary: "Describes the emerging
    use of collaborative scenario planning practices in urban and regional
    planning, and includes case studies, an overview of digital tools, and a project
    evaluation framework. Concludes with a discussion of how scenarios can be
    used to address urban inequalities. Intended for a broad audience"—Provided by publisher.
Identifiers: LCCN 2019051425 (print) | LCCN 2019051426 (ebook) |
    ISBN 9781558444003 (paperback) | ISBN 9781558444010 (adobe pdf) |
    ISBN 9781558444027 (kindle edition) | ISBN 9781558444034 (epub) |
    ISBN 9781558444041 (i book)
Subjects: LCSH: City planning. | Regional planning.
Classification: LCC HT166 .G646 2020 (print) | LCC HT166 (ebook) |
    DDC 307.1/216—dc23
LC record available at https://lccn.loc.gov/2019051425
LC ebook record available at https://lccn.loc.gov/2019051426

Composed in Minion by Westchester Publishing Services in Danbury, Connecticut.
Printed by Puritan Press, Inc. The paper is Rolland Enviro100.

MANUFACTURED IN THE UNITED STATES OF AMERICA

Contents

Part 4. Transformation and Conclusions

Preface

Challenges Facing Contemporary Planning

Cities today face two primary planning challenges: how to transform themselves to realize sustainability goals and how to plan for uncertain external forces, like climate change and new technologies. Many cities in the United States and elsewhere in the developed world are dissatisfied with their current state: they have environmental and public health burdens because transportation systems are auto dependent. They have low densities and high demand for housing, but municipal codes inhibit redevelopment. Widely dispersed residences, shops, and workplaces reduce accessibility and increase traffic congestion, pollution, and energy use. Income disparities grow and exacerbate inequality among neighborhoods. Cries for change question cities' infrastructure decisions, land use patterns, and public policies, and demand better methods to plan for the transformation of cities. Although dissatisfactions are growing, they are not universally shared, and we are far from agreement about how, or even whether, to balance environmental, economic, and equity goals (Campbell 1996).

In addition to cities' internal transformations, external uncertainties proliferate. The most prominent future uncertainty is climate change. Its ongoing, historically unprecedented effects vary with geographic location: different cities face sea-level rise, intense hurricanes, flooding, heat waves, droughts, and more (Moriarty and Honnery 2015). Planning assumptions have been upended, requiring new definitions of floodplains and coastal adaptations that respond to shifting conditions. Compounding climate science's inherent uncertainty are the unknown levels of future greenhouse gas emissions—and therefore the future climate conditions for which planners must prepare. Scholars of climate-adaptation planning have concluded that this requires ending "the deeply embedded practice of planning for one future" (Woodruff 2016, 445), and they argue that scenario planning holds unrealized promise to incorporate climate uncertainty into plans (Stults and Larsen 2018).

Another notable source of external uncertainty for cities is new technologies. Mobility services like car sharing, bike sharing, and ride sharing are new forms of urban transportation. "Smart city" technologies, especially automated vehicles, also have major uncertainties.

Practitioners and scholars who focus on urban transformation, resilience, and related technologies have realized that long-term decisions must recognize the unique structure of each city—containing natural, human, and technological systems—and the uncertainties each faces. Changing a city is not simply a matter of updating government policies or regulations; instead, it requires coordinating the decisions of many actors. For example, switching from auto-oriented to pedestrian- and bicycle-oriented development requires building new transportation systems, changing real estate development practices, redesigning streets, reforming zoning rules, and rethinking cultural values. Decisions that shape cities are made by their diverse residents and organizations. Government itself is composed of a collection of institutions with different scales, mandates, and interests. Similarly, pursuing resilience and responding to technological changes requires greater attention to uncertainty, which traditional planning methods neglect.

Meeting these challenges requires breaking away from past planning approaches. In this book, I argue for planning based in the theory of *complex systems*, which provides a way to understand cities and how they react to changes, and for embracing broad *collaboration*, necessary to clarify goals and create knowledge. This planning involves deep analysis of uncertainty via multiple scenarios to define a vision and enable wiser decisions, resulting in *strategic plans*. Unlike project plans, which contain "blueprints of the intended end-state of the physical environment" (Mastop and Faludi 1997, 819), a strategic plan is a frame of reference for future decision making. Spatial strategic planning is "a public-sector-led socio-spatial process through which a vision, actions, and means for implementation are produced that shape and frame what a place is and may become" (Albrechts 2004, 747). Strategic plans describe a shared vision, coordinate the decisions of participants, and recommend actions under different future conditions. Project participants are stakeholders and citizens. To include relevant groups, strategic planning projects typically engage with *stakeholders*, which I define as representatives of organizations, interests, or communities. I use the term *citizens* to describe those with a moral or political right to contribute to decisions that affect residents of a project's area, not those with legal national citizenship status.

Creating strategic plans is a relatively uncommon activity for many urban planning professionals. Only some U.S. states mandate that their cities create such plans (often called master plans or comprehensive plans). Even when planning mandates exist, a strategic plan might more closely resemble a project plan, with long lists of specific proposals and policies. Miller's (2009) interesting analysis of the types of professional urban plans shows that many have relatively short time frames. Scenario planning may not make sense for these plans. A scenario-based strategic plan is more appropriate for vision, framework, comprehensive, system, and redevelopment plans and for those with long time horizons and low or moderate detail. Writing long-range strategic plans is relatively unusual today, but Myers and Kitsuse (2000) argue that they have a role in the history and identity of the professional planning field that is disproportionate to other professional tasks, such as reviewing development proposals.

Scenario planning is a method of long-term strategic planning that creates representations of multiple, plausible futures of the system of interest. Scenario planning originally arose in military and corporate strategies. Urban planning is a professional field concerned with the physical development of many types of places. I combine these in the term *urban scenario planning*. Examples of urban scenario planning are at all spatial scales, although it has been adopted most widely for regional planning. This book focuses on scenario planning methods to create strategic plans to aid city stakeholders making decisions with long-term repercussions. In this book, I use *city* to refer to any inhabited place (regardless of political boundaries or incorporation) and *place* to refer to the geography being planned, whether a corridor, district, municipality, or other jurisdiction, region, or rural area.

Urban scenario planning has two related approaches: *Normative projects* use scenarios to define a preferred future for a place, enriched through careful analysis and the consideration of alternatives. *Exploratory projects* use scenarios to develop deeper insights into emerging trends and issues or inform specific decisions through the use of multiple scenarios. To illustrate the value of using scenarios to consider uncertainty in more concrete terms, the next section of this preface describes planning in two places that experienced demographic and economic uncertainties. Planners in Dresden, Germany, used traditional planning methods anchored in a single forecast of future population to make decisions about the city's spatial development. As a result, their plans were blindsided, first by population and economic decline and then by stabilization and growth, which resulted in mismatches between the city's actual population and its housing and infrastructure. By contrast, planners in Gwinnett County, Georgia, recognized major uncertainties that would affect the future of their county; consequently, their plan centered on scenarios of the city's options, which prepared them for economic vicissitudes. The preface closes with a description of the book's structure and which chapters may be of most interest to different audiences.

Frequently misunderstood to be an academic exercise at the margins of urban planning, scenario planning is, rather, a reinvention of long-range strategic planning and holds the potential to reanimate planning's progressive spirit and empower practitioners and citizens to better address the unprecedented challenges that lie ahead for our cities.

Planning With and Without Scenarios

Dresden, like many other cities in the former East Germany, experienced dramatic economic and demographic shifts after the fall of the Berlin Wall in 1989 and German reunification. Thorsten Wiechmann's (2008) case study of the city's planning after reunification reveals the drawbacks of traditional planning, which ignores uncertainty. Wiechmann divides the city's evolution after 1990 into three phases: During the first phase (1990–1995), the city made optimistic assumptions for urban growth after reunification, inspiring a large amount of new housing and commercial construction at the city's periphery. However, the city experienced population loss, with nearly 60,000 people departing because of the country's struggling economy. Housing vacancy rates climbed and abandoned industrial sites became brownfields. By the next phase (1996–2001), the reality of population declines had become apparent, and the city in 1996 adopted a zoning plan that assumed continued population decline. Though two subsequent redevelopment plans in this phase were slightly more optimistic, they still predicted population stabilization at historically low levels. During this period, the city demolished nearly 6,000 housing units, in keeping with the assumption they would not be needed in the foreseeable future. In the final phase (2002–2008), however, new industries in the region and an influx of people to historic neighborhoods around the city center resulted in population growth. Newer plans forecast continued growth, but the city by 2008 was experiencing uneven development, "areas of shrinkage and decline" were near "prospering and wealthy communities" (Wiechmann 2008, 442). Figure 1 shows the city's steep population decline and surprising resurgence, as well as the population forecasts of several plans.

Wiechmann observes that the demographic and economic trends affecting the city were "very hard to predict if not completely unforeseeable" (2008, 443). One lesson is that a linear trend extrapolation "is very likely to lead to counterproductive strategies," because the only constant for Dresden during these periods was changing trends. He therefore advocates planning with "strategic flexibility" to ensure that plans can adapt to change and urges planners to pursue preparedness, robustness, and resilience instead of drawing up plans that assume one trend (443). Although Wiechmann does not mention scenario planning specifically, scenarios can be useful in exactly this type of situation to create plans that prepare for various economic and demographic futures. More broadly, scenarios call attention to uncertainty, including the possibility of long-term population decline, which can jump-start discussions about adapting to a new reality, too easily ignored when planning is based on fixed forecasts.

Gwinnett County, Georgia, in the metropolitan Atlanta region, illustrates the use of scenarios to create plans that address demographic and

Figure 1 Actual Population in Dresden, Germany, and Projections of Plans over the Years

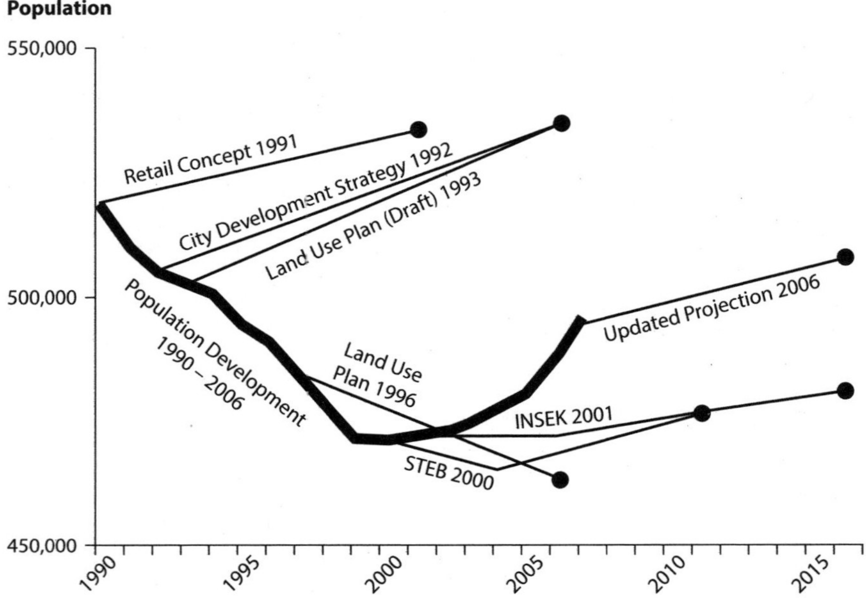

Based on Wiechmann (2008, fig. 5). © Taylor & Francis Ltd., www.tandfonline.com and www.informaworld.com.

economic uncertainty head-on. Gwinnett County boomed in the 1990s and early in the next decade, adding about 450,000 people to reach a 2010 population of 805,321. Much of this growth came from typical suburban-style development. By the middle of the first decade of the 2000s, however, county leaders had realized they were entering a new stage of development: once overwhelmingly white, the county rapidly diversified after 2000 and became home to large communities of African Americans, Hispanics, and immigrant communities of many nationalities (Ehrenhalt 2012). Worsening traffic congestion, changing preferences in commercial and housing markets, and increasing redevelopment meant that the county faced not only a more uncertain future but also new issues on the planning agenda.

Therefore, when county officials embarked in 2006 on a project to update the county's unified plan (which simultaneously functions as the comprehensive, housing, and transportation plans required under state and federal law), they developed, with the help of consultants, contrasting scenarios to explore the interplay of economic, demographic, and land use change. The resulting *2030 Unified Plan* (Gwinnett County 2009) includes regional and countywide economic and demographic forecasts that superficially resemble those of a traditional plan. However, the document is careful to note that these projections do not describe an inevitable or even likely future; instead, they highlight some of the key trends and issues the county *may* face.

To develop the plan, the project hosted workshops, established an advisory committee, ran focus groups with specific minority communities, and conducted interviews to further explore the diverse concerns and goals of stakeholder groups. Using decision-focused scenario construction (see chapter 4), the project produced four plausible scenarios for the county's future: Middle of the Pack, Regional Slowdown, International Gateway, and Radical Restructuring. These scenarios differed in the growth or decline in population and jobs, in land use patterns, and in options for where public transit, roads, and sewer infrastructure should be expanded. The Radical Restructuring scenario, which focused growth in a few large cities within the county, was abandoned as implausible because it required many decisions that local elected officials were unlikely to make. The other three scenarios were converted into maps showing their spatial patterns. Figures 2 and 3 show the Middle of the Pack and International Gateway maps, respectively, which emerged as the scenarios of greatest interest. Future population changes for different areas were then estimated through an allocation procedure, and the resulting patterns were further analyzed to understand their impacts on the county. That analysis included traffic modeling to explore congestion and fiscal modeling to explore the effect of each scenario on public budgets. Table 1 shows selected quantitative indicators, or measurements, for the two scenarios and base conditions in 2005.

The two scenarios were used to generate a list of policies needed to make each more achievable or to diminish potential negative impacts. Ultimately, planners identified International Gateway as the preferred scenario; however, they also retained the Middle of the Pack scenario, because planners recognized that the actions and growth needed for the preferred scenario might not materialize. Planners concluded, "By evaluating a

Figure 2 Middle of the Pack Scenario for Gwinnett County, Georgia, in *2030 Unified Plan*

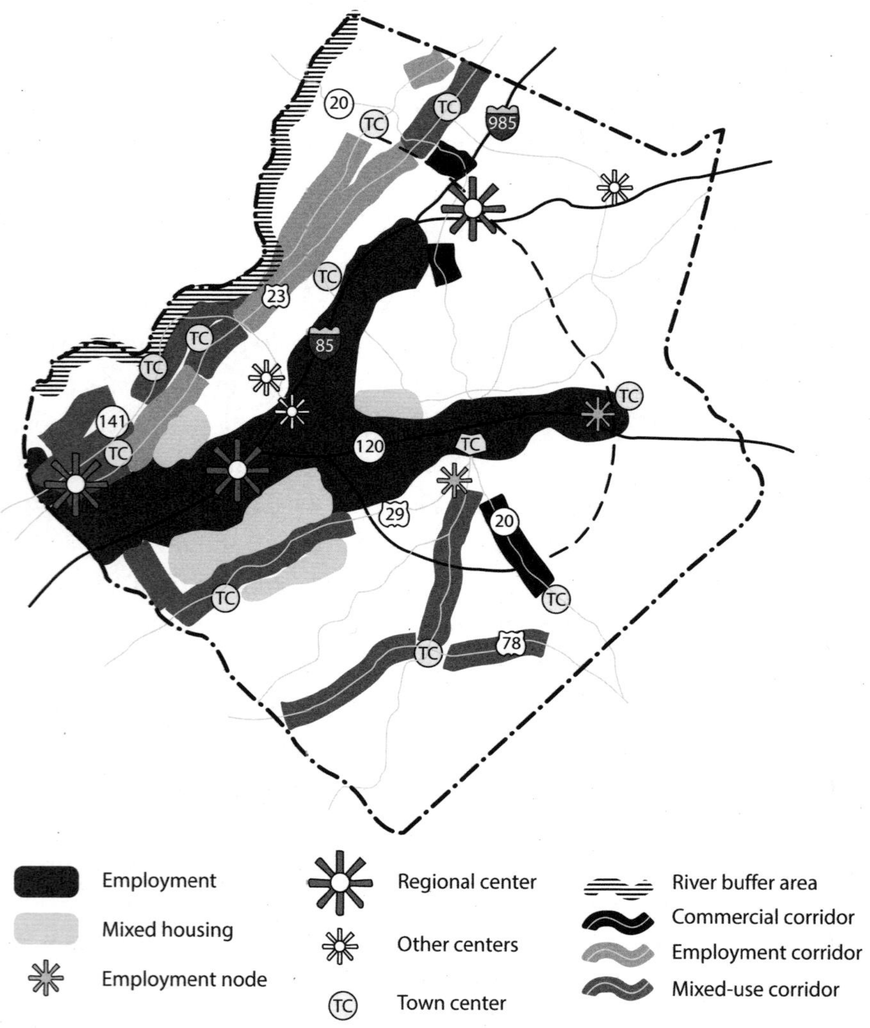

Gwinnett County (2009).

plausible range of futures and their related policies, Gwinnett . . . acquired a ready repertoire of responses to inform decision makers if future conditions play out in ways that veer off from the course assumed by the adopted plan," a flexibility that was ultimately "one of the major payoffs of engaging in scenario development and testing" (Gwinnett County 2009, 71).

Figure 3 International Gateway Scenario for Gwinnett County, Georgia, in *2030 Unified Plan*

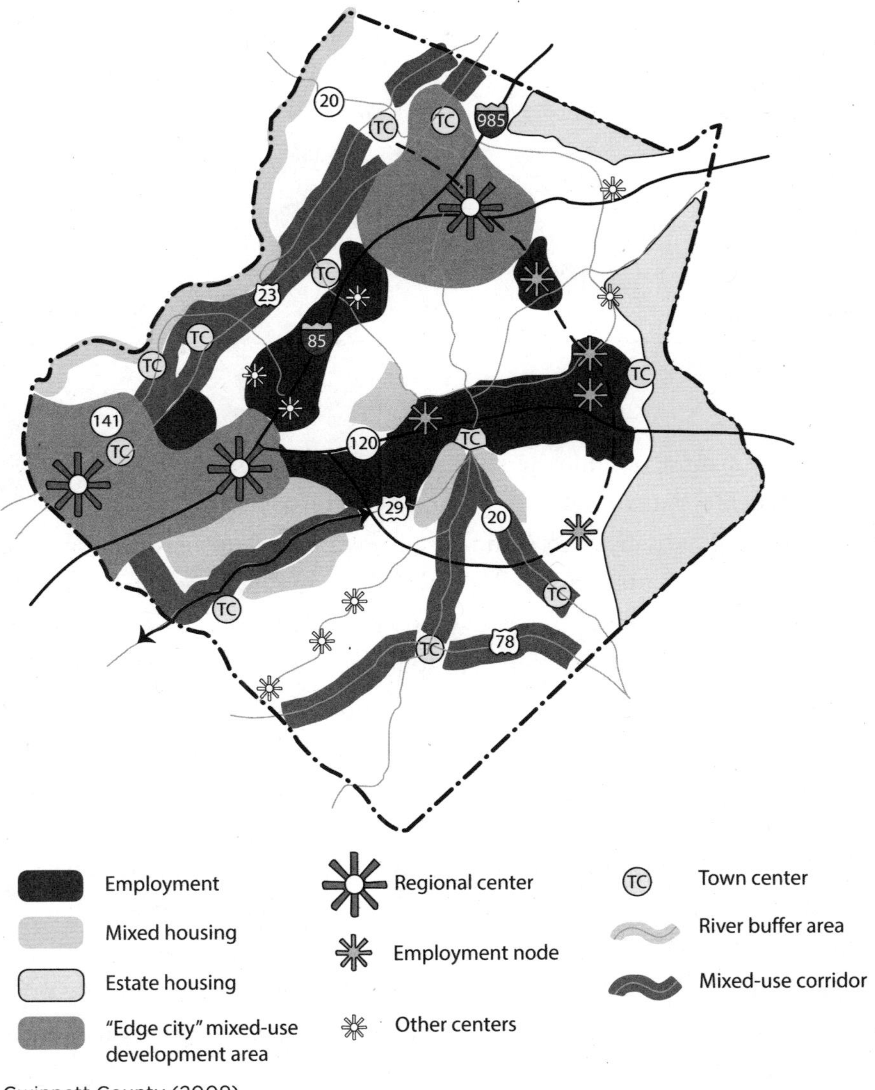

Employment

Mixed housing

Estate housing

"Edge city" mixed-use development area

Regional center

Employment node

Other centers

Town center

River buffer area

Mixed-use corridor

Gwinnett County (2009).

When the Great Recession hit around the time of the plan's completion, the county already had an actionable lower-growth scenario that contained relevant analysis and recommendations. With the return of economic growth, the county can again pursue its International Gateway

Table 1 Select Scenario Indicators in Gwinnett County *2030 Unified Plan*

	Base Conditions, 2005	Middle of the Pack Scenario	International Gateway Scenario
Population	719,349	1,040,000	1,150,000
Employment (jobs)	316,472	487,000	594,950
Housing (units)	246,140	369,168	410,378
Roadways (lane miles)	2,662	2,953	3,549
Revenue ($)	n/a	1,025,000	1,090,000
Expenditure ($)	n/a	1,028,000–1,109,000	1,028,000–1,045,000

Source: Gwinnett County (2009).

scenario for an economically sustainable development pattern based on regional centers anchored in new, mixed-use districts.

Planning activities are complex endeavors and not easily judged as simple successes or failures. Indeed, Wiechmann describes some laudable ideas and initiatives in Dresden's plans that planted seeds of revitalization, even without formal scenarios to guide them. Similarly, Gwinnett's scenarios could be criticized for having a limited topical range, for not considering many environmental impacts, and for continuing to promote resource-intensive suburban-style development. However, Gwinnett's unified plan has several advantages: Its recommendations are not as vulnerable to changes in trends, and it explicitly describes scenarios for how the county can accommodate different levels of growth. Created with the extensive participation of diverse stakeholders, its scenarios and analysis reflect equally diverse concerns and priorities. And by engaging directly with competing visions and values, it links community goals with concrete decisions. In sum, Gwinnett's unified plan is likely more useful in guiding the county through its future than a traditional plan would be.

Book Overview

The way we plan our cities must change—and this book shows a promising way forward. Scenario planning has been used in urban planning for about two decades, so why is a book needed now? First, most urban scenario planning projects have been normative projects for regional transportation–land use plans, leading to a strong association between those plans and urban scenario planning. But urban scenario planning is useful in many other types of projects, such as the exploratory projects discussed by Hopkins and Zapata (2007). Second, scenario planning is used widely in other fields, but this book describes the tools and approaches practitioners use to create urban scenarios and discusses scenarios' theoretical underpinnings, which have been neglected in the planning literature. Third, urban scenario planning is relevant to the planning challenges of today.

The three chapters in part 1 establish the theoretical perspective of the book. Chapter 1 introduces systems thinking and collaboration, the basis of urban scenario planning. Chapter 2 defines scenario planning, drawing on foundational management literature, and describes its history, its theory, and criticisms of it. Chapter 3 discusses how urban scenario planning builds on, and in some ways rejects, ideas from established methods of long-range urban planning like forecasting, strategic planning, visioning, and consensus building.

The three chapters in part 2 provide an in-depth discussion of urban scenario planning practice. Chapter 4 covers the three major approaches to urban scenario planning and illustrates with several cases. Chapter 5 describes the digital tools used for scenario building and analysis. Chapter 6 discusses the qualities of effective scenario practice, including how practitioners design scenarios, incorporate digital tools, engage stakeholders in collaboration, and compare scenarios by using indicators.

The three chapters in part 3 discuss how urban scenario planning projects should be evaluated by practitioners and researchers. Chapter 7 considers how success is defined from the perspectives of planning evaluation and scenario theory. Chapter 8 provides a literature review of all existing empirical evaluations of scenario projects, describing a wide range of outcomes that researchers have measured. Chapter 9 then presents a novel evaluation framework, building on chapters 7 and 8, and reports an empirical validation of the framework applied to three projects.

Finally, part 4 looks to the future. Chapter 10 considers how scenario planning practices might address deep-seated social problems, such as racial segregation and inequality. Chapter 11 revisits the book's goals, outlines the research needed to advance the practice, and comments on the book's implications for planning education.

The book features detailed discussion of several scenario projects, beginning in chapter 4. I present three in greater detail to illustrate three types of typical urban planning practices and how practitioners tailored the methodology to them. The *Futures 2040: Metropolitan Transportation Plan* for the Albuquerque, New Mexico, region illustrates the use of scenarios for regional transportation and land use planning that incorporates an analysis of climate change. The Sahuarita Exploratory Scenario Project applies exploratory scenarios to community-scale comprehensive planning. Finally, the Austin Sustainable Places Project uses scenarios for land use planning for neighborhood or district plans in several communities outside Austin, Texas, facing growth pressures. Two cases, the *Futures 2040* plan and the Austin Sustainable Places Project, use typical tools. I studied them intensively and have thus collected interviews, surveys, and photographs, and I participated in workshops. The Sahuarita Exploratory Scenario Project uses no technical tools at all, and my study of it is based on case materials and interviews provided by participating professionals. All three projects occurred long enough ago that some follow-up is possible, which I report in chapter 9 in the discussion of how to evaluate scenario planning project outcomes. All three are real-world projects, under the constraints of typical planning resources and timelines, and therefore have strengths and weaknesses to learn from.

I envision three audiences for this book. The first is planning practitioners; those unfamiliar with scenario methods can use the book as an introduction to the topic, especially chapters 2, 4, and 6. Practitioners with some experience in scenario planning may be interested in exploring its theoretical assumptions (chapter 2), tools (chapter 5), evaluation methods (chapters 7–9), and potential use for social good (chapter 10).

The second audience is students and scholars researching and teaching planning practice, since the book discusses planning theory (chapters 1 and 3), digital tools (chapter 5), and evaluation (chapters 7–9). Although not formatted as a textbook, the book roughly follows the structure of the semester-long graduate course in scenario planning I developed at the University of Michigan, and it could be used as a textbook for graduate courses on planning practice, methods, theory, or applied urban geographic information systems and modeling.

The third audience is public citizens and urbanists, especially those dissatisfied with their cities or the methods by which those cities are planned. Because the book is primarily aimed at the first two audiences, casual readers may encounter passages where the discussion is too detailed for their purposes. Scenarios provide activists a valuable method for proposing and analyzing changes, as well as building a consensus for action among diverse perspectives, and I hope this text is useful in those regards, especially in light of popular books about cities that describe problems but not solutions or that promote particular urban-form ideologies or policies in isolation. This book encompasses a *planning* perspective on cities: problems are interconnected, decisions are made wiser by careful analysis, and conflicting views can be clarified and sometimes resolved through deliberation. Cities' problems are too large—and planning practices in too many places are too timid—to rely on professional reform alone to make urgently needed changes to policies and institutions.

I call for better planning in cities everywhere, and I hope this book can provide guidance. Planning is not the top-down implementation of a utopian vision; rather, it is a painstaking, long-term project of studying existing and anticipated problems, taking progressive actions to ameliorate them, and keeping in mind uncertainty about the future. City planners must grapple with complex legacies of our society. Some may encounter tremendous resistance to their efforts and even professional risk. But asking what form of civilization we aspire to can unleash a virtuous process of progressive improvement in any city.

Chapter Summary

- Many cities wish to transform themselves and realize sustainability goals, or they must plan for uncertain external forces like climate change and new technologies. Urban scenario planning can be useful in both these situations because it integrates discussions of desired futures with rigorous technical analysis.

- Urban scenario planning practices generally view cities as complex systems requiring collaboration among diverse people.
- Planning in Dresden, Germany, and Gwinnett County, Georgia, shows that having multiple scenarios can improve decision making under uncertainty by prompting people to consider several possible futures and by fostering inclusive dialogue.

FOUNDATIONS

1 The Kind of Problem a City Is

In her classic book *The Death and Life of Great American Cities*, from which this chapter takes its title, Jane Jacobs argues that cities are systems of organized complexity. Scenario planning, which treats the intrinsic complexity and uncertainty in city planning in multiple scenarios, rests on assumptions about urban planning methods that are radically different from the methods presented in many planning textbooks today and criticized by Jane Jacobs in the past. In this chapter, I explain how Jane Jacobs's ideas relate to the argument that planning addresses uniquely difficult problems. Next, I show that Jacobs's and scenario planning's premise is that the city is a complex system, which provides insights for how cities should be understood and planned. Finally, I discuss how collaborative planning theory provides guidance for planning within the complex system of urban governance. I argue that ideas on complexity and collaboration, developed subsequently to Jacobs's work, supply the foundational theories Jacobs lacked in 1961 and follow in her intellectual tradition.

Although Jacobs's ideas have been further developed by more recent work, her core argument remains valid. This chapter begins with a brief discussion of her ideas, which even today have not been fully incorporated into common planning approaches. *The Death and Life of Great American Cities* draws on biology for categorization of problems. At first, Jacobs argues, science excelled at problems of *simplicity* concerning a limited number of variables, such as an elegant formula used to describe the physical motion of objects. Next, investigations of *disorganized complexity*, such as the behavior of gases, led to the development of statistical methods to make inferences about large collections of similar individual units. However, neither approach proved sufficient for the life sciences and the *organized complexity* in "organisms that are replete with unexamined, but obviously intricately interconnected, and surely understandable, relationships." Calling her book "one manifestation of that idea," Jacobs argues that studying organized complexity "depends on the microscopic or detailed view, so to speak, rather than on the less detailed, naked-eye view suitable for viewing problems of simplicity or the remote telescopic view suitable for viewing problems of disorganized complexity" (Jacobs 1961, 438–439).

In her view, urban planning experts relied too often on flawed assumptions and on the less detailed view of disorganized complexity, resulting in fundamental misunderstandings about the nature of cities. Indeed, her book famously critiques the "expert" principles that at the time shaped urban planning and renewal, which swept away complex and dense neighborhoods, replacing them with homogeneous, single-use districts. Ordinary city residents, she believed, held deep and useful insights into cities that planning experts ignored.

Despite paying lip service to some of the concepts in Jacobs's work, many modern planning methods perpetuate the top-down approaches to planning she despised. For example, the classic U.S. text *Urban Land Use Planning,* in its fifth edition by 2006, describes land use planning as beginning with quantitative forecasts of population and employment growth that "must be accommodated in the land use plan" (Berke and Kaiser 2006, 119). The book's main advice is to use technical exercises to determine the amount and location of land and infrastructure needed to satisfy forecast growth. Although the fifth edition briefly mentions scenarios and discusses mixed-use development, the recommended planning approach favors single-use districts that separate residential and commercial activities—exactly the style of planning Jacobs criticizes. Public participation activities, if they are conducted at all, seek input about vague "values" or solicit feedback about options designed by planners; they do not build consensus for the future of the community.

Communities in the United States have grown increasingly frustrated by planning that applies a conventional set of land uses. Dating from a simpler post–World War II society, this approach facilitates rapid suburbanization through a narrow menu of options such as subdivisions, strip malls, and office parks. Today, however, these landscapes are considered sprawling, low-density development that is detrimental to natural systems and lacks many valuable qualities of older cities. This planning presumes the future will be just like the past and therefore ignores the needs of communities facing an uncertain future or a future they wish to change. This type of planning does not meet the two major challenges presented in the preface to this volume: urban transformation and growing uncertainty. Traditional planning methods have long been inadequate in places with declining populations, but today *all* cities grapple with novel uncertainties.

The Unique Context of Planning

Jane Jacobs is responsible for urban planning's paradigm shift. This section sketches out her revolutionary thinking in more detail and considers why her ideas about complexity have not had the same impact as other parts of *The Death and Life of Great American Cities* have had. Her book's introduction includes a sharp criticism of mainstream urban planning of the day; in particular, she argues that the ideas of Daniel Burnham, Le Corbusier, and Ebenezer Howard—three seminal figures in planning history who promoted grand designs for cities—were flawed. Their top-down design prescriptions, she writes, led to an ideology of decentralization, suburbanization, separation of land uses, and isolation of cultural facilities. To Jacobs, these ideas, taken together, constitute nothing less than the death of a city.

Jacobs also correctly observes that focus on the physical form of the city held sway in the professional field at the time. Although urban planning was a more intellectually diverse field than she portrays in her book, the future was still commonly envisioned as low density and auto oriented. In sum, "the principles of sorting out—and of bringing order by repression of all plans but the planners'—have been easily extended to all manner of city functions, until today a land use master plan for a big city is largely a matter of proposed placement . . . of many series of decontaminated sortings," a term that exhibits the contempt Jacobs held for the practice of spatially separating the jumble of uses in older urban neighborhoods that typically included a mixture of residences, stores, and other destinations (Jacobs 1961, 25).

Many urban planners in Jacobs's era did not understand or appreciate the older historic neighborhoods that filled U.S. cities, which she corrects through her detailed description of Greenwich Village and how its design fostered a lively urban community. Jacobs argues that the neighborhood's density, diverse land uses, small blocks, and older buildings—seen by many planners at the time as obsolete—supported a vibrant social and economic life that many newer planned areas could not. Although scholars have since raised important caveats about and criticisms of her arguments, she helped millions understand the nature and benefits of urban life (for caveats, see Page and Mennel 2011). Her ideas generated tectonic shifts in what many came to perceive as a "good" city, and she helped inspire two major reform movements. Today, the Congress for the New Urbanism promotes a return to denser, more pedestrian-oriented cities, which has led many cities to overhaul their zoning codes to foster neighborhoods similar to those Jacobs describes (Duany, Plater-Zyberk, and Speck 2000; Ellis 2002). The contemporary smart growth movement pursues similar aims, promoting dense, walkable cities but also adding the complementary goals of protecting critical environmental areas and agricultural land (Calthorpe and Fulton 2001; Daniels 2001).

As influential as Jacobs's ideas about cities have proved, her perspective on cities as complex systems has not been widely adopted in planning. How planning practices should change to accommodate her alternative perspective is not clear, and Jacobs herself provides few answers, ending her chapter about how cities should be governed and planned on a pessimistic note. Observing that U.S. metropolitan areas are generally fragmented across government levels and departments—and city governments are often fragmented themselves—Jacobs concludes, "We have no practice or wisdom in handling big metropolitan administration or planning" (1961, 427). Her general silence on the organization and role of government functions has led some to describe her underlying political philosophy as libertarian (Montgomery 1998). However, Jacobs was no doubt aware of the many public services that made Greenwich Village life possible—the subway, public utilities, public education, social services, and more—and she also understood the broad-scale planning required to create and maintain them. We should not confuse her silence on how collective action can support a lively urban community with a libertarian-style position in favor of radically limited government.

Another reason Jacobs's ideas had limited impact on contemporary urban planning is that theories of complex systems were then in an early stage of development. Tellingly, she relied on an account by a biologist in describing her ideas; available work on complexity and systems analysis was at the time ill equipped to address systems like cities, where human behavior and perceptions are critical ingredients. Since complexity theory arose in the physical sciences, where quantitative approaches reign, its application in planning tends to be dominated by quantitative modeling that neglects the rich qualitative dimensions of cities (Skrimizea, Haniotou, and Parra 2018).

Some planners use quantitative modeling of cities that is inspired by complexity theory, but planning that is exclusively quantitative has weaknesses, as a landmark article explores. In "Dilemmas in a General Theory of Planning," Horst Rittel and Melvin M. Webber (1973) argue that, unlike problems of engineering, problems of the social system, the subject of planning, are "wicked" problems. Rittel and Webber argue these problems are ill defined, involve normative judgments about values, have an indefinite list of solutions that cannot be fully tested, and have other unique qualities. Like Jacobs, Rittel and Webber present no clear path for planners to follow; their only sure conclusion is that "planning is a component of politics" (1973, 169) because it involves making inherently political value judgments. However, they admit they "have neither a theory that can locate social goodness, nor one that might dispel wickedness, nor one that might resolve the problem of equity that rising pluralism is provoking" (169). Their article effectively marks the death of the idea that systems thinking and quantitative modeling could provide a firm basis for planning, and it leaves open the question of whether or how planning can address these wicked problems at all.

Cities as Complex Systems

Advances in systems theory, as well as planning theory, provide useful intellectual perspectives on these problems. This chapter does not attempt to describe the long history of systems thinking in planning; instead, it presents a snapshot of current ideas to illustrate their consequences for planning methods. Urban planners have long viewed cities as systems, defined by *Merriam-Webster* as "regularly interacting or interdependent group[s] of items forming a unified whole" (http://merriam-webster.com/dictionary /system). Cities contain many natural and artificial systems, most obviously physical networks, such as the transportation, water, and utility systems (Wachs 2009). However, more abstract legal, institutional, and social systems and even less visible ecological systems are just as important. Figure 4, from a work discussing urban resilience, shows how such governance networks—encompassing the institutions of society—interrelate with the more easily measured and observed systems of material, energy, and infrastructure (Meerow, Newell, and Stults 2016).

The dense interconnections among these elements historically have provided the rationale for comprehensive planning, as illustrated in figure 5, created by the urban planner Peter Calthorpe: travel behavior, building performance, land consumption, and infrastructure costs are all linked. By placing urban form at the center, Calthorpe takes the position of an architect and planner. But the relationships shown in this figure nonetheless go in multiple directions; urban form is itself influenced by fiscal, transportation, and environmental factors.

The fundamental insight of Jacobs and of Rittel and Webber is that cities are not merely very large, very complicated systems, and they do not function as such. Jacobs observes that a city's evolution is not only the work of designers but also often the product of a subtle interplay between its form and social life. A few small changes could spark an economic resurgence in one area, whereas a seemingly similar area might stagnate. Theorists have come to call these *complex systems*, defined by Zellner and Campbell (2015) as

> composed of multiple, often heterogeneous parts that selectively interact with each other, giving rise to a coherent organization with its own attributes, behaviors and trajectory. A complex system is adaptable

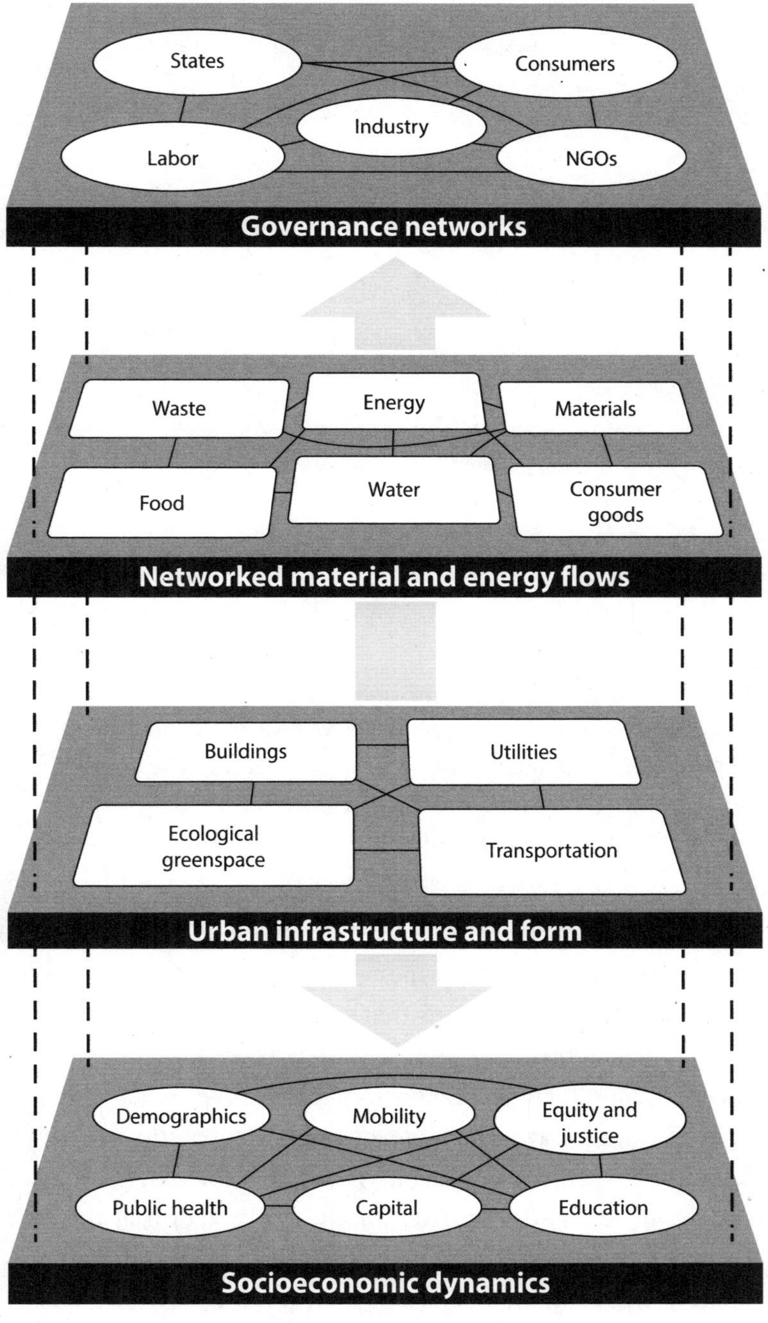

Meerow, Newell, and Stults (2016, 45). With permission, © Elsevier.

Figure 5 A Systems Perspective on Urban Form and City Performance

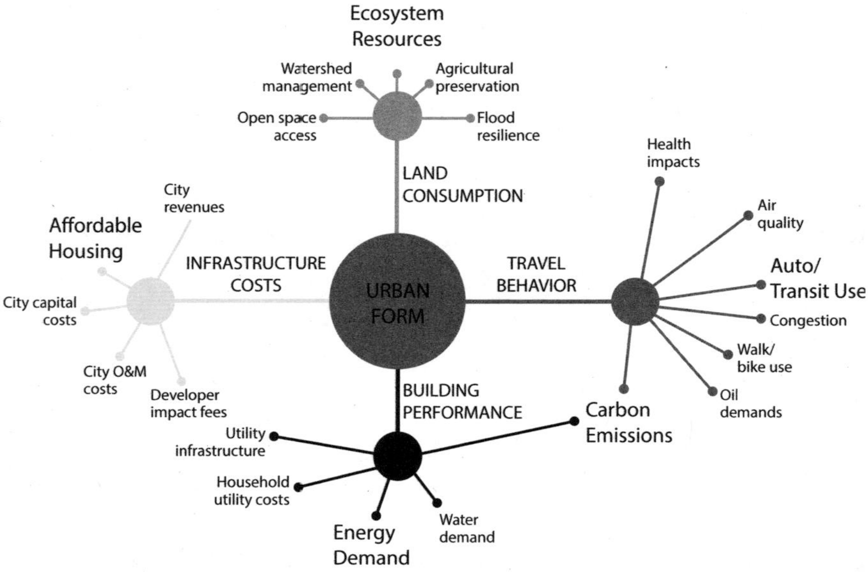

Courtesy of Peter Calthorpe.

and robust, retaining its integrity and coherence over long periods of time, even when its constituent parts cease to exist (e.g., people leave the city, buildings are demolished, new officials are elected). The system's ability to self-organize despite constant change relies on the selective and decentralized flow of matter, energy and information among its parts. (459)

This definition calls attention to several of the properties that distinguish a complex system from other types of systems. First, complex systems exhibit *self-organization*, meaning that order appears among multiple interacting parts without resulting from centralized coordination. Second, they are *robust*, or retain their general form over time, even when they undergo changes. Third, they are *adaptable*, having the capability to change over time to better fit their environment. Within this context, the flow of information among residents is crucial for the organization of the city. Complex systems theorists often make two further distinctions: between a *closed* system (a self-contained object, such as a machine or organism) and an *open* system (an object subject to change by its external environ-ment) and between *artificial* and *natural* systems. Marshall (2012) argues that a city is an open system with artificial components, although cities of course also contain natural ecosystems.

The observations of Rittel and Webber suggest there are major differ-ences between city systems and natural ones. They also find that a city's residents conceptualize problems differently among themselves and prior-itize different goals. Cities are therefore dual systems in that they contain both their own complexity and the complexity contained within the minds of their residents (Portugali 2011; 2016). Therefore, the most important ele-ments that explain a city's operation are not the physical infrastructure systems or natural systems but instead the intangible culture, thoughts, norms, and institutions that shape the decisions and behavior of residents, whose actions and decisions ultimately shape the city's physical and natu-ral systems.

Viewing the city as a complex system has profound consequences for how it should be planned, highlights the obstacles facing any effort to change a city, and calls into question whether large-scale attempts to change are desirable. Since cities are produced and reproduced over time by a vast set of forces, changing their structure may require changes to institutions and culture, as well as infrastructure and buildings. Furthermore, even if these changes are possible, they are difficult. Marshall (2012) describes three forms of ignorance predicted by complex systems theory: First, unlike closed systems, complex systems are not fully knowable, because they are open to outside influences, are produced through the decisions of many people, and evolve over time. Knowledge about cities is necessarily always partial owing to our limits of observation and their ongoing evolution. Second, as Rittel and Webber also observe, the precise effects of any in-tervention on the city are also unknowable. Assessing an effect requires determining what would have occurred without the intervention. Com-plexity theory also says that small changes may produce significant, un-predicted effects on a system. Third, because the optimal (or desired) future state of the city system is unknowable, what is desired today will likely change in the future.

> All three types of unknowability suggested here mitigate against effective planning: one could say that unknowability is the enemy of planning. The challenge of planning becomes one of how to intervene in or attempt to organize a largely artificial open system where there is not full knowledge of the system; where even if the current state is known, the outcome of intervention is unforeseeable; and even if outcomes were reasonably foreseeable, the optimal outcome would not be specifiable in the first place. (Marshall 2012, 201)

It is little wonder, then, that planning has not been eager to adopt complexity theory. Theorists do, however, point out that "complexity sciences do not validate the principle of laissez-faire as a means to effectively not plan a prosperous future," because there is no guarantee that cities will evolve in socially desirable ways—and because there is plenty of historical evidence that they will not (Skrimizea, Haniotou, and Parra 2018, 130). Without planning of any type, cities may stumble into avoidable problems like the tragedy of the commons, or they may evolve in a direction serving elites (Skrimizea, Haniotou, and Parra 2018). If any one of several futures is possible and if social actions influence what futures come to pass, some form of planning seems possible (Byrne 2003, 174). Byrne calls for planning that uses "appropriately chosen theories, methods, and tools, acknowledging the evolutionary nature of socio-spatial change and accepting its limitations" (10). To that end, he urges planners to embrace uncertainty and calls for an adaptive form of planning that "formulates a both responsive and proactive integrated strategy constructed by a number of individual spatial-temporal planning solutions that aim to address specific situations" (13). More knowledge does not necessarily reduce the uncertainty embedded in complex spatial problems, but the most appropriate form of planning in this view would make basic uncertainties transparent and recognize planning as occurring in an evolving, decentralized system.

In addition to being adaptive, taking specific actions, and carefully monitoring results, planning for a complex system must consider long-term consequences and anticipate the effects of decisions for three reasons. First, as previously noted, planning aims to inform decisions that are unavoidably long term, such as new infrastructure development or land use changes. Despite cities' many uncertainties, we can draw on a substantial body of knowledge to anticipate the long-term effects of key planning decisions. Ignoring this knowledge would be tantamount to making big decisions in a state of willful ignorance. Second, although the future is unknown, many specific uncertainties can be identified and the consequences of possible futures at least partially anticipated. Third, investigating the consequences of decisions is not the only function of planning: this information can also clarify visions and goals, identify indicators for how best to measure progress toward these goals, and develop durable concepts to guide action.

The picture that emerges is a form of planning that looks into the future and draws on the best knowledge available to inform decisions and actions. Given the reality of complex systems, this type of planning must be conducted with humility, or a readiness to adjust assumptions and predicted outcomes as needed. In *Human Nature and Conduct*, the philosopher John Dewey distinguishes between a *planned* society—where central authorities coordinate all activities—and a *planning* society. In the latter, the purpose of planning is not to realize or control a specific future but rather to make more intelligent, progressive decisions today, especially those likely to have long-term consequences. Such planning is indispensable for any society that seeks self-determination. In Dewey's words, "Memory of the past, observation of the present, [and] foresight of the future are indispensable. But they are indispensable to a present liberation, an enriching growth of action" (1922, 265). As chapter 2 explains, scenario planning is a methodology for identifying and exploring selected uncertainties. Apart from analysis, scenario planning projects produce other valuable results, such as improving a city's ability to understand and respond to events, to define which goals to pursue, and to decide how to measure collective progress. Exactly how planning can bring about these valuable social outcomes, however, is not described in complexity theory, which is ill equipped for social analysis. We therefore turn to collaborative planning theory for this important aspect of planning.

Planning as Collaboration Within a Complex Social System

Understanding cities as complex systems is only one part of explaining their nature. Because planning is conducted by groups of people, it requires organizational guidance. How people involved in planning should act within their social context raises profound, challenging questions beyond the scope of complexity theory:

- Many different future cities are possible and desired. How can we reconcile residents' diverse values and opinions and define shared goals?
- Cities are complex, large, and unique and therefore cannot be planned by referring exclusively to universal conceptual models. How can we create the specific knowledge about each city needed for planning?
- Cities are created by the actions of many individuals and organizations. How can their decisions be coordinated to pursue shared goals?
- Complex systems are capable of remaining unchanged but *also* of transforming into new forms. How can planning be conducted in a way that pursues desired transformations of, for example, physical form, institutions, and social relations?

All these questions are addressed by a set of ideas now known as collaborative planning theory. Like the literature on complex systems, that for collaborative planning theory is large and diverse, and it has evolved over the last nearly 30 years (Goodspeed 2016a). As in the previous section, the purpose here is to set forth the basic perspective from a contemporary viewpoint, not to provide a detailed genealogy of the ideas. I focus on how the ideas are useful for evaluating, analyzing, and fostering innovation in planning practices.

Before embarking on a more detailed discussion of collaborative planning theory, I compare this theory with the idea of complex systems and consider whether the two are, in fact, compatible. Systems theory's roots in the physical sciences, which use quantitative modeling, have led to a presumption that experts have an exclusive role in defining the models. This tradition was the implicit target of Rittel and Webber's critique, which was motivated by planners' neglect of the distinct type of system that a city comprises and by failure to appreciate the multiple perspectives of city residents. In the years since their work, theories have been adapted and elaborated to understand systems with a strong social component. Complexity theorists today argue that the theory of complex adaptive systems can be applied to systems with quantitative and qualitative dimensions (Portugali 1999).

The strongest endorsement for a potential link between complexity theory and collaborative planning comes from the theorists Judith E. Innes and David E. Booher, who argue in a series of publications that collaborative planning theory is well suited to complexity (Innes and Booher 1999a; 1999c; 2000; 2010). Complexity theory upends the desirability of top-down planning and also describes how "adaptive changes within a system can grow from learning generated by the individual interactions in the networks of system participants" (Innes and Booher 1999c, 148). As we see later, their research focuses on fostering such learning.

One other important comparison should be made between the two theories. Complex adaptive systems theory, being based in science, is a positive theory—that is, it describes how the world works but does not compare or judge. This is a major weakness from a planning perspective. Collaborative planning theory is positive *and* normative; it allows analysis and hypothesis formation and provides guidance for improving social practices to increase desirable outcomes. The following presentation of collaborative planning theory explains how it has been applied at different scales and summarizes current empirical and theoretical work.

The most logical place to begin is with researchers who have used collaborative planning theory to analyze dialogue and deliberation among stakeholders, planners, and others. Their work forms the basis of planning practice and it illustrates some of the ideas widely shared by collaborative planning theorists. The touchstone for such researchers is Jürgen Habermas's *Theory of Communicative Action* (1984; 1987), which Innes argues likely "provide[s] the principal framework for the new planning theory" (1995, 186). Writing in the critical social tradition, Habermas observes that different forms of rationality dominate in different areas of society: cognitive-instrumental rationality is the domain of science and technology, moral-practical rationality is the domain of law and morality, and aesthetic-practical rationality is expressed through the arts. Unlike grand social theorists like Max Weber or Émile Durkheim, whose insights Habermas seeks to build on, he is dissatisfied by critiques that remain at the broad societal scale. Could individuals' actions, he asks, perhaps be questioned or even changed through small-scale interventions and thus affect abstract patterns?

To link individual action and society at large, Habermas observes that everyday conversations between people can bring together the different ways of reasoning that are so often separated in our culture. This connection is especially important, Habermas believes, because social institutions (which he calls the system), such as law and government bureaucracies, tend to be permeated by impersonal cognitive-instrumental rationality at the expense of the rich personal insights rooted in alternative forms of rationality needed for a fuller perspective on any issue.

In contrast to "the system," Habermas calls the reality created through conversation and communication the lifeworld. Although social systems are always present in this lifeworld, participants in a dialogue are free to discuss or ignore aspects of the system or interject their subjective perspectives. Therefore, he concludes that the lifeworld exists in a state of "half-transcendence," because it can be present when the system is reproduced or when elements of the system are questioned and transformed (Habermas 1987, 120–126). The conceptual heart of communicative rationality lies in Habermas's description of the types of deliberation most likely to result in such transformations and breakthroughs: every competent speaker should be allowed to take part in the discourse; all speakers should be allowed to question any assertion; all speakers should be allowed to introduce any new assertion; all speakers should feel free to express their attitudes, desires, and needs; and no speaker may be prevented from exercising these principles (Habermas 1990). According to Habermas, the obstacles to this type of conversation are formidable, since distortion can have many sources, such as coercion, lying, or incomprehensibility. However, the liberating potential of deliberation lies in settings that minimize distortions and pursuit of an ideal of open dialogue.

In accordance with these ideas, the planning theorist John Forester elaborates on Habermas's discourse ethics (attributes of conversation that minimize distortions) and provides a more detailed analysis of power. Forester posits that power can be wielded during planning discussions in the three ways proposed by Steven Lukes (1974): by promoting formal decisions, setting the agenda, and influencing the broader ideological context of debate. In Lukes's view, a plurality of interests and perspectives is unavoidable, which leads Forester to argue that Lukes's theory can be used to help planners identify distortions and to guide critical practice to counteract them. The specific ethics proposed by Habermas are comprehensibility (clear statements), sincerity (the speaker's trustworthiness), legitimacy (appropriate relationship to context), and truth (the accuracy or validity of the claim) (Forester 1989, 144). Forester argues that professionals such as planners have a special responsibility, as they are often able to recognize and take action to counter systemic distortions at different levels (150–151). Using the insights of critical theorists, Forester describes how planning practitioners can work to mitigate the societal divisions—such as through discussion and broader organizing practices—to bring stakeholders to the table and reveal the deceit and misinformation often peddled by the powerful.

Forester's work has revolutionized the analysis of planning practice by introducing an ethics framework that illustrates how practitioners' daily decisions relate to broader social issues. Other scholars have developed similar ideas at higher levels of analysis; Innes and Booher, for instance, studied mainly large, multiyear projects with standing stakeholder committees (Booher and Innes 2002; Innes and Booher 1999a; 1999b; 1999c). Investigating how such groups operate and how stakeholder groups can create solutions through extended deliberations, their empirical research culminates in what they call the DIAD model, which, like Forester's research, takes work by Habermas and other social theorists as a starting point. Achieving collaborative rationality within a planning process requires diverse, interdependent interests and authentic dialogue, or DIAD (Booher and Innes 2002). If these criteria are met, planning can result in the system adapting accordingly—namely, by stakeholders developing shared identities and meanings and by models using new heuristics and making innovations (Innes and Booher 2010).

One strand of their work observes that collaboration frequently obtains agreement on which indicator to measure to understand whether goals are being met. Drawing explicitly on complexity theory, they suggest that an indicator might describe overall system performance, provide feedback on particular policies or programs, or generate rapid feedback to inform day-to-day decision making (Innes and Booher 2000). Another scholar working in this tradition, Richard Margerum (2002; 2011), develops practical insights from empirical cases. As described in chapter 3, these ideas led to methods of organizing stakeholders to achieve consensus.

Finally, whereas Forester's insights may apply very broadly, the models of stakeholder deliberation described by Innes, Booher, and Margerum are often quite different from the specific institutional contexts in which planners work. These contexts are often organized around zoning and development review processes in which legally required procedures may hinder open-ended stakeholder deliberation. One scholar interested in the scale of planning institutions is Patsy Healey, whose book *Collaborative Planning* (1997) combines ideas from Habermas, the sociologist Anthony Giddens, and other institutional theorists to propose how such institutions can be made more collaborative.

The planning field has by no means accepted these ideas as uncontroversial. Their complexity and normative dimension have made them unpopular in academia: some consider their claims relatively untested, and others have questioned their usefulness or validity or claimed their tenets are specific to liberal democracies (Huxley and Yiftachel 2000). However, scholars have taken up these questions, documenting the development of consensus using surveys (Deyle and Slotterback 2009; Schively 2007), applying collaborative planning theory to the global south (Fahmi et al. 2016), testing the theory in the arena of transportation planning (Deyle and Wiedenman 2014), making theoretical contributions by exploring epistemological issues (Goldstein 2010), relating the theory to ideas of the public good (Mattila 2016), and developing substantive criteria to judge the outcome of collaborative dialogue (Sager 2013). The literature contains no clear-cut refutation of collaborative planning theory, but further research is needed to refine and rigorously test the ideas of its first generation of theorists.

One issue debated within collaborative planning theory is whether a single public interest exists. Habermas's theory calls attention to the diversity of societal perspectives and the role of deliberation in establishing shared knowledge and understanding. He discusses how powerful entities—government bureaucracies, companies, and legal systems—develop their own ways of looking at the world. His ideas suggest that we should expect to encounter quite diverse viewpoints but also that overcoming these differences is possible at certain times. On the basis of her case research, in which groups of stakeholders with many positions carried out extensive negotiations, Innes (1996) argues that discussion groups often do discover shared public interests. Other theorists have taken more nuanced views. For instance, Forester, informed by his analysis of power, more detailed than Innes's, describes a progressive form of professional practice and suggests a world where shared goals may be continually debated and contested, but he never claims such practice would identify the public interests. Therefore, collaborative planning theory would seem to suggest a corresponding pluralist picture of society because it anticipates diverse perspectives that are never fully reconciled.

Finally, here I provide general approaches to the four questions in planning practice that open this section. Collaborative planning theory maintains that achieving some form of consensus about values and goals is possible through deliberation—perhaps on the overall vision but also on other elements such as the indicators to evaluate performance. Discussion is also the basic mechanism for gathering and applying the knowledge needed for tackling a problem, although that mechanism has been relatively neglected by collaborative theorists (Goodspeed 2016b). Beyond the consensus and epistemological dimensions, involving participants gives rise to the pragmatic need to coordinate across diverse actors. Inspired in part by these ideas, chapter 3 describes some of the methods planning practitioners have created to identify stakeholders and bring them to a common table for deliberation. Collaborative planning theory, however, provides few answers to the final question of how to organize discussion of a city's evolution.

Conclusion

This chapter begins by considering the perspectives contained in two classic urban planning works: In seeking to understand how cities function, Jane Jacobs argues that, as systems of organized complexity, cities cannot be planned effectively through top-down designs, which in her era too often ignored cities' intricacies. Rittel and Webber agree that cities are systems, but they make the important point that cities combine complex features with the human dimension, resulting in what they call "wicked problems." I have argued that all three scholars were limited by the state of theory in their day, which is particularly evident in their lack of professional prescriptions. I then elaborate on Jacobs's basic perspective by drawing on two complementary theories: a theory of the city (complex systems theory) and a theory that planning can be conducted from within a city in a way that engages directly with conflicting values, multiple forms of knowledge, and various actors (collaborative planning theory).

Next, we turn to the focus of this book: scenario planning methodology, a promising approach to considering the future of complex systems.

Chapter Summary

- In her classic book *The Death and Life of Great American Cities*, Jane Jacobs argues that cities are a problem of organized complexity. Subsequent developments in the areas of complex systems and collaborative planning theory have clarified how this insight should influence planning practice.
- As complex systems, cities develop their own self-organization and retain their general form over time, but they also have the capacity to adapt. Qualitative concepts and residents' perceptions are existing ingredients to urban systems that cannot be ignored in planning.
- Because complex systems can react to changes in unpredictable ways, plans cannot—and should not—represent a fixed goal. Instead, planning shapes cities by fostering intelligent decisions, learning, and consensus among residents.
- Collaborative planning theory provides advice about how professionals can organize deliberation and stakeholder engagement to generate consensus and foster urban change.

2 Scenario Planning Defined

As chapter 1 notes, scenario planning is distinct from other planning approaches. This chapter builds on this book's basic definition of scenario planning: *long-term strategic planning that creates representations of multiple, plausible futures of a system of interest.* This chapter describes what all scenario planning projects have in common, despite their varied project goals, geographic scales, types of scenarios created, and processes. After briefly outlining the methodology's origins and discussing its theoretical underpinnings, the chapter reviews the basics of scenario planning, how scenarios are defined and created, and the types of scenarios that practitioners create to analyze specific issues and uncertainties. Finally, it introduces the main questions about the methodology that planners raise.

Origins of Scenario Planning

Scenario planning is best understood through its historical origins. Two key figures contributed to its development: Herman Kahn and Pierre Wack. Born in New Jersey to Eastern European immigrants in 1922, Kahn studied physics at the University of California at Los Angeles and served in the U.S. Army. After World War II, he worked for the RAND Corporation, where he participated in the creation of the hydrogen bomb. During the Cold War, his primary focus at RAND was military strategy. He became known for his explorations of types of nuclear wars to determine how best to promote deterrence and preparedness. In his 1962 book *Thinking About the Unthinkable*, for example, Kahn notes, "Thermonuclear wars are not only unpleasant events; they are, fortunately, unexperienced events, and the crises which threaten such wars are almost equally unexperienced. Few are able to force themselves to persist in looking for novel possibilities in this area without aids to their imaginations" (1962, 143).

In his book, Kahn proposes one method to plan for such unprecedented events: scenario creation, or "an attempt to describe in more or less detail some hypothetical sequence of events" (1962, 143). Kahn argues that creating scenarios has several advantages: First, they call attention to the large range of possibilities that the future holds, which was especially appropriate for nuclear wars, "unexperienced events." Second, scenarios force the planner to explore details and dynamics of the system and help identify critical choices. Third, scenarios illuminate interactions among elements. Fourth, they identify questions that might otherwise be ignored. Fifth, when crises occur, decision makers can refer to relevant scenario analysis already completed. Kahn further contends that exploring scenarios—such as those holding the potential for an accidental war—motivated RAND to examine new issues, such as improving command-and-control systems. He describes integrating scenario thinking into war-and-peace games, wherein a group of people would consider a hypothetical series of events, and argues that "the serious, even if temporary, consideration of extreme examples jerks us out of our peaceful world and stimulates our imaginations," helping identify basic principles or options for use in real-world decision making (Kahn 1962, 175).

Although the RAND Corporation bristled with systems analysts and their quantitative skills, Kahn looked to the nearby moviemaking industry for creating military strategy in a world where new technology equipped combatants with weapons of unprecedented destructiveness. Kahn believed that creating imaginative scenarios in the same way a screenwriter develops plot alternatives could help in considering the future and its potential for nuclear warfare (Kahn 1962). Some thought his work—which, for example, proposed that the United States could win a nuclear exchange with the Soviet Union, even if it resulted in massive destruction—made nuclear war more likely. Others, praised his work. They saw his shocking accidental-war scenarios as presenting a strong case for full disarmament (Menand 2005). For his part, Kahn insisted scenarios, although not predictions, were useful in preparing the nation for an uncertain future.

Kahn used scenarios as many futurist thinkers do, but it is hard to see how his idiosyncratic methods might be adapted to other questions. In addition, his description of the scenario planning method in *Thinking About the Unthinkable* is sketchy and incomplete. His work established the utility of scenarios for issues whose future can be somewhat anticipated in the present. New technologies often exist long before they enter wide use, and Kahn's analysis focused on the consequences of using a technology—thermonuclear weapons—that had never been used in warfare. He also called attention to the value of considering alternative chains of events to anticipate future situations. Kahn's notion of scenarios is therefore evocative—but still incomplete. To become an established methodology, scenario planning needed better-defined elements, a clearer overall process, and application to more routine forms of decision making.

These three elements came together at Royal Dutch Shell, the oil and gas company where Pierre Wack and colleagues applied scenarios to their corporate strategic planning. In two influential 1985 articles, Wack lays out the company's scenario approach (Wack 1985a; 1985b). Like Kahn, Wack believes the true value of scenarios is in the development of abstract insights: "Scenarios deal with two worlds: the world of facts and the world of perceptions. They explore for facts but they aim at perceptions inside the heads of decision makers. Their purpose is to gather and transform information of strategic significance into fresh perceptions. . . . When it works, it is a creative experience that generates a heartfelt 'Aha!' from your managers and leads to strategic insights beyond the mind's previous reach" (1985b, 140). Instead of relying on forecasts, which he sees as an inferior substitute for careful thinking, Wack thinks managers should explore outside forces by creating scenarios about the future.

The starting point for scenario creation on any topic is to separate *predetermined* elements from *uncertain* elements. In the scenarios of the oil industry that Wack describes, the predetermined elements were the 1973 oil crisis and the economic stresses it had created (1985b). The key uncertainty was how the economy would evolve—a long-term recession, constrained growth, or boom and bust. Wack proposes that there should be at least three and never more than four scenarios for any project: "first the surprise-free view . . . and then two other worlds or different ways of seeing the world that focus on the critical uncertainties" (Wack 1985b, 146). Wack calls these macroscenarios. Scenarios more focused on particular issues come out of macroscenarios. For example, macroscenarios of the world economy led to more detailed scenario analysis of specific decisions facing Royal Dutch Shell.

Wack argues, "Central to decision scenarios—indeed the basis for their success or failure—is the microcosm of the decision makers; their inner model of reality, their set of assumptions that structure their understanding of the unfolding business environment and the factors critical to success. A manager's inner model never mirrors reality; it is always a construct" (1985b, 150). During times of rapid change and increased complexity, he argues, managers' mental models can become a hazard; the ultimate value of scenarios therefore comes from the "reperception" of reality. Managers can then use more specific scenarios to evaluate the company's strategic vision or the "structured view of what you want your company to be" and help managers in option planning (147).

The Royal Dutch Shell scenario methodology is described in several books: Peter Schwartz's *The Art of the Long View* (1991); Kees van der Heijden's more scholarly *Scenarios: The Art of Strategic Conversation*, in its second edition by 2005; and a highly practical handbook by Ralston and Wilson (2006) describing further refinements by the consulting organization Global Business Network (GBN), which began scenario planning in 1987.

Van der Heijden's insightful account most clearly describes the concept of scenario planning regardless of its field of application, and the next section draws on it. Box 1 summarizes some of the major ways fields other than urban planning use scenarios.

The Basics of Scenario Planning

The essence of scenario planning is a careful analysis of what is certain and uncertain about the future. As we have seen in chapter 1, uncertainty has too long been ignored in planning, which has resulted in plans that fail when their underlying assumptions are violated. Plan failures have concrete, not theoretical, consequences: homes flooded because they were

BOX 1 Scenarios in Other Fields

Developed for war planning and then refined for corporate strategy, scenario planning methods have been adopted by several fields related to—but distinct from—urban planning. Urban planners may encounter or collaborate with people from these fields.

Climate Change. The Intergovernmental Panel on Climate Change (IPCC) has long used scenarios to characterize uncertainty in future greenhouse gas (GHG) emissions. Whereas scenarios in earlier reports were original research, the IPCC's Fifth Assessment Report uses four scenarios, called representative concentration pathways (RCPs), drawn from the existing scientific literature. These RCPs characterize alternative-future scenarios for GHG emission mitigation, atmospheric concentrations, air-pollutant emissions, and land use (Moss et al. 2010; the numbers describe time series of GHG emissions and the resulting atmospheric concentrations). The four RCPs are the strident mitigation scenario (RCP2.6), two intermediate scenarios (RCP4.5 and RCP6.0), and one scenario with very high GHG emissions (RCP8.5) (IPCC, Pachauri, and Meyer 2014). However, the IPCC stresses that each scenario makes distinct socioeconomic assumptions, so the differences among them are not only the result of degree of mitigation (Moss et al. 2010). These four scenarios form the basis of the IPCC's analysis of ecological changes projected to result from climate change.

Environmental and Ecosystem Research. Scenarios are widely used in ecological research, especially to incorporate human behaviors and choice into environmental analysis (Oteros-Rozas et al. 2015). Peterson, Cumming, and Carpenter (2003) argue that scenario planning for conservation offers benefits, including increased understanding of key uncertainties, incorporation of alternative perspectives into conservation planning, and greater resilience of decisions to surprise. In the environmental field, scenarios are generally used to explore uncertainties that are outside managers' control, and Peterson, Cumming, and Carpenter suggest that adaptive management is more appropriate in situations in which direct

Box 1 *Cont'd*

control exists. One exception to this approach is Alberti (2016), who advocates using scenarios to incorporate urban issues more fully into ecological analysis.

The Millennium Ecosystem Assessment, conducted from 2001 to 2005, raised the profile of scenarios in the environmental field. This large-scale scientific project, somewhat similar to the IPCC's, was called for by United Nations Secretary-General Kofi Annan in 2000 to "assess the consequences of ecosystem change for human well-being and the scientific basis for action needed to enhance the conservation and sustainable use of those systems and their contribution to human well-being" (Assessment 2018). The project culminated in three major reports (Carpenter and Group 2005; Chopra and Group 2005; Hassan et al. 2005), and one had four detailed scenarios: Global Orchestration, Order from Strength, Adapting Mosaic, and TechnoGarden (Carpenter and Group 2005). These scenarios were qualitative and quantitative. In conjunction with this project, 18 official and 15 associated assessments were conducted for regional ecosystems, based on the global scenarios or developed on their own (Biggs et al. 2007; Bohensky, Reyers, and Van Jaarsveld 2006).

Landscape Design and Geodesign. Landscape architecture and the emerging related field of geodesign make use of scenarios, primarily using them to explore design alternatives and to link designs with analysis (Flaxman 2009; Slotterback et al. 2016; Steinitz 2012). In landscape design, normative scenarios illustrate the environmental consequences of design choices (Nassauer and Corry 2004). Geodesign's scenario planning practices have many similarities to those in urban planning, but geodesign begins with design choices, whereas urban planning typically starts with key uncertainties. The two are not mutually exclusive, though, and these two communities have great potential for constructive collaboration.

built in areas that were thought to be safe from storms, public funds wasted on infrastructure to accommodate growth that never materializes, or a mismatch between the types of housing units available and what people prefer. Furthermore, planning that ignores uncertainty tends to perpetuate the status quo.

Scenario planning methodology, by contrast, identifies, prioritizes, and analyzes the most important uncertainties facing complex adaptive systems like cities. Analysis of forces within a city explores not only what *might* change but also what *could* change to further the community's goals for transformation. An analysis focused on external uncertainties improves preparedness for changes in the broader environment and thus allows cities to improve their resilience to foreseeable events with uncertain ramifications.

The first step in developing scenario planning as a concept was an analysis of what can be known about the future; the scenario practitioner and theorist Kees van der Heijden argues that lack of knowledge is the most easily solved source of uncertainty about the future. Scenario projects, in his view, should begin with an analysis of context, which often continues as the focus and questions are refined. The remaining forms of uncertainty are *predetermined* factors, which are things that will remain unchanged in the future, and *uncertainties*. In the short term, predetermined factors dominate; therefore, forecasting may be appropriate. Van der Heijden describes forecasting as the illumination from headlights when driving through a snowstorm at night: the headlights reveal only a bit of the road, a short-range view that does not allow the driver to prepare for the journey ahead (2005, 96). Wise drivers rely on their headlights but also consult other sources of information about the route, such as maps or their own knowledge of curves and potential obstacles. In the very long term, uncertainty overwhelms predetermined elements, and planning is impossible. Between the two is a zone of predictability but also considerable uncertainty—the realm where scenario planning is valuable, seen in figure 6.

Thus far, the description of uncertainties has been quite abstract. Schwartz (1991) and other scenario practitioners describe the uncertainties that could have a big impact on a project as driving forces, or forces in

Figure 6 The Balance of Predictability and Uncertainty over Time, and the Associated Planning Methods: Forecasting (F), Scenarios (S), and Hope (H)

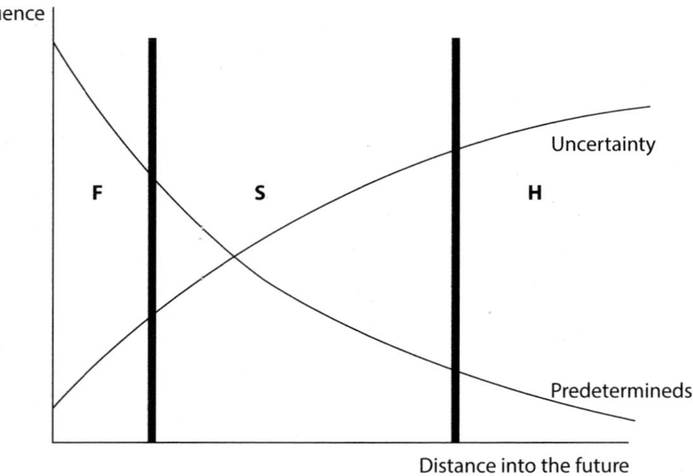

Based on Van der Heijden (2005). © John Wiley & Sons Ltd.

society, technology, economics, politics, and the environment. For public sector applications, Avin (2007) advises including transportation and infrastructure within the technology category and including governance and fiscal structures within the politics category.

Scenario planning addresses two out of four types of uncertainties: *Risks* are uncertainties that can be analyzed using historical data and described using statistics. They can be estimated quantitatively, and forecasting makes sense for them. Van der Heijden, however, cautions against excessive reliance on forecasts, because "people settle into a routine implying that the historical situation will continue forever" (2005, 95). This leaves people unprepared when the trends break. The second type cannot be assigned a numerical likelihood. Van der Heijden calls these structure uncertainties, but I use the term *scenario uncertainties* to maintain consistency with the terminology in Walker and colleagues (2003). The other two types of uncertainties, which are not included in scenario planning, are *recognized ignorance*, some of which can be addressed through research, and *total ignorance*, or the profound uncertainty of what we "do not even know that we do not know" (Walker et al. 2003, 13).

Whereas forecasting aims to predict a single value, scenario planning aims to discover a possible future, not only a value but also a description of the world that explains how it was achieved. Therefore, scenarios require structures that explicitly include *predetermined elements*, shared by all scenarios in a project, and *scenario uncertainties*, which vary among scenarios. Distinguishing these elements can be complex and is the focus of the scenario-building process. Predetermined elements typically are slow-changing phenomena like demographics and infrastructure and may also be more abstract issues like firmly held political preferences. Deciding on the predetermined elements to include also depends on the project goals. The total number of households and jobs to accommodate is usually a predetermined element in transportation–land use plans, because the plan's purpose is to deal with that growth. Of course, a planning project on whether a certain transportation infrastructure should be built may consider scenarios with different amounts of growth, such as the Gwinnett County scenarios described in the preface to this book.

The scenario funnel (or cone) in figure 7 is, like figure 6, organized along a timeline, beginning at the tip in the present. The entire cone represents plausible futures that share predetermined elements. For any scenario project—even one with a topical focus and a set of predetermined elements—many plausible scenarios can be created. For that reason, scenario practitioners create several scenarios that together provide a sense of the full scope of plausible futures under predetermined elements and scenario uncertainties. Each scenario reflects uncertain trends, events, or decisions along the path from the present to the future. The diagram also suggests the importance of a timeline in scenario structure: many scenario projects pay relatively little attention to when specific uncertainties occur, because their goal is to evaluate long-run consequences that do not rely on exact timing. However, some planning contexts benefit from much closer attention to the precise pathways taken. For example, early decisions in water planning (to build a dam, for example) can affect subsequent choices. Water planning involves large, irreversible infrastructure decisions, resulting in more narrowly defined options and quantitative indicators that can be used to make decisions (Haasnoot et al. 2013; Quay 2010). In other contexts, however, it may be difficult or impossible to clearly define

Figure 7 The Scenario Funnel

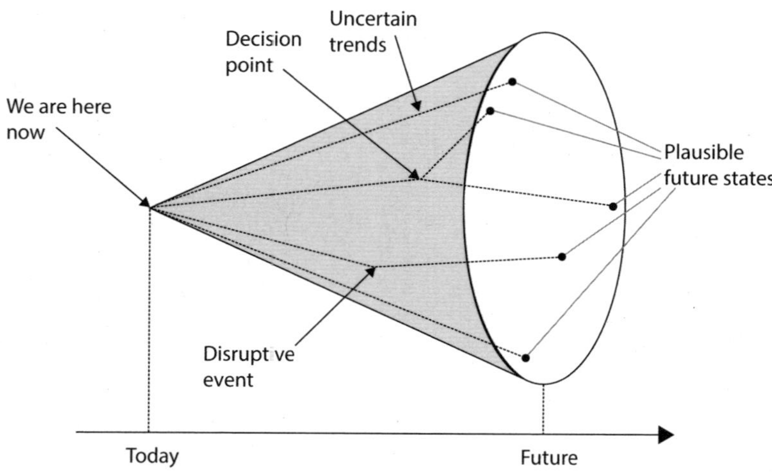

Based on Timpe and Scheepers (2003).

pathways or to know what indicators should be used in key decisions, but even in those cases it is possible to describe a range of plausible scenarios.

Scenario practitioners vary widely in how they conceptualize scenario structure. According to some management theorists, such as Schwartz (1991) and Van der Heijden (2005), a narrative story can represent structure through a qualitative discussion about how things are connected. Different scenarios are thus described by different stories, all of which share certain assumptions but differ in critical uncertainties.

For problems for which there is a good deal of scientific knowledge about causal relationships, though, scenario structure may be better represented by models. These range from conceptual models sketched on flip charts to elaborate quantitative computer models based on cutting-edge scientific knowledge. Because models are so often used to implement the structure of urban scenarios, Walker and colleagues' (2003) uncertainty framework, for analysis of uncertainty in model-based decision support, is useful to explain the ways models represent structure and create scenarios. Walker and colleagues also argue that uncertainties exist in several locations in modeling projects: First, there is *contextual uncertainty*, or how the system will be defined. Second, a model's *structural uncertainty* refers to different interpretations about how a system should be represented. Third, even given a specific context and model structure, model *inputs and parameters* represent additional uncertainties. Therefore, the approach to analyzing structure depends on decisions about the location of the uncertainties under consideration. If they concern the context itself—the natural, technological, economic, social, and political structure of society—then technical models may not be appropriate. Such uncertainties can be analyzed through more qualitative techniques like narratives and cognitive maps (e.g., Jetter and Schweinfort 2011). In other cases, multiple quantitative models may be used to explore different model structures, yet practitioners should remain aware of the limits of knowledge and limitations of quantified uncertainty (Maier et al. 2016). Finally, in some cases planners may vary their inputs into an accepted model in order to understand possible outcomes for a system in which both context and model structure are well known.

In summary, scenario planning involves the creation of multiple scenarios that share predetermined elements but differ in key regards, called scenario uncertainties. All scenarios have a structure that establishes their plausibility: At one extreme, a scenario structure may be a written story describing a chain of events. At the other, formal conceptual or quantitative models may describe different scenarios; however, what model is appropriate depends on the context, structure, input, and parameter uncertainties in a project.

Types of Scenarios

Scenario planning methods have been applied in many different ways and in many different contexts, but scholars have introduced two helpful typologies for all fields. I use these typologies to explain scenario planning practices in the next chapter. In the first typology, Van Notten and colleagues (2003) propose that scenario projects differ in three dimensions: project goal, process design, and scenario content. *Project goals* can range from exploration to decision support and involve choices about norms, vantage points, focus (e.g., on an issue, area, or institution), timeline, and spatial scale. *Process design* refers to the coordination and use of quantitative and qualitative data, stakeholder workshops, and other research activities from highly intuitive qualitative approaches to formal analytic and quantitative approaches, although many projects combine elements of both. Finally, *scenario content* can be simple to complex, depending on the level of detail in each scenario. In a review of futures studies literature, Bishop, Hines, and Collins (2007) describe ways to create scenario content, many of which have not yet been used in urban planning.

The Van Notten typology does not address scenario type. To fill this gap, Borjeson and colleagues (2006) propose a typology of six scenario types in three categories, shown in table 2. *Predictive* scenarios answer "What will happen?" and are either forecasts or what-if scenarios. *Explorative* scenarios answer "What can happen?" and are external or strategic or have elements of both types. *Exploratory* has become the preferred term for this type of scenario, and I use it instead of *explorative* in the following. *Normative* scenarios ask, "How can a certain target be reached?" and are preserving, transforming, or elements of both. In Borjeson and colleagues' explanation, each type can combine quantitative and qualitative elements and include several representations of system structure.

Although urban planners use all three types of scenarios, they use more exploratory and normative scenarios and fewer predictive scenarios because those are generally short term. Isserman (1984) argues that planners should use normative or contingency forecasts to help change the direction of current trends or prepare for anticipated events. Therefore, although many

Table 2 Scenario Types

Category	Principal Question	Types	Directional Focus
Predictive	What will happen?	Forecasts	External
		What if?	External and internal
Explorative	What can happen?	External	External
		Strategic	Internal, under influence of external
Normative	How can a specific target be reached?	Preserving	External and internal
		Transforming	Internal

Source: Borjeson et al. (2006, table 2).

projects may include a current-trends scenario, most focus on normative or exploratory scenarios. I reproduce Borjeson and colleagues' typology here because it is useful and widely cited, but from the perspective of scenario theory, a predictive scenario is impossible, given that the future is unknown. At first glance, a current-trends scenario might be interpreted as a prediction. But because predictive scenarios typically describe a widely disliked outcome, they likely do not describe the most likely future, because communities will probably act to avoid them. Therefore, a current-trends scenario should be considered as an exploratory scenario that investigates the consequences of certain assumptions, typically the long-term consequences of current regulations and trends.

Questions

A substantial scholarly literature has developed about scenario planning in the several fields where it has become an established methodology. Because of the diversity and complexity of scenario planning practices and the different outcomes practitioners seek to achieve with them, however, there is remarkably little consensus about the precise nature of the method. This section introduces three broad questions that have been raised about scenario planning and points to the chapters that address them.

Does It Work?

The first and most intuitive question asks, Does scenario planning work? This question has proved tricky, because definitively answering it requires determining the indicators and outcomes for, respectively, measurement and evaluation of scenarios. Indicators and outcomes, in turn, reflect project contexts and perspectives. In a U.K. climate scenario project, Hulme and Dessai (2008) observe that judging the success of that project's scenarios depends on their aims: predicting, deciding, or learning by participants in the scenario creation process. Hulme and Dessai conclude that the value of scenarios lies primarily in decisions and learning, because scenarios that contain accurate predictions but are ignored are not valuable. However, they note that the three aims are interrelated, since the effect on decisions and learning assumes a degree of confidence in the predictive accuracy of the scenarios.

Even if indicators for an evaluation can be decided on, empirical evidence is often lacking. Rebecca Hendrick, a public administrator, writes about strategic planning methods, of which scenario planning is a subset, as used by government agencies. She concludes that, although scholars have documented the popularity of strategic planning, the literature is still based largely on surveys and isolated case studies, so scholars do not know "the level or extent to which [strategic planning] is implemented, how it is used, and whether it is effective. We know even less about how its implementation, use and effectiveness are likely to change under different governing circumstances, and we know nothing about its negative effects" (Hendrick 2010, 222). She thus urges scholars to improve the scope of case studies and to conduct syntheses of the existing literature, which has not yet been done for scenario planning.

To answer whether scenario planning works, first, chapter 7 describes how urban planning improves decisions and how the goal of improved decision making aligns with the existing performance principle in the urban planning evaluation literature. Second, chapter 8 reports the results of synthesizing empirical research on scenario planning's effectiveness in the urban planning, management, and environmental fields. Although considering very diverse projects, these studies consistently find evidence of learning among the people involved in scenario projects, but they also see mixed results in longer-term impacts on decisions and institutions.

Finally, chapter 9 presents my framework for evaluating the outcomes of urban scenario planning projects, as well as empirical results I obtained through follow-up evaluations on scenario projects presented in methodological case studies in chapter 4. Retrospective interviews showed that the projects had modest but tangible impacts extending beyond ephemeral learning: recommendations adopted in subsequent plans, a right-of-way reserved during a land subdivision, and ongoing implementation work to redesign a major public space.

Much more research is needed in this area of inquiry, an issue I cover in the conclusion. In addition to conducting studies that seek to evaluate different outcomes, evaluation research must be more tightly linked to the scenario planning methods used if it is to inform practice.

Is It Worth the Effort?

Closely related to the first question is whether scenario planning's outcomes justify its expense. Such a cost-benefit perspective has been especially important in the management field, because scholars seek to discern the financial value of scenario planning—or other forms of strategic planning—relative to firms' bottom lines (e.g., Phelps, Chan, and Kapsalis 2001).

This question has been less influential in urban planning, whose practitioners already understand the value of planning and recognize that its value is often widely shared and that plans are prepared to address public problems or respond to legal mandates. It is not irrelevant to urban planning, however, because urban scenario planning has developed a reputation as a complex, comparatively costly form of planning. Although potentially more expensive and difficult than conventional urban planning methodologies, practitioners often find that it yields superior outcomes: a more rigorous, effective, and long-lasting plan. Like any method, scenario planning can be tailored to fit the resources available. I address this question in chapter 6 with empirical evidence on the expense of scenario planning and in chapters 7–9 with additional information.

Does It Perpetuate the Status Quo?

This question arises out of concerns that are more philosophical and political than practical. Scenario planning has earned a reputation as a technocrat's tool because of its long use by the military and large corporations, association with specialized jargon, and frequent use of complex analyses and modeling. As a consequence of its often-elitist method of application, scenario planning can generate scenarios that reflect creators' priorities and perspectives, instead of any transformative vision. Scenario planning can thus entrench the status quo by "anticipating and counteracting crises and threats" that threaten powerful interests instead of questioning their place in society (Sandberg 1976, 257).

Within the urban planning field, this question calls to mind two important, related historical legacies that may explain the impetus for the question. The first legacy is planning professionals' actions in the urban renewal era: under modernism's intellectual influence, planners and city leaders across the United States constructed urban freeways; demolished wholesale low-income, often African American neighborhoods; and built monotonous public housing (Anderson 1964; Hirsch 1983; Klemek 2011; Sugrue 2005). In many cases, these interventions had devastating effects on communities (Fullilove 2004). Although the era was not without its successes—and although historians like June Thomas (1997) have shown that urban planners often resisted the program of urban renewal—the urban renewal campaign nonetheless left a suspicion of large-scale planning among planning professionals. Scarred by the experience, many communities turned in the ensuing decades to alternative modes of practice like participatory or incremental planning, which seemingly avoided the hubris and risk of the urban renewal era.

The second legacy is the long-standing association between urban computer models and problematic decisions. As is explained in chapter 1, such modeling was associated in part with a broader, overly quantitative interpretation of complexity theory, which was often reductive and divorced from practical problems. The failure of several ambitious, comprehensive urban modeling efforts in the 1960s that had ties to urban renewal agendas led to a deep skepticism of modeling, summarized by Douglass B. Lee Jr.'s influential article "Requiem for Large-Scale Models" (Lee 1973). For many planners, the link between the use of urban computer models and problematic decision making persists. Conventional transportation demand models used in planning today, for example, are the intellectual heirs of the quantitative analysis in transportation studies in the 1950s and 1960s conducted in Chicago and other cities that recommended building major freeways through neighborhoods without fully considering the effects of these decisions.

This question is the most wide ranging and expansive, and I incorporate it in this book in three primary ways. First, grounding urban scenario planning practice in collaborative planning theory not only provides normative guidance to practitioners about how to plan in an effective way but also equips them with a critical perspective to recognize and address statements that misinform or manipulate. Second, practitioners can extend the logic of collaboration to include digital scenario tools and ensure the tools serve project goals without imposing planners' assumptions. Chapter 5 discusses model approaches, including transportation demand models, and chapter 6 has tool-use guidelines. Finally, I concede that the specific advice and cases I provide are not always satisfying, and chapter 10 thus considers how urban scenario planning can be more transformative and how it can help address the United States' systemic racial inequality.

Although the book describes scenario planning—and to a certain degree promotes it—it does not do so uncritically. This chapter is cautiously optimistic about scenario planning: it holds potential for urban planning, but it must be used in nuanced, context-specific ways. The book's more specific goal is to foster reflective practice that uses the most appropriate method for a given planning context by presenting critical ideas and perspectives on scenario planning alongside current planning practice.

Conclusion

Originally developed as a war-planning tool, scenario planning methods were popularized as a tool for corporate strategic planning. Today, they have been widely adopted in many fields to analyze significant uncertainty. This chapter describes scenario projects, regardless of the area of application, as sharing a focus on analyzing uncertainties and representing system structure appropriately to ensure plausibility. In the unique nature of urban planning, those scenario projects involve extensive public participation, which is needed to define key values and goals. In addition, they may draw on participation tools, computer models, and more diverse scenario types. Two general categories for scenario projects in urban planning are normative projects, which define a community's desired goal, and exploratory projects, which enable communities to develop deeper insights into trends and prepare for uncertain futures.

Chapter 4 delves into how these two types of projects are conducted, describing practice guidebooks and cases.

Chapter Summary

- Scenario planning involves creating multiple scenarios, constructed by combining predetermined elements and scenario uncertainties, which are foreseeable uncertainties that cannot be accurately predicted.
- Depending on the nature of the uncertainties under consideration, scenarios can be represented as qualitative narratives or in conceptual or computer models.
- Uncertainties are generally broad trends, such as the rate of economic growth, population change in an area, or cultural shifts, but in some cases they can be defined as specific decisions.
- Categories of uncertainties examined by scenarios include society, technology, economics, politics, and the environment. For public sector plans, practitioners often include transportation, infrastructure, governance, and fiscal structures.
- Although many different types of scenarios are possible, a leading typology groups them into three categories: predictive (what will happen), exploratory (what can happen), and normative (how a specific target can be reached).
- Questions raised about scenario planning are (1) Does it work? (2) Is it worth the effort? and (3) Does it perpetuate the status quo? The book answers them throughout in its descriptions of collaborative planning theory, in chapters 7–9 on evaluating outcomes, and in chapter 10 on transformative scenario practice.

3 Competing Approaches

As described in chapter 2, scenario planning arose largely from military and corporate strategic planning practices. Planning practitioners applying the method to urban planning for cities have had to adapt the method to their unique needs. This chapter describes several approaches to scenario planning, presented in roughly chronological order of emergence in the urban planning field. As we see in the following, although each has useful elements, none is suited for the two challenges to long-term urban planning—transformation and uncertainty—raised in the preface. Still, they provide many valuable ideas that have been incorporated into scenario planning practices.

Forecasting

Forecasting creates predictions about the future, both quantitative and qualitative. Historically, quantitative forecasts of population and employment lay at the heart of many urban plans, and this section describes the debate around such forecasts before turning to a broader discussion of whether some people have special insights into the future.

The classic textbook *Urban Land Use Planning* only briefly mentions scenario use, such as for facilitating public participation (Berke and Kaiser 2006, 307). Estimating "how much land will be required in the future to accommodate the anticipated future population, economy, and environmental processes" is central to the land use planning method it describes. But quantitative forecasts have often simply been wrong. Dresden, Germany, the dramatic example of forecasting discussed in the preface of this book, resembles many cities that face uncertain demographic futures (Wiechmann 2008). The difference between forecast and reality for any shrinking city that plans on the basis of a single, optimistic forecast is no mere theoretical concern. At a minimum, flawed forecasts reduce the usefulness of the plans they inspire; more seriously, they may lead to flawed decision making, such as investments in unneeded infrastructure or mismatches between the supply and demand of public services.

One of the most incisive criticisms of the injudicious use of quantitative forecasts was made by Andrew Isserman (1984). Too often, he argues, planners base their work on others' projections and calculation methods, and that reliance overlooks assumptions underlying the projections. Isserman advocates instead for three types of forecasts: a *pure forecast*, or a statement of the most likely future; a *contingency forecast*, a description of possible futures, given different events; and a *normative forecast*, which describes an attainable desirable future. Since what is forecast may not always be desirable, "the objective of planning may be to change that future . . . and prevent it from occurring" (215). For this type of planning, he argues, "methods must be developed to think about the future systematically—to structure thought processes, to gather information, to stimulate imaginations, and to focus inquiry" (213). Isserman briefly mentions scenario writing, but he provides only tentative suggestions. Use of scenarios in urban planning was limited at that time.

How well has Isserman's critique stood the test of time? On one hand, his criticisms of the unthinking use of projections (or others' forecasts) remain valid. On the other hand, his alternative framework remains anchored in a forecasting paradigm, since it retains the belief that a pure forecast is possible in planning. Forecasting methods have in the ensuing years grown increasingly complex, but their performance remains dismal. A U.S. Federal Reserve study found that predictions of important economic indicators had considerable uncertainty; Robert Samuelson, in his summary of its findings, concludes that "the future—not all of it, but much of it—is too complex to be predicted" and that too often "people wrongly think the future will resemble the past" (Samuelson 2017). Scenario planning theorists agree not only on the futility of forecasting beyond the short term but also that the use of forecasts at all can be harmful. Corporate scenario planner Pierre Wack argues that managers should not rely on forecasts, because they are "someone else's understanding and judgment crystallized in a figure that then becomes a substitute for thinking"; instead, they should use scenarios to "develop their own feel for the nature of the system, the forces at work within it, the uncertainties that underlie the alternative scenarios, and the concepts useful for interpreting key data" (Wack 1985b, 89). In later work, Isserman promotes exactly this type of thinking, describing a case in which no pure forecast was present but forecasting to explore possible scenarios could still prove useful (Isserman 2007).

Although forecasting in urban planning has been associated with quantitative estimates, futurists have a long history of making qualitative and other forecasts. A method of systematically consulting experts to develop qualitative forecasts, the Delphi method, was developed by the RAND Corporation in the 1950s. A diverse group of experts are consulted on a topic. In several successive rounds, views are shared anonymously in the group. One well-known Delphi study predicted development of a universal language and weather control by 2000. In light of this and other inaccurate predictions, RAND researchers conclude that "while Delphi can provide a disciplined reification of conventional wisdom, it does not provide any guarantee that the output will bear any relation to how the future unfolds" (Lempert, Popper, and Bankes 2003, 17).

One of the most scientifically rigorous investigations into predicting the future was the Good Judgment Project, conducted by the researchers Philip Tetlock and Barbara Mellers with a group of collaborators at the University of Pennsylvania. In previous research, Tetlock found that foreign affairs experts and pundits on geopolitical events generally perform no better than random guesses (Tetlock 2005). In the Good Judgment Project, Tetlock and his collaborators recruited thousands of people from all walks of life for an online prediction competition. Prediction accuracy for future events of a small number of participants was much better than average. The top 60 participants were called superforecasters and made predictions 30 percent more accurate than those of career intelligence analysts.

Researchers found that several factors improved forecasting accuracy: Despite Tetlock's earlier work that cast doubt on expert forecasts, intelligence and domain expertise were important to explain who was a superforecaster. Participants who practiced making predictions, were more open-minded, worked in teams, deliberated longer, received training in probability, and revised their predictions if they obtained new information performed better than others (Frick 2015; Mellers et al. 2015; Tetlock and Gardner 2016).

What should we conclude from this research? On one hand, good judgment about the future is a real characteristic that can be cultivated through developing expertise and deliberating with others and through being open-minded. On the other hand, an entire research project on predicting probabilities of specific events found that even the best forecasters were often wrong. The laws of probability dictate that correctly making a group of forecasts will be harder than making an individual forecast, meaning even superforecasters struggle to predict entire scenarios. Likewise, scenario planning, which involves many of the same activities that this research found to increase ability to predict the future, should also not base a plan on any one person's prediction.

How does forecasting stack up against the two planning challenges framing this book—urban transformation and growing uncertainty? First, some elements of forecasting may aid construction of alternative scenarios for urban transformation, especially Isserman's concepts of contingency and normative forecasts, because they add rigor and clarity to plans. For example, a normative population forecast for a city hoping to increase its population would provide numbers for the required in-migration and birth and death rates. Second, for external uncertainties, forecasting is not only irrelevant but also potentially harmful. The use of a single pure forecast disregards the empirical evidence that forecasts are often inaccurate, and it leads to planning that ignores the potential for dramatic changes in the very measures being forecast. Most importantly, pure forecasts may distract planners from considering causes of quantifiable changes, such as economic or social trends. As Isserman partially anticipated in 1984, practitioners have developed methods that seek a more expansive view than narrow quantitative analysis allows.

Strategic Planning

Strategic planning attracted attention in the private sector and evolved there for corporate and organizational planning (Mintzberg 1994). It began to find its way into urban planning in the 1980s (Bryson and Roering 1987; Kaufman and Jacobs 1987; Sorkin et al. 1984). The core of organizational strategic planning is consideration of an organization's internal characteristics, such as the organization's mission and values, and external characteristics, such as regulations and laws. This process results in plans focused on particular issues, goals, and objectives rather than on a comprehensive overview of all activities. Organizational strategic planning leads to internal analysis of the organization's strengths and weaknesses. Its external analysis considers trends and external mandates affecting the organization and lists emerging opportunities and threats. The result is analysis of strengths, weaknesses, opportunities, and threats (SWOT), which identifies strategic issues, or "fundamental policy questions affecting the organization's mandates, mission, values, product or service level and mix, clients or users, cost, financing, or management" (Bryson and Roering 1987, 11). Strategic planning often involves an analysis of organizational stakeholders (Bryson 2004b). These plans typically include a limited set of goals and measurable objectives, pursued through programs, policies, and actions. Strategic planning therefore contrasts with the wider scope of comprehensive planning, discussed in chapter 1.

Although a few cities created strategic plans that closely followed private sector templates, strategic planning ideas have typically filtered into urban planning in a more nuanced way (Kemp 1992). Many plans incorporate the concrete focus on specific issues implied by the standard structure of strategic plans: goals, strategies, and clearly defined objectives and implementation steps. The scholar Louis Albrechts argues that European plans increasingly moved away from traditional comprehensive land use planning in the 1990s to include more strategic characteristics, combining a concrete vision with short-term actions (Albrechts 2004; Albrechts and Balducci 2013). His concept of strategic spatial planning is a more flexible theoretical approach to practice than its predecessors: "Strategic spatial planning is not a single concept, procedure, or tool. . . . It is a dynamic and creative process" (Albrechts and Balducci 2013, 19). As a result, post-Albrechts practitioners must look elsewhere for specific guidance for conducting planning projects.

Ultimately, strategic planning provides useful but incomplete concepts for urban transformation. Although a scan of external strengths and weaknesses may draw attention to uncertainties facing an organization, strategic planning's emphasis on qualitative methodologies to guide organizations makes it silent on the more complex forms of analysis needed to understand how external forces may affect cities. Urban plans often require much more rigorous definitions and analysis of scenarios (Bryson 2004a).

Similarly, strategic planning methods do not fully address how to generate a shared vision for the future that is truly different from the past. In fact, the organizational orientation of strategic planning may result in a shortsighted perspective on the potential for long-term changes and external impact. Visioning, the next approach, has been used for precisely that purpose: whereas forecasting and strategic planning typically remain firmly embedded in the present, visioning asks communities to look toward and imagine the future.

Visioning

As with forecasting, creating a community vision has been a long-standing element in many planning approaches, and the term *vision* is used widely in planning. However, whereas planners were once expected to formulate the vision in the first plans written, the term has increasingly taken on a social dimension alongside shifts toward greater public participation. In their content analysis of interviews and planning documents, Shipley and Newkirk (1999) find approximately 20 definitions for *vision* that they further divide into substantive and procedural categories. They discuss some examples of visioning in professional practice and note that these projects typically get community members involved in defining a shared vision, described in words and also often in pictures (Shipley and Newkirk 1998; Walzer 1996).

An influential approach for visioning became known as the Oregon model, developed by Steven Ames (Ames, American Planning Association, and Oregon Visions Project 1993). This method asks five questions:

- Where are we now?
- Where are we going?
- Where do we want to be?
- How do we get there?
- Are we getting there?

It emerged as a popular planning technique in the 1990s, and visioning explicitly invited communities to enter into a discussion of normative values, arguably neglected by more technical or practical forms of planning (Walzer 1996; Walzer and Hamm 2012). Strategic planning upheld the importance of vision, but its methods—focused on a single organization with a small set of stakeholders—made it poorly suited for hosting broader conversations. To fill that gap, planners in the 1990s began to combine participatory methods with creative, aspirational discussions; however, these projects typically resulted in vague outputs, and they thus limited enthusiasm of or guidance for participants to move toward implementation activities. Shipley points out that these practices rest on many untested assumptions, and he finds evidence of mixed success in more detailed empirical research on five such projects (Shipley 2002; Shipley et al. 2004). The Oregon model suggests but does not fully describe how to ground visioning discussions in much more specific analyses of trends in an area. Furthermore, a common weakness of visioning projects is their limited analysis of the feasibility and internal consistency of a vision or the steps needed to achieve it. In a largely negative discussion of the Atlanta Vision 2020 Project, Amy Helling (1998) argues the costly project failed to yield significant results or a clear plan of action because of emphasis on process outcomes and consensus and de-emphasis on substantive expertise. She concludes that planners using visioning should proceed with caution.

In addition to these drawbacks, visioning is an incomplete technique. The method's internal focus can neglect powerful external forces that influence a community's ability to reach its desired vision and its resilience in meeting those forces. Furthermore, because it reaches for a single vision, differing perspectives can be lost or glossed over, and the final version may describe an implausible future with internal contradictions, such as low taxes but high-quality public services. For these reasons, visioning strikes many in planning as a Pollyannaish exercise that distracts attention from the real conflicts cities face. In response, the final approach considered here—consensus building—draws inspiration from theories of negotiation and aims to resolve specific conflicts rather than defining a single shared forecast, goal, or vision for a city.

Consensus Building

The advent of collaborative planning theory in the 1990s coincided with planning practices that shifted to reflect the theory's emphasis on deliberation and that can be analyzed at two levels. First, the theory provided a new perspective on planning practices, including activities that might otherwise appear unchanged, such as facilitating informal negotiations about proposed real estate developments. Forester (1989) argues persuasively that planners' power comes from their central role in a discussion among a broader set of players. Consequently, planners can ensure that all voices are heard, rebut misinformation or falsehoods, and convene key stakeholders, even while performing conventional professional activities. The activities his theory calls for depend on the local context.

Second, collaborative planning theory has inspired entirely new approaches to planning practice that break from traditional approaches. These are described abstractly by Innes and Booher's DIAD (diverse, interdependent interests and authentic dialogue) model, in which planning convenes all the relevant stakeholders, organizes a collaborative dialogue among them, and facilitates the necessary technical analysis and information gathering (Innes and Booher 2018). One of the most influential and widely used models of how to put DIAD into practice is the consensus-building approach (CBA), a dispute-resolution method developed over many years by Larry Susskind and collaborators. Susskind and Jeffrey L. Cruikshank set forth the method in *Breaking Robert's Rules* (2006). CBA identifies relevant stakeholders in a public dispute, brings them to the negotiating table, facilitates a negotiation, and creates agreement (Susskind, McKearnan, and Thomas-Larmer 1999). Important features of CBA include seeking the authorization of powerful decision-making entities for the process and using neutral conveners and facilitators. The method has been applied at different scales and in various settings and is now widely taught in professional graduate school programs.

In many ways, CBA has been a groundbreaking extension of the principles of mutual-gains negotiation to the complex, multiparty situations that abound in urban planning. It remains an indispensable tactic when parties are at a costly impasse or when inaction may result in lengthy legal and political battles or in lost opportunities for the community. CBA also provides a practical, concrete avenue for involving stakeholders in complex decision making in a constructive—rather than adversarial—way. However, as an abstract method of negotiation, CBA contains nothing specific to urban planning. In fact, Susskind, who has spent his career at MIT's Department of Urban Studies and Planning, views himself as belonging to the transdisciplinary field of dispute resolution, and most planning processes today do not closely follow CBA.

Still, many aspects of the CBA model have become mainstream in planning practice, including proactively seeking out nontraditional stakeholders, organizing stakeholder committees to discuss issues and provide input, and ensuring that meetings are facilitated well. Therefore, the influence of consensus building has probably been broader than one might first assume. CBA alone may not be appropriate for creating urban plans, however, because of practical constraints on time and resources and because creating an urban plan is about more than resolving disputes—it is also about engaging with the future. In fact, a research project led by Susskind and doctoral student Danya Rumore applied collaborative principles to the problem of coastal climate adaptation planning and used a wide array of techniques, including climate forecasts and role-playing (Rumore, Schenk, and Susskind 2016; Susskind et al. 2015).

Taking Stock

Thus, by the late 20th century, urban planning had developed at least four alternative planning approaches. Although the preceding discussion began to compare and find similarities among them, the overall picture is one of significant diversity, because each approach has complex sets of assumptions about the goals, context, and purpose of planning and of plans. This section argues that these four approaches are not merely alternative tools for professionals to deploy; rather, they rest on important assumptions about the nature of society and the purpose of planning itself. Although each approach contains valuable elements, each is incomplete for long-range urban planning. Although urban scenario planning selectively draws on all four, they are used in specific ways.

The analysis begins with the extent to which scenario planning approaches are consistent with the ideas of complexity theory and collaborative planning theory introduced in chapter 2. First, conceptually, all four are compatible with a complex systems view of cities. The holistic, problem-focused perspectives of visioning and consensus building encourage planners to consider the interplay of multiple issues. Similarly, although forecasting is occasionally used to analyze issues in isolation, Isserman (2007) shows how forecasting can explore interconnections between issues, and there is already a tradition of systems modeling in forecasting (Smith, Tayman, and Swanson 2001). Systems thinking is also often used in strategic planning to help set priorities for action.

The four methods place their emphases in different places, as seen in table 3. Consensus building and visioning primarily create an internal consensus among participants, whereas strategic planning and forecasting

Table 3 Time, Orientation, and Focus of Four Common Planning Approaches.

		Emphasis	
		External Trends	**Internal Consensus**
Outlook	Present	Strategic planning	Consensus building
	Future	Forecasting	Visioning

call attention to external trends. Of course, divisions are not absolute; strategic planning can incorporate a good deal of discussion about internal issues, such as an organization's mission and vision. Considering these distinctions in light of Habermas's theory of communicative action, we see that consensus building and visioning apply to what Habermas calls the social world (the interpersonal relationships between people and their underlying assumptions and knowledge), whereas forecasting and strategic planning are to a greater extent concerned with the objective world (the physical reality of cities).

The four methods' social and temporal outlooks provide another means of comparison. As discussed, collaborative planning theory describes a pluralist world composed of people and organizations with diverse perspectives, and it suggests a method for resolving disputes. Strategic planning, through its focus on defining a shared organizational mission and its assumption of differing external interests, is also compatible with a pluralist view. However, this is not the only way to view society; some see it as essentially about conflict, whereas others presume harmony (Sandberg 1976). In its focus on creating a single outlook, visioning necessarily involves ironing over those fundamental disagreements. Similarly, pure or normative forecasts require an accepted set of variables and assumptions.

These differences have consequences for the temporal orientation of each method. Although consensus building places the discussion of competing perspectives at the center of planning, it is largely silent on how and by whom the future should be analyzed, leading to a stress on negotiations about near-term decisions. Although strategic planning emphasizes establishing clear goals and focusing analysis on specific issues, its ability to clarify community values is poorly developed, leading to largely short-term actions. In contrast, both forecasting and visioning explicitly incorporate discussion of the future.

Urban planning today faces a quandary: despite the field's rich methodological toolbox, each of the approaches described here has well-documented weaknesses. Furthermore, differing perspectives and tools make it hard to combine them fluidly. As chapter 4 shows in more detail, scenario approaches developed in planning practice draw on some planning traditions and reject others. Scenario planning makes use of forecasting and visioning to construct alternative futures that are always plausible and sometimes desirable. If the alternative futures in multiple scenarios differ in their views of the future, that may reveal conflicting values and important decision-making trade-offs that fuzzy visions obscure. Finally, scenario projects seek to integrate mutual understanding among participants with robust analysis of external conditions. Good urban plans must simultaneously address how residents conceptualize and shape their city and how external forces outside anyone's control will affect the city.

The next chapter presents scenario planning as a route to a good urban plan.

Chapter Summary

- Urban scenario planning projects draw extensively on four related approaches: forecasting, strategic planning, visioning, and consensus building.
- Scenario planning rejects the notion that forecasting can predict a most likely future; instead, it argues forecasting can only describe outcomes based on different assumptions.
- The outcome of visioning may resemble a normative scenario, but scenario planning projects typically feature greater analysis of uncertainties, more detailed and consistent scenarios, and intertwined desired and undesirable—yet possible—futures.
- Scenario projects often adopt the techniques of consensus building, but they explicitly include discussion and analysis of long-term issues, which consensus building does not.

PART 2

URBAN SCENARIO PLANNING PRACTICE

4 Scenarios in Urban Planning

Previous chapters sketch out the maturation of scenarios in corporate strategic planning and underlying ideas of scenario methodology but probably raise as many questions as they answer. How do the abstract principles of scenario planning integrate with professional goals? How do urban planners involve key stakeholders and individual citizens in creating and using scenarios? How do planners reconcile the exploratory and visionary nature of scenarios with practical and legal mandates to define realistic plans that can be implemented? This chapter answers these questions. The first two sections discuss when scenarios are most valuable for urban planning and introduce a framework for urban scenario planning projects that organizes the remainder of the book. The remaining sections describe the two categories of scenario methods in urban planning practice, normative and exploratory, with examples of each.

Urban Planning with Scenarios

Avin and Dembner (2001) find three important differences between scenario use by businesses and by urban planners. Businesses seek their own survival and prosperity, can use flexible strategies, and can pursue a single business idea. Urban planners pursue the public good, must implement policies, and must reconcile diverse and often conflicting goals and ideas. Of course, urban planners also construct *urban* scenarios that describe particular places through representation, analysis, and visualization. Urban planning practitioners have adapted scenario methods from the business world. This section explains these unique approaches.

In what cases should practitioners use scenario planning? Scholars have long noted that uncertainties—the central focus of scenario methods—are an important dimension of planning. Christensen (1985) observes that planning depends on knowing the problems that stand in the way of a goal and knowing their solutions (she describes solutions as technology). If both are known, programming, or the routine application of existing solutions to problems, is all that is needed. If only one is known, bargaining (to clarify goals) or experimentation (to clarify solutions) is called for. When both are unclear, professionals must navigate a chaotic environment and determine both the substance of a problem and participant preferences. Although this framework usefully separates practice contexts, it does not consider external uncertainties. Building on these and other ideas about uncertainty in planning, Abbot (2005) proposes organizing planning uncertainties into five categories:

- *External uncertainty*, or uncertainty about the wider environment of planning.
- *Chance uncertainty*, or unknowable one-off chance events that affect the city or problem being addressed.
- *Causal uncertainty*, or uncertainty about the situation's causal relationships.
- *Organizational uncertainty*, or uncertainty concerning the motivations and actions of participating organizations.
- *Value uncertainty*, or uncertainty about the values and aspirations of the people and groups involved.

The South East Queensland 2001 Project, an ambitious regional planning project in Australia, used scenarios to navigate these uncertainties (Abbot 2009). In the Queensland project, Abbot explains, the scenario creation exercise successfully addressed external, value, and causal uncertainties. Local officials doing subregional planning, however, tended to prefer better-known local plans over the project's regional scenario. Abbot's framework also reminds us that all planning is vulnerable to chance events, not easily anticipated, even though planning must by necessity focus on

Table 4 Conceptual Framework for Futures Planning

| | | Likely Futures | |
		Known	Unknown
Key issues and problems	Known	Analyzing options	Defining futures
	Unknown	Defining problems	Building scenarios

Source: Avin (2007, 113).

known unknowns. Some call these "black swan" events, which challenge existing assumptions (Taleb 2007).

In what circumstances, then, is scenario planning most valuable? This is ultimately a matter of judgment, but Avin (2007) suggests three rules of thumb that are broadly compatible with the theoretical insights Abbot describes. First, because scenario planning analyzes medium- and long-term trends, scenario projects should be future oriented and concern issues and decisions over at least ten years. Second, it is useful when significant changes (that is, external uncertainties) seem likely and when there is a need to consider their effects. Third, it is beneficial when stakeholders are heterogeneous and hold differing values and views (covered by Abbot's concepts of organizational and value uncertainty). Avin suggests using a conceptual matrix, shown in table 4, as a diagnostic tool during the project-scoping phase. The matrix has two dimensions: the degree of uncertainty about the future and the uncertainty about key issues and problems. When both are known, scenarios are unnecessary, and planners can proceed to analyzing options. When one or both are unknown, scenario planning may be beneficial. When there is only one unknown—Avin calls these "defining futures" and "defining problems" (2007, 113)—scenarios can clarify a community vision or come to key agreement on problems. When both are unknown, Avin suggests that a full-blown scenario process can address both needs simultaneously.

Other aspects of project context may also come into play. Volkery and Ribeiro (2009) argue that scenarios can be used in two ways in public policy contexts: early in the policy-making process, they argue, scenarios can stimulate debate about an issue and facilitate stakeholder engagement. Later on, when specific policies are under consideration, more direct scenario-based decision support can analyze specific options and inform implementation activities. As this chapter shows, scenarios' uses roughly align with this continuum in urban planning.

Avin (2007) asserts that creating planning scenarios follows two parallel tracks (figure 8). One is analytic and explores trends from a technical point of view, constructs plausible scenarios, and evaluates them. The other track involves a dialogue among stakeholders about goals and objectives, which define desired futures. Avin's model provides a useful starting point for discussing how business scenario planning is adapted for urban planning: A business's scenario planning has only itself for a stakeholder. Scenario-based urban planning, in contrast, has many stakeholders whose participation is closely linked with research and technical analysis, and it may use evaluation criteria to compare scenarios.

A typical outcome of urban scenario planning is that stakeholders adjust their beliefs and behavior "when they are shown an analysis of the outcome of their particular, cherished futures" (Avin 2007, 110). When stakeholder positions are hardened, the project can still clarify the choices facing the community. Avin's process model for exploratory projects is described later in this chapter.

Figure 8 Avin's General Framework for Urban Scenario Planning

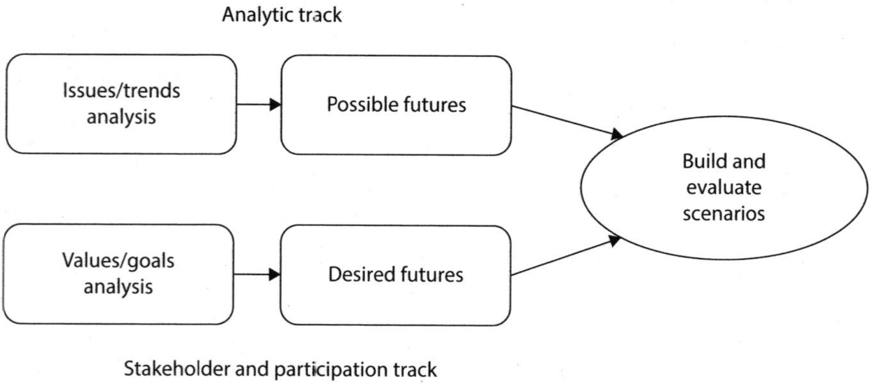

Based on Avin (2007).

Scenario Planning Project Typology

Thus far, this chapter has focused on the theoretical question of when scenarios should be used for urban planning, not the crucial question of how. In the world of corporate strategic planning, scenarios narrowly focus on the firm's prosperity, with goals set by consultants and executives in the comfortable confines of the boardroom, although the best consultants advise their clients to include diverse participants because of the benefits their involvement can bring.

Urban planning is clearly different: it necessarily encompasses a broader array of participants, a broader choice of scope and outcomes, and various organizational and funding models.

A typology (figure 9) of components for urban scenario planning projects formally defines the key dimensions of urban scenario planning projects. This typology is based largely on that proposed by Chakraborty and McMillan (2015) but with my modifications and additions (table 5). Six of the components in the figure describe aspects of a project that are largely key decisions made by the professionals involved: the organizational structure, goal, scenario tools, scope, scenario types, and participation extent. As shown in the figure, four are linked to other categories: Scope and organizational structure are part of the project's financial resources and information infrastructure. Scenario tools and participation extent relate to the process's engagement mediums and stakeholder involvement. The typology has four types of outcomes: improved decisions, learning, institutional change, and system change, which are not in Chakraborty and McMillan's typology.

Chakraborty and McMillan's (2015) typology uses "outcome" to describe the project's result of awareness, vision, or policy recommendations. I rename it the "goal" in adding a category for broader outcomes. I also add a component for information infrastructure, which includes indicators, data, and computer models that provide context for a planning project. I add a double-ended arrow underneath the components to indicate that complex systems and collaborative planning theories extend throughout professional practice and undergird it.

Figure 9 A Scenario Planning Typology for Urban Planning

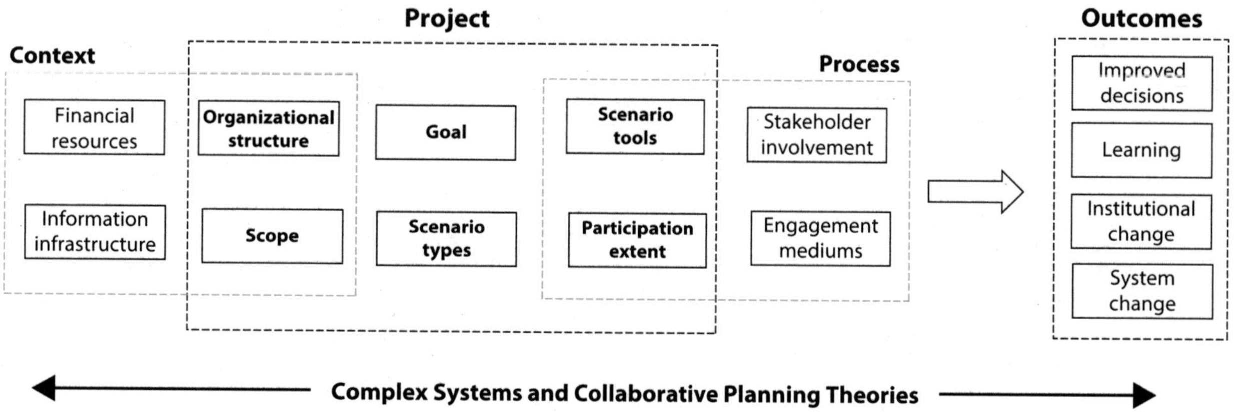

Based on Chakraborty and McMillan (2015).

Table 5 Scenario Typology for Planning Practitioners

Category	Component	Subcomponents	Description
Context	Financial resources	• Fundraised • Opportunity-based • Statutory or recurring	Project funding and other resources used
Context	Information infrastructure*	• Computer models • Data • Indicators	Existing information resources for a project to use
Project	Organizational structure	• Loose coalition • Strong leader • Unitary	Relationships among participating organizations
Project	Scope	• Comprehensive • Problem-oriented • Single-issue	Project breadth or focus
Project	Scenario type	• Explorative • Normative • Predictive	Primary type of scenario used
Project	Goal*	• Awareness • Policy recommendation • Vision	Intended project result or product
Project	Scenario tools	• Computer modeling • Planning support system • Qualitative	Tools used to create and analyze scenarios
Project	Participation extent	• Inform only • Joint fact-finding • Seeking feedback	Nature of involvement by participants
Process	Stakeholder involvement	• General public • Government agencies • Interest groups	Types of participants in the process
Process	Engagement mediums	• Hybrid • Web-based • Workshops	Medium of participation activities
Outcomes	Improved decisions*	• Minimize bias • Strategy insights • System insights	Specific ways scenarios can improve decisions
Outcomes	Learning*	• Collective • Community • Individual	Learning elicited by scenario projects
Outcomes	Institutional change*	• Community capacity • Policies, programs, and practices • Shared mental models	Institutional changes resulting from scenario projects
Outcomes	System change*	• Behavior change • General plans, laws, regulations, and implementation • Goal performance	System changes resulting from scenario projects

Source: Chakraborty and McMillan (2015), except for components marked with an asterisk, added by author.

Although it is a useful tool for analyzing and comparing projects, this typology does not explain how projects are integrated into specific planning contexts, and it does not describe the planning process followed. Furthermore, although Chakraborty and McMillan acknowledge relationships between these components, they do not explain the most prevalent models for scenario planning, which integrate choices about scenario types, participation extent, scenario tools, and goals. This section addresses this by describing two types of scenario projects, defined by their separate goals.

The two popular types of scenario projects are (1) *normative* projects, which define a community's preferred vision; and (2) *exploratory* projects, which cultivate foresight and learning among participants. Some exploratory projects focus on specific decisions, whereas others have broader goals.

Most projects that use scenarios in urban planning are normative projects. This preponderance is probably due to the well-established tradition of visionary planning, as well as planners' mandate in many situations to define a single preferred plan. All scenario projects that focus on defining a preferred vision assume that participating stakeholders have the ability to make decisions to realize that desired scenario, although scenarios do consider internal and external drivers.

Two normative projects are described in more detail later in this chapter: *Futures 2040* is a regional transportation plan for Central New Mexico. Although this project resembles those of many other regions, it also incorporates a novel analysis of climate change. The Austin Sustainable Places Project, for districts within four exurbs of fast-growing Austin, Texas, shows that normative land use scenarios can be created at a much smaller scale. Using tools different from the regional projects and smaller budgets, this project illustrates how the methods can be translated to the context of district-scale land use planning.

Exploratory projects explore possible futures without necessarily considering how desirable they are from a normative point of view. Planners conduct these projects when they want to deepen their understanding of external forces, by definition not controlled by participating stakeholders. Unlike decision projects, which structure the process of creating a conventional plan, exploratory scenarios are typically conducted separately from that process. Sometimes they occur at the start of a planning project to identify emerging issues and trends to inform the project, such as the Denveright project described by me elsewhere (Goodspeed 2017) or the DVRPC Greater Philadelphia Futures Group (DVRPC 2014b; 2016). Other projects take place after a plan has been created in order to inform implementation. In the third case discussed in this chapter, the Sahuarita Exploratory Scenario Project, the community used exploratory scenarios to facilitate analysis of their general plan's policies amid possible futures. Finally, exploratory projects are sometimes conducted independently of other planning projects to develop scenarios that spark broad public discussion about what the future might hold.

Some exploratory projects focus on specific decisions. Planners often need to know whether a decision should be contingent (made only in specific cases) or robust (made under multiple scenarios) (Chakraborty et al. 2011). Therefore, decision projects often do not identify a preferred scenario but rather evaluate a decision in light of the scenarios considered. This type of project is most applicable when the most important uncertainties are external and therefore out of the project participants' hands.

This chapter's three cases are summarized in table 6.

Normative Projects

The best-developed normative practice model is the transportation–land use plan. Transportation–land use scenarios have two variants: projects creating local land use scenarios and projects using a scenario approach known as *backcasting*.

Scenario planning has been widely used for transportation–land use plans and transportation plans, and two publications provide useful practitioner guidance for them. *The Scenario Planning Guidebook*, published by the Federal Highway Administration (FHWA 2011), advises states' departments of transportation and metropolitan planning organizations. It proposes a six-phase process that asks:

- How should we get started?
- Where are we now?

Table 6 Three Scenario Planning Cases

	Sahuarita Exploratory Scenario Project	Futures 2040: Metropolitan Transportation Plan for Central New Mexico	Austin Sustainable Places Project
Project type	Exploratory	Normative	Normative
Project goal	Awareness	Vision and policy recommendations for regional transportation plan	Vision and policy recommendations for district plan
Stakeholder engagement	Government agencies and interest groups	Government agencies and interest groups	General public
Scenario types	Exploratory	Predictive, normative	Exploratory, normative
Scenario uncertainties	• Amount of support for public financing • Water resources • Access to state trust land • Ability to attract workforce • Availability of recreation • Willingness to create financial tools	• Land use location and types • Transportation infrastructure	• Land use location and types
Scenario tools	• Qualitative narratives • Qualitative analysis	• Computer model (urbanism) • Geographic information system	• Computer model (Envision Tomorrow) • Geographic information system

- Who are we and where do we want to go?
- What could the future look like?
- What impacts will scenarios have?
- How will we reach our desired future?

Each project may have a unique topical scope, but the project sponsor is assumed to be a public agency. The FHWA advises planners to create a baseline scenario that describes what the future would look like if current trends and policies continued, followed by a set of alternative scenarios. The scenarios are compared using indicators, and a preferred comprehensive vision is created, along with a set of strategic actions and performance measures. A follow-up guidebook published in 2017 describes in more detail how scenario planning can be used to meet planning goals (Ange et al. 2017).

Although the 2011 FHWA guidebook has popularized scenario ideas, its 30-page length limits its treatment of many issues. *Oregon Scenario Planning Guidelines*, issued by the Oregon Department of Transportation (2017a) and weighing in at over 240 pages, provides much more detailed guidance on how metropolitan areas in the state can create transportation–land use scenarios. Like the California Sustainable Communities and Climate Protection Act of 2008, Oregon's Sustainable Transportation Initiative created by Senate Bill 1059 of 2010 requires the state's two largest metropolitan regions to conduct scenario planning for meeting statewide greenhouse gas (GHG) emission reduction goals and encourages other urban regions in the state to do the same. This guidebook proposes a six-step process:

- Create a framework for the scenario planning process.
- Select evaluation criteria.
- Set up for scenario planning: evaluation tools, data, and building blocks.
- Develop and evaluate base-year conditions and reference case.
- Develop and evaluate alternative scenarios.
- Select the preferred scenario.

Although broadly similar to the FHWA guidance, Oregon's guidebook is much more specific and tailored to the state's unique planning context. It advises planners to define a base-year scenario and then a reference scenario, which represents the continuation of current trends and policies. It recommends developing up to three alternative scenarios, describing transportation–land use options for each and comparing their evaluation criteria. Finally, from the three alternative scenarios, planners should develop a scenario that describes the region's preferred vision for the future. From the preferred scenario, planners then develop implementation activities.

In keeping with its focus on GHG emissions, the guidebook describes specific tools, particularly the Metropolitan GreenSTEP model, for considering the impact of regional policies such as new taxes or tolls. It also describes computer models that planners can use to create more detailed patterns of land use and transportation, which are then used to refine the assumptions in the GreenSTEP model. Figure 10 illustrates the recommended scenario development process.

The *Futures 2040* metropolitan transportation plan for the Albuquerque, New Mexico, region is another transportation–land use scenario project, and it provides a framework for incorporating additional issues. The region had experienced a dramatic slowdown in economic growth after the 2008 recession. When the metropolitan planning organization (MPO) for the region launched a planning process to create its 2015 long-range metropolitan transportation plan (MTP) in 2013, planners realized that several converging trends would make scenarios a valuable component of their plan. As preferences and needs of millennials and of aging baby boomers changed, interest grew in more walkability and expanded transit service in the region. The financial stress many communities were experiencing created greater interest in addressing congestion through changes in land use instead of costly infrastructure investments. In fact, a simple scenario analysis in the MPO's previous MTP, from 2011, had shown that a com-

Figure 10 Overview of the Scenario Development Process in the *Oregon Scenario Planning Guidelines*

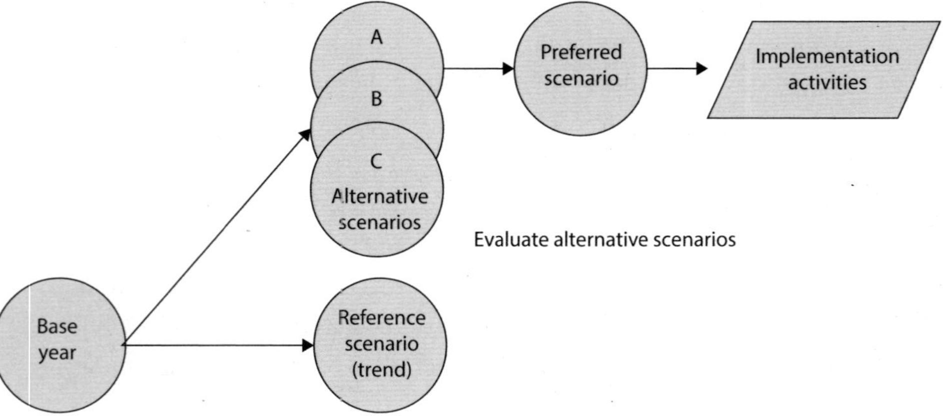

pact land use pattern could greatly reduce automobile congestion. Finally, there was a growing awareness that climate change would result in a complex set of new future conditions, including changes to temperature and rainfall, with important consequences for the region. As a result, the MPO applied for and received a grant from the Volpe National Transportation Systems Center to conduct what would be known as the Central New Mexico Climate Change Scenario Planning Project. This project created alternative scenarios for the official MTP, and it also conducted novel in-depth analysis of the effects of climate change on the region (Lee et al. 2015; MRMPO 2015; Rasmussen et al. 2015).

To create and refine the scenarios, the MPO formed the Land Use and Transportation Integration Committee, comprising representatives from member jurisdictions and other stakeholders, like the New Mexico Department of Transportation and area transit providers (MRMPO 2015). To complement the work of this committee, the MPO reached out to interests not typically involved in planning activities such as public health advocates, housing specialists, and developers. Their input was used to develop a list of key regional challenges and needs, including climate change and resiliency, economic development, more housing and transportation options, balance of jobs and housing, shared and active places, historic and rural preservation, and water resources. Some of these issues then inspired the design of the project's alternative scenarios, and others informed the analysis conducted on them. In three intensive workshops, draft scenarios and related climate change analyses were presented and discussed.

Overall, the project's use of scenarios followed the model described by the *Oregon Scenario Planning Guidelines*, since the aim was to produce a preferred scenario for the MTP. To complement an existing-trend scenario, the project developed three alternatives: Allowable Uses, which illustrated the result of current trends on the basis of existing policies; Emerging Lifestyles, which provided more compact development and transit options; and Balancing Housing and Jobs, which addressed traffic congestion crossing the Rio Grande by adding jobs to predominantly residential areas west of the river. Scenarios used a combination of UrbanSim (to simulate land use change), Cube Voyager (to simulate travel demand and congestion), and other software tools to compute performance measures for comparing the

Table 7 Illustrative Performance Measures on Preliminary 2040 Scenarios for Central New Mexico

Category	Performance Measure	Unit of Analysis	Scenario Difference from 2012		
			Allowable Uses (%)	Emerging Lifestyles (%)	Balancing Housing and Jobs (%)
Accessibility	Proximity to activity centers	Households within 1 mile of activity center	76	73	78
Land use	Proximity to key corridors	Employment within 500 feet of key corridors	17	21	29
Mobility (highway)	Vehicle miles traveled	Total per day	56	49	57
Mobility (public transit)	Ridership	Daily boardings	31	36	29
Mobility (river crossings)	River crossings	Daily number of vehicle trips	47	40	38
Economic competitiveness	Average commute time	Minutes	103	44	63
Safety	Crash rate in high-risk locations	Crashes per 100 million VMT	86	88	87
Sustainability and resiliency	Greenhouse gas emissions per capita	Daily CO_2 equivalent per capita (kg/day)	–5	–14	–7

Source: Lee et al. (2015, 106).

scenarios (table 7). The alternative scenarios were developed by changing zoning assumptions and stipulating development incentives for certain areas (MRMPO 2015).

The MPO organized workshops where municipal and stakeholder representatives were able to review and provide comments on the preliminary scenarios (figure 11). Using feedback from workshop participants,

Figure 11 Stakeholder Workshop in Albuquerque, New Mexico, Part of
Futures 2040: Metropolitan Transportation Plan for Central New Mexico

the agency developed the Preferred scenario, which combined elements of
the Emerging Lifestyles and the Balancing Housing and Jobs scenarios. The
Preferred scenario identified several key locations where changes were anticipated: transit nodes, commercial corridors, and other activity centers.
The plan anticipated coordinating new development, new transportation,
and infrastructure upgrades in these locations. To use as a comparison, Allowable Uses was renamed the Trend scenario. Analyses compared the Preferred and Trend scenarios, including their effects on accessibility, land use,
highway mobility, and sustainability and resiliency, as seen in table 8.

One notable feature of this project is its attempt to analyze scenarios
in light of climate change, as Rasmussen and colleagues (2015) describe.
Analysts working on that element of the project developed a tool that summarized the climate projections released by the Intergovernmental Panel
on Climate Change (IPCC), which had been spatially downscaled by the
federal Bureau of Reclamation. The analysis compared the future period

Table 8 Illustrative Performance Measures on Final Scenarios

	Performance Measure	2012	Trend Scenario	Preferred Scenario
Accessibility	Population proximate to activity centers	51,840	91,578	116,695
Land use	Population proximate to key corridors	72,202	102,426	126,902
Mobility (highway)	Vehicle miles traveled	1,850,00	2,90,00	2,762,00
Sustainability and resiliency	Residential water consumption (million gallons/year)	56,607	82,075	76,753

Source: MRMPO (2015).

of 2025–2055 against the baseline period of 1950–1999 with a data set that included 112 general-circulation model runs, using nine models and three emissions scenarios. The IPCC emissions scenarios were high, or the current path (A1B); medium (A2); and low (B1) with results divided into five categories according to the amount of warming and the predicted change in precipitation for the region. In short, all climate scenarios showed warming, with inconsistent predictions about whether overall levels of precipitation would increase or decrease. Monthly average temperatures, number of extreme hot days, heat waves, monthly precipitation change, extreme precipitation, and drought indicators were also computed. Separating results from model runs that used each of the three emissions scenarios may have resulted in more useful results for the future, because it became increasingly clear that emissions would not follow the low-emissions scenario.

After analyzing the climate data, the MPO concluded that the region should minimize carbon dioxide emissions and plan for a future with greater risks of droughts, wildfires, and floods (Lee et al. 2015; MRMPO 2015). These goals were linked to the scenarios through five performance measures: the amount of development in flood-risk, fire-risk, and crucial-habitat areas; per capita water consumption; and overall carbon dioxide emissions. Although both the Trend and Preferred scenarios moved in unsustainable directions, the Preferred scenario performed better on all metrics. For example, the modeling estimated that, under the Trend scenario, carbon dioxide emissions would increase by 42 percent over 2012, whereas in the Preferred scenario, they would increase by only 30 percent. Dramatic growth in development in floodplains and lands vulnerable to wildfires under both scenarios further highlighted the need for greater effort to limit those risks.

A growing number of MPOs are using scenarios to introduce three major changes to the way they plan transportation. First, their scenario planning considers more than just transportation planning. In California and Oregon these include GHG emissions, and in the *Futures 2040* plan it includes locally relevant measures like the number of crossings of Albuquerque's congested bridges over the Rio Grande. Second, instead of viewing their role as accommodating inevitable sprawl, MPOs can use transportation–land use scenarios to show that regional stakeholders have the power to realize better outcomes through coordinated land use and transportation decision making, a topic discussed in Ewing and Bartholomew (2019). Third, the *Futures 2040* project illustrates the potential for scenario methods to consider emerging uncertainties; in this case, they showed how climate change could influence transportation and land use systems in the future.

Austin Sustainable Places Project

The Austin Sustainable Places Project applied scenario methods in a setting much different from *Futures 2040*'s, a regional transportation–land use scenario project with wide scope and complexity and supported by funding and analytic models from its MPO. This project in four exurban communities (Hutto, Lockhart, Dripping Springs, and Elgin) surrounding fast-growing Austin, Texas, resulted in four small-scale land use plans. The project was led by the Capital Area Council of Governments, which selected the four communities and secured a grant from the U.S. Department of Housing and Urban Development's Sustainable Communities program. Led by planners from the Capital Area Council of Governments, the project team comprised McCann Adams Studio, a local urban planning firm; a group of University of Texas faculty and students, led by Robert Paterson; Fregonese Associates, a consultant; and local planning staff.

The project took a similar planning approach in each of the four communities. Local participants gathered for three participatory events: a visioning meeting to introduce the project and seek specific feedback, a workshop in which participants created preliminary land use scenarios, and a workshop to review and provide feedback on preliminary plans. The scenarios were created and analyzed using the Envision Tomorrow software, written by Fregonese Associates with assistance from the University of Texas. The projects' final reports presented the scenarios and specific implementation recommendations, including changes to zoning and other local ordinances (for more background, see Goodspeed 2013 and Minner 2015).

Since the workshops, one in each community, were a unique feature of this project, we consider them in greater detail. They began with several short orientation presentations about the background of the project, and they transitioned to a hands-on activity conducted in parallel at several tables; figure 12 shows the Dripping Springs session. Each group received a set of colored stickers representing land use types such as single-family residential or urban mixed use. The groups affixed the stickers to a large paper map of the study area. They also recorded other ideas, such as future roads or paths, by writing notes directly on the maps. At each table, a staff member entered the land uses from the physical paper map into Envision Tomorrow. The software estimated future population and fiscal impact of the development, calculated from assumptions about the land use types. At the conclusion of the activity, the groups shared highlights from their discussions.

As documented elsewhere (Goodspeed 2013; 2015), the participants and planners reported that the Envision Tomorrow tool created a connection between the qualitative activity and the quantitative indicators. In several cases, participants were surprised by how much development was forecast for their community, and they had hard conversations about where this development should occur. In addition, a survey documented extensive social learning among the participants, including on the perspectives of others (Goodspeed 2013).

Figure 12 Scenario Creation Workshop in Dripping Springs, Texas, Part of the Austin Sustainable Places Project

Many of the important outcomes of these workshops were not from the software. For example, at the Lockhart workshop, participants coalesced around adding more mixed-use development to their traditional downtown and reconfiguring an existing central square to be more pedestrian oriented. In Hutto, the community brainstormed how a proposed road could improve connectivity and be designed to ensure appropriate vehicle speeds. After the workshops, professional planners reviewed the ideas and proposals generated by workshop participants, produced a final plan based on the workshops, and included further analysis in the final meetings and project report. With a more limited budget and much simpler tools than the *Futures 2040* Albuquerque project, the Austin applied scenario approaches to routine local land use planning. Chapter 9 discusses what was learned through follow-up interviews four years later with the local planners involved in these projects as part of research on how scenario planning should be evaluated.

Visioning and Backcasting for Transport

One common problem with vision projects is that, because scenarios are developed by analyzing current conditions, the results may not achieve stakeholder goals. This often occurs in transportation, a large and growing source of GHG emissions (Geurs and Van Wee 2004). The *Futures 2040* project just described is typical; even its Preferred scenario involved only modest reductions in per capita GHG emissions, and the scenarios did not show dramatic sustainability improvements.

In response to this problem, David Banister and Robin Hickman developed a scenario planning methodology they call Visioning and Backcasting for Transportation (VIBAT), which has been used in the United Kingdom, Canada, Australia, and India (Banister and Hickman 2013; Hickman and Banister 2014). VIBAT adapts backcasting methods developed in the futures studies literature to the problem of achieving a transportation system with much greater sustainability than today's system. The starting point, as in transportation–land use scenarios, is to analyze a business-as-usual projection—that is, the anticipated future scenario if no major policies change. Strictly speaking, this scenario does not provide a forecast, because current policies are likely to change over time. Instead, as in transportation–land use scenarios, effects of existing policies are extrapolated into the future. Next, VIBAT projects develop a scenario of a desired vision of a sustainable transportation system and then a set of policies needed to reach the desired future, as seen in figure 13. Hickman and Banister conclude, "Backcasting can thus be viewed as a normative scenario, but with an additional and explicit step in the development of the pathway back from an image or scenario of the future to the present" (2014, 78).

The VIBAT method shares many similarities with other approaches, shown in figure 14. Hickman and Banister advise organizing the process around three workshops with policy makers and participants, who all participate in every stage. A parallel set of technical activities draws on participant input to define and evaluate possible scenarios. To develop the vision scenario, workshop participants explore key driving forces and define four future scenarios, which are then combined with policy packages

Figure 13 Scenarios in the Visioning and Backcasting for Transportation Method

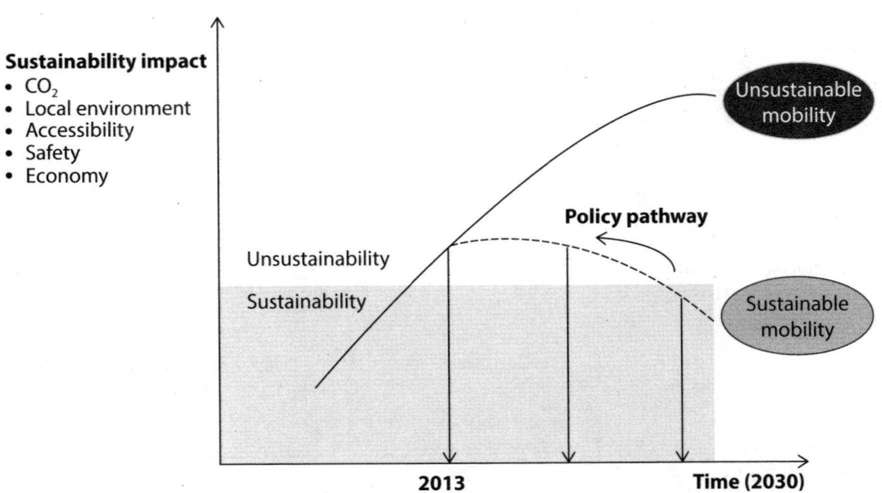

Based on Hickman and Banister (2014). With permission, Routledge via Copyright Clearance Center, Inc.

to analyze their environmental performance. The primary concern of these VIBAT projects is to reduce GHG emissions, although many also use multicriteria appraisal to analyze scenario effects on, for example, accessibility, local environments, and public safety. The VIBAT method is motivated by the authors' belief that "dominant trends, such as the rise in [carbon dioxide] emissions, need to be broken, indeed reversed" (Hickman and Banister 2014, 82); the process is therefore designed to result in visionary scenarios that are linked to the concrete policies needed to achieve them. The VIBAT method assumes that participants have a strong desire for transformational change and a narrow focus on a few quantitative outcomes. Because these conditions are not present in most planning contexts, the method is not described here in further detail, but it may be useful in communities that have already developed a strong consensus for change.

Exploratory Projects

When participants in the planning process control major uncertainties at the heart of the scenarios—such as the locations of new development

Figure 14 VIBAT Scenario Building and Backcasting Study Process

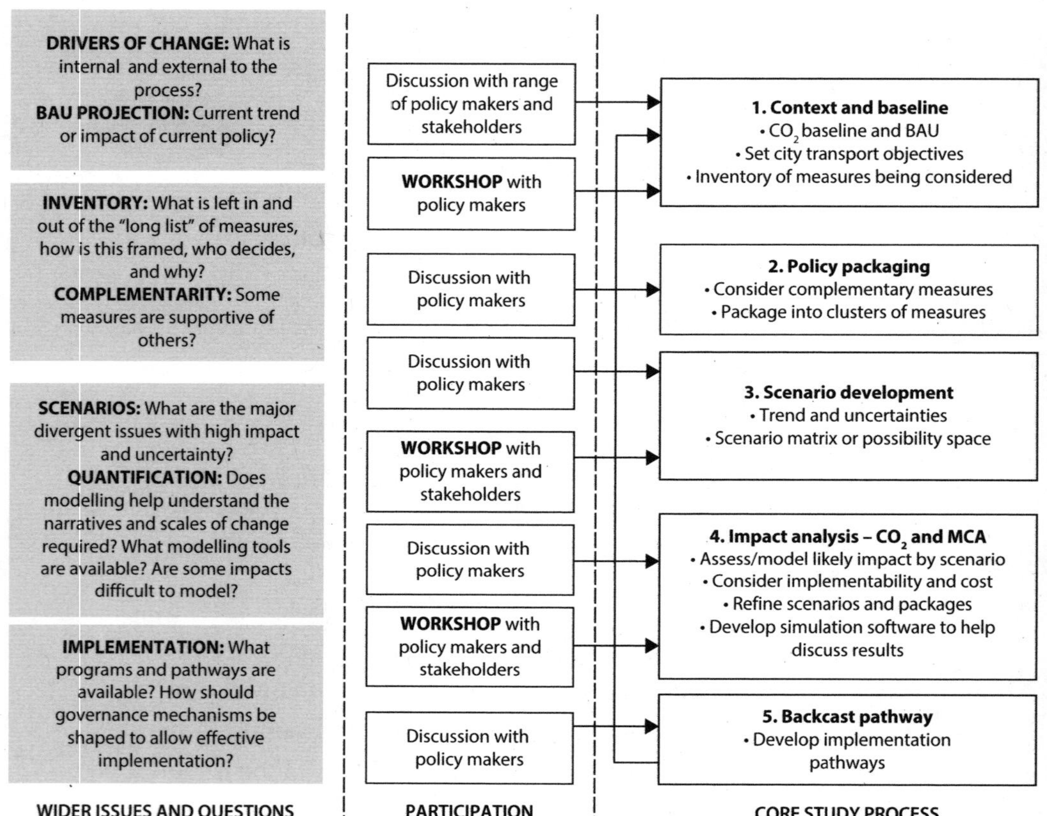

Based on Hickman and Banister (2014). With permission, Routledge via Copyright Clearance Center, Inc.

or transportation infrastructure—normative projects are a powerful method for defining a desired future and developing the more specific plans and policies needed for implementation. In many cases, however, the important uncertainties are beyond planners' control. One example is automated vehicles, which have been the subject of several exploratory scenario projects (see box 2). These cases call for exploratory scenario planning, introduced in this section. The following section discusses more specific versions that seek to more closely integrate exploratory scenarios and decision making.

Exploratory scenario planning draws on the intuitive logics method, which has been widely used in corporate strategic planning (Huss and

BOX 2 Using Exploratory Scenarios to Understand Automated Vehicles

In recent years, no new technology has attracted greater interest among urban planners and the general public than automated and connected vehicles (AV/CVs), which have potentially profound consequences for cities and society (Taiebat et al. 2018). AV/CVs have many uncertainties, however, including when they will be ready for the commercial marketplace, who will own and operate them, and with what regulations and infrastructure policy makers and planners should respond (Taiebat et al. 2018). As a result, AV/CVs have generally been excluded from formal transportation plans, even as planners closely follow the development of the technology (Guerra 2015). The deaths of Tempe, Arizona, pedestrian Elaine Herzberg (struck in 2018 by a self-driving vehicle owned by Uber; Wakabayashi 2018) and Tesla owners Joshua Brown (Vlasic and Boudette 2016), Gao Jubin (Boudette 2016), and Walter Huang (Siddiqui 2019)—who died in 2016 and 2018 crashes that occurred while they were using their vehicles' autopilot mode—further call into question the future of this technology.

Their many uncertainties make AV/CVs ideal subjects for qualitative exploratory scenarios, which can be applied to topics not yet defined enough for quantitative analysis. Two projects to develop such scenarios, although research studies, illustrate how this might be done. Anthony Townsend's report *Re-Programming Mobility: The Digital Transformation of Transportation in the United States* uses a scenario method developed at the University of Hawaii to create four imaginative narrative scenarios about AV/CV technologies' evolution (Townsend 2014). Instead of creating scenarios for only two key uncertainties, this method involves four categories of scenarios: growth (or an extension of current trends), collapse, constraint, and transformation. Set in four U.S. cities, the imaginative scenarios contrast ways AV/CV technologies may be deployed.

Box 2 *Cont'd*

- Atlanta 2028 (growth): Large-scale deployment by a single company results in renewed sprawl, urban decentralization, and undermined transit ridership.
- Los Angeles 2030 (collapse): A lack of adequate coordination results in a flood of vehicles with poor interoperability, reducing walking and causing greater congestion.
- New Jersey 2029 (constraint): AV/CV technologies for bus rapid transit encourage redevelopment of suburbs around existing centers.
- Boston 2032 (transformation): AV/CV technologies that primarily automate urban logistics networks result in greater urban density.

Presented in creative 10-page descriptions, these scenarios build on readers' understanding of current AV/CV issues through entertaining narratives. They nonetheless verge on science fiction and thus provide little concrete guidance for short-term planning actions.

A more policy-relevant example is described in the 2015 Texas A&M Transportation Institute report *Paths of Automated and Connected Vehicle Deployment* (Zmud et al. 2015). This analysis is anchored in a literature review, from which the authors identify 16 uncertainty factors concerning the future of AV/CVs. Factors include the market demand for AV/CV technology, the speed of maturity of the underlying technologies, and public support for new infrastructure. The authors develop two scenarios: The Revolutionary Path is a realistic series of events leading to more rapid adoption of significant numbers of self-driving vehicles. The Evolutionary Path envisions slower adoption of AV/CV technologies. After sharing their scenarios with officials at different state departments of transportation, the authors developed a series of recommendations on how transportation agencies can prepare for the future, regardless of which scenario occurs: establishing external stakeholder groups, building new skills among their staff, designating a staff member to monitor and coordinate AV/CV activities, and more. These suggestions describe practical steps that would likely improve an organization's ability to understand and react to these technological changes and that are not always taken by government agencies focused on present mandates and concerns.

The scenarios resulting from these projects give users specific knowledge about the current nature of these technologies, as well as a fuller understanding of their potential development and consequences. For highly uncertain issues like AV/CV, these two types of knowledge are invaluable for making informed short-term decisions based on a broad understanding of potential consequences and not unduly influenced by narrow viewpoints.

Honton 1987). Unlike methods incorporating quantitative analysis, this method is intuitive because it relies on a purely qualitative exploration to develop the scenario logics (Bradfield et al. 2005). Most associated with the Shell Corporation, consultants from SRI International, and the Global Business Network, the basic method has been applied, relatively unaltered, to urban planning contexts. This section first summarizes it and then discusses how the method is used in urban planning contexts. The last section describes a full application of this method.

Schwartz (1991) distills the intuitive logics method into eight steps. In the first step, planners identify a focal issue or decision and, in the second, inventory key forces in the local environment. In the third step, planners identify important trends (i.e., driving forces) in the macroenvironment that influence the factors identified in the second step. Fourth, planners rank these driving forces by their importance to the focal issue or decision and by the degree of uncertainty surrounding them.

In step five, planners translate the driving forces into "logics," or alternative narratives about the future for a given uncertainty, which provide the basic structure of the scenarios. Although Schwartz suggests that the scenario drivers can be organized along a spectrum, in a matrix, or in other ways, probably the most common approach is to select two that form an axis, which results in four scenarios described by the four possible combinations (Ramirez and Wilkinson 2014).

In step six, they flesh out the scenarios by developing a narrative and incorporating discussion of the issues identified so far, and the seventh step applies the resulting scenarios to the original focal issue or decision. The eighth step is to select leading indicators or signposts that may suggest which of the scenarios are closest to the course of events. The much more detailed account provided by Ralston and Wilson (2006) has many more concrete suggestions for how to follow this same basic approach, including the exact structure and goals of each stage of the process.

Valley Futures Project

An application of the intuitive logics method to urban planning came in the first years of the 21st century, when the Great Valley Center, a California nonprofit, commissioned the Global Business Network to work with participants and create qualitative scenarios for California's Central Valley in a project known as the Valley Futures Project (Cummings 2007; Ogilvy and Smith 2004; Smith 2007). The project leaders interviewed potential participants and selected a diverse group of roughly 25 in each of the project's three subregions of the Central Valley. In two workshops, each lasting two days, the participants in each subregion created four scenarios, for a total of twelve. Table 9 summarizes the four scenarios created by the group convened in the San Joaquin Valley. The scenarios emerged from two primary uncertainties: whether external influences on the region would be positive or negative and whether social conditions would improve or worsen. These far-ranging scenarios illustrated to participants how investments in certain industries with short-term payoffs, such as hazardous waste processing and chemically intensive agribusiness, could result in detrimental long-term consequences. The Tale of Two Valleys scenario explored the consequences of socioeconomic polarization and how ignoring it might undermine regional attractiveness for residential and commercial development.

The Great Valley Center then conducted extensive outreach and education activities, including media coverage of the scenarios (Cummings 2007). The Global Business Network's Ogilvy and Smith (2004) conclude that applying this method and other public sector exploratory scenario planning projects requires greater attention to project framing and goals and to the diversity of participants' perspectives, experience, and priorities

Table 9 Valley Futures Project Scenarios

Scenario	Narrative Excerpt	Conclusion Example	Indicator Example	Strategic Option Example
New Eden	"We didn't stop doing agriculture . . . but we did it differently, with more biotechnology and less water. . . . We learned how to farm in ways that are now setting a new standard for the rest of the world."	Out-migration by people who can leave leads to a decline in local tax revenue.	Increasing unemployment rates and bankruptcies	Level the educational playing field, decrease differences among school districts, and maintain standards for teachers.
Toxic Gold	"But then some of those dumps started leaking . . . [and] we noticed peculiar pockets of cancer."	Short-term benefits must be balanced against long-term results.	More hazardous waste dumps proposed or sited in the valley	Encourage scientific studies on efficient and ecofriendly uses for waste by-products.
Rosa's World	"Once class tensions flared into violence, most of the remaining [people] . . . fled to the coast or the Sierras. . . . The San Joaquin Valley now looked like some of the poorest parts of Mexico."	Air quality implementation must be enforced.	Poor air quality, higher asthma rates, and other health problems	Implement strategic economic development plan that progressively builds on the valley's strengths: first warehouses, then light manufacturing, and then high-tech industries.
A Tale of Two Valleys	"A high school education wasn't enough to gain admission into the information elite, so most Mexican immigrants had to settle for low-paying service work."	Ethnic and class divisions pose risks to the region's success.	Latinx college graduation rates	Develop programs to educate newcomers about political and judicial systems.

Source: Great Valley Center (2006).

than is needed in the private sector. Although the scenario narratives in the cases they consider identify some indicators and strategic options, the narratives require further work as abstract qualitative exercises before they can be effectively applied to decision making on specific plans, policies, or actions. An interesting follow-up study conducted by Zapata (2013), discussed in greater detail in chapter 9, found mixed evidence of project success, with participants reporting some individual learning but with fewer reports on organizational outcomes than had been hoped, because of a lack of follow-up.

Sahuarita Exploratory Scenario Project

The Sahuarita Exploratory Scenario Project used intuitive logics methods very similar to those of the Valley Futures Project, but it sought to connect scenario activities much more closely to typical local-government decision making. The Town of Sahuarita, located 15 miles south of Tucson, Arizona, launched the project while working on three planning processes: a 10-year general plan, a transportation plan, and a proposal to annex state trust land adjacent to the existing town center (Marlow et al. 2015). The project's objectives were to facilitate a dialogue about trends affecting the town, develop an understanding of possible futures, and inform the selection of strategies for the general-plan update. The project began with a round of 24 interviews to identify residents' perspectives and generate a preliminary list of driving forces. Fifteen people participated in the first project workshop, in May 2014, identifying driving forces in, making refinements to, and developing the basic storylines for the resulting scenarios. Instead of picking only two driving forces, the group deliberated about all possible combinations of five driving forces, each of which had two possible outcomes. Participants voted on combinations to create the scenarios. This resulted in four scenarios, summarized in table 10; participants then selected goals and policies from the draft general plan to test against them. Eighteen people at a workshop in December 2014 discussed how the strategies fared under each of the four scenarios and what could be done to overcome barriers or take advantage of opportunities. From this exercise, the group identified robust strategies that would work well across a wide range of

Table 10 Summary of Assumptions in Scenarios Created
for Sahuarita, Arizona

Scenario	Water Supply Availability	Availability of State Land	Ability to Attract Workforce	Willingness to Create Financial Tools for Infrastructure
Low Support for Public Financing	Adequate	Low	High	Low
Constrained Water Resources	Inadequate	High	High	High
Overcoming All Barriers	Inadequate	Low	Low	High
The Best Bedroom Community	Inadequate	Low	Low	Low

Source: Marlow et al. (2015).

futures, incremental or flexible solutions to implement under certain conditions, and hedge strategies to fall back on if worst-case futures occurred. The discussion led to several insights about the town: it may need to question its goal of economic self-sufficiency, increase its collaboration with outside partners to overcome barriers to achieving its goals, and more concretely, form its own water utility (Marlow et al. 2015).

Nearly four years after the project's conclusion, in June 2017, I conducted a phone interview with the town's planning director, Sarah More. She reported that it had been valuable and was still influencing follow-up activities. She said, "Having the conversation, having people think about running out of water, not annexing land, fiscal constraints to implementation, etc., has had a lasting benefit on strategic planning of the community." In the wake of the project, the general plan focused on greater mixed-use development in one area and water and wastewater treatment, which remain the subject of ongoing discussions with county officials. The project also encouraged the town to apply for a U.S. Economic Development Administration grant to develop more areas for technology companies. Although More believed the project was valuable, she thought it should have been done before the general-plan update.

Exploratory Projects Focused on Decisions

Some exploratory projects generate multiple scenarios for creating plans and making decisions while accepting that the participants can only influence—not control—which scenario actually occurs. The primary purpose of creating multiple scenarios is to inform decision making by stakeholders, who do not pick a single preferred scenario; still, such projects do not avoid the question of values and preferences. The urban planner Uri Avin took a diverse array of projects and developed a model for creating scenarios that incorporates both objective trends and values that shape the scope, nature, and evaluation of the resulting scenarios.

As described earlier, the heart of Avin's model is a dual process that simultaneously explores the stakeholder values and empirical trends affecting the project area (Avin 2007; Avin and Dembner 2001), summarized in figure 15. Project goals and objectives are developed simultaneously with research into trends, and both are used to create scenarios. Participants list their diverse values and create scenarios by brainstorming driving forces, grouping similar forces, and analyzing their degree of uncertainty. Forces and values are clustered to create contrasting scenarios, which may remain brief qualitative descriptions or be developed into specific proposals. Avin (2007) argues that creating the scenarios is fundamentally a creative design process, and he shows how the results from a brainstorming exercise can be organized into a matrix to create alternative scenarios. The scenarios are then compared according to a set of common evaluation criteria.

Project participants may want to identify their preferred scenario, but Avin advises against that, because scenarios reflect external uncertainties. Instead, he suggests choosing *actions* leading in a preferred direction, which may or may not be sufficient to lead to a scenario because they also describe internal uncertainties. Avin next advises planners to "monitor events regularly to make sure that your actions are effective and that your target scenario remains valid. . . . Options explored in discarded scenarios may regain their relevance. Above all, good scenarios are durable learning resources. They must be preserved along with the preferred plan" (Avin 2007, 133).

Figure 15 Avin's Scenario-Building Process

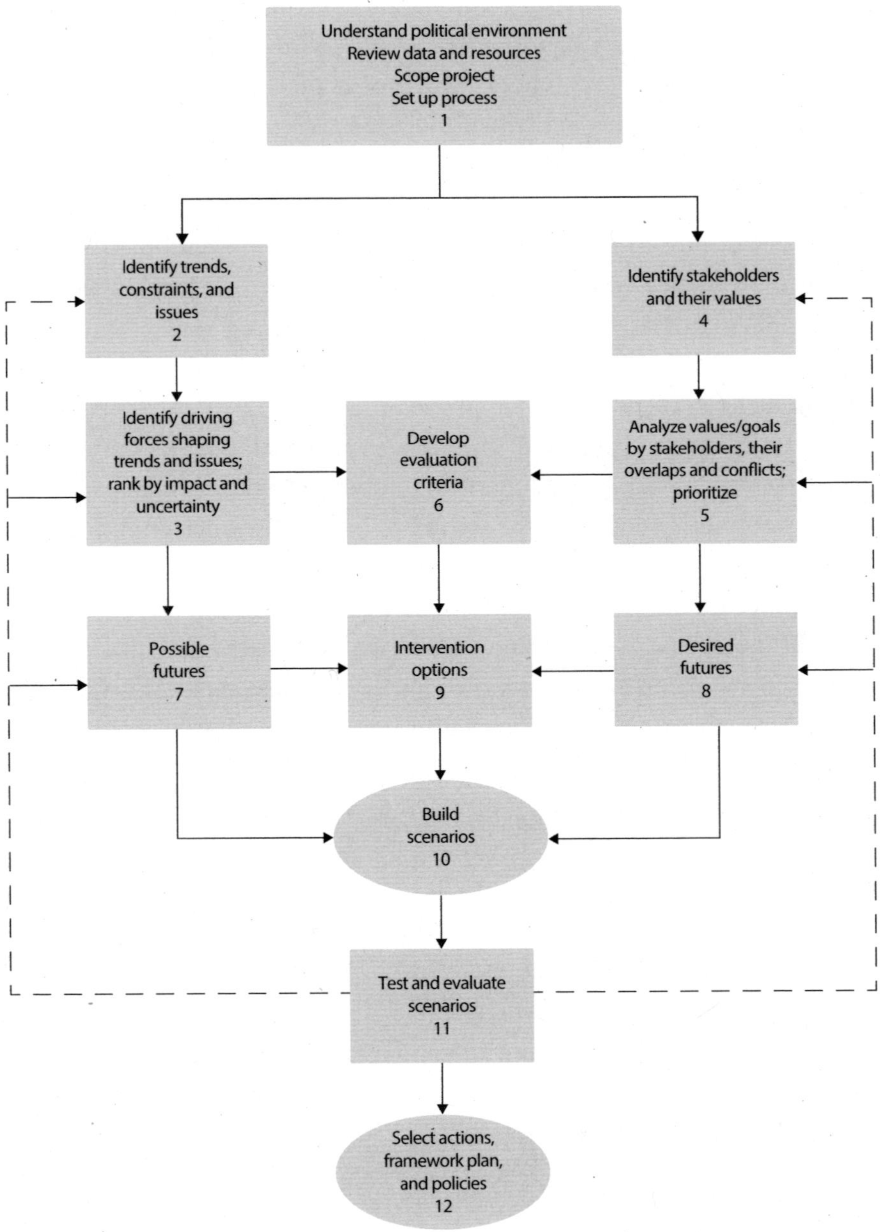

Based on Avin (2007).

Two of Avin's prominent planning projects, although not presented as full case studies here, nonetheless illustrate how this model can be applied to diverse planning settings. The first is the Gwinnett County project described in the preface to this book. This project produced scenarios of macroeconomic conditions, and when the 2008 recession hit, local planners found the plan's low-growth scenario useful for navigating this challenging period. When growth returned, county officials and stakeholders directed growth toward certain areas to realize the International Gateway scenario. In a place with a long history as a predominantly white suburb, this scenario notably embraces the county's growing ethnic and racial diversity and describes how these trends can underpin an economic-development strategy.

A stakeholder group with support from the Maine Department of Transportation, Maine State Planning Office, and the U.S. Department of Transportation conducted the second Avin project, which culminated in the *Gateway 1 Corridor Action Plan* (Gateway 1 Steering Committee 2009). State Route 1 runs along Maine's scenic Midcoast region, but in the first years of the 2000s, its increasing traffic, strip-style development, and disjointed coordination among jurisdictions led local stakeholders to launch a project to analyze these issues and guide planning responses. They developed three scenarios: Full Wind, Riding the Current, and Perfect Storm. After determining that Riding the Current was the best representation of the business-as-usual outcome, they compared it with current conditions along multiple measures of effectiveness. They determined that a "community-centered corridor" would perform best and created a set of action strategies to implement it (Gateway 1 Steering Committee 2009).

Avin's model is suitable for contexts with many conflicting issues and many uncertainties, but practitioners have developed decision-focused models for better-defined planning situations. Two examples at different spatial scales illustrate decision-focused models: Chakraborty and colleagues (2011) advocate constructing a scenario from a limited set of external options combined with internal options. In a case study, they compare the performance of transportation investments under macroeconomic scenarios for the Baltimore-Washington region and argue that such a comparison allows decision makers to determine which options are *robust* (i.e., perform well across different possible futures) and which are *contingent* (i.e., should be implemented under only certain future conditions). Unlike Avin's approach, however, this academic analysis avoids engaging with the conflicting values that underpin disagreements about which transportation investments to prioritize and which metrics to emphasize in decision making.

Applying exploratory scenario techniques does not always require using complex analytic models. A project led by Richard Norton that uses scenarios to conduct planning for coastal resilience illustrates how the same logic as used by Chakraborty and colleagues (2011) can be applied at the municipal scale to analyze issues (Norton et al. 2019). In this project, the primary external uncertainties considered are Great Lakes water levels and storm intensity, both of which are uncertain because of climate change. The scenarios are defined as a combination of assumptions about climate futures and local decision options: (1) current conditions; (2) future development reflecting growth under current rules; and (3) future development under revised local rules for best management practices (e.g., excluding the most vulnerable land from development). For each combination of future conditions and management options, the planners compute a set of indicators, including land area, parcels, and the number of structures damaged by waves or flooding (Norton et al. 2019). Implemented on a modest budget and using relatively routine forms of geographic information system analysis, Norton's project shows that even stripped-down scenario methods can generate useful insights. The narrow focus of the project on specific hazards and management options means that it does not engage the broader set of issues of land use planning, including questions of community identity and the economic and social impacts of land use decisions.

As we have seen, decision projects vary considerably. They include both Avin's complex, multifaceted projects and the topical, analytic projects described by Chakraborty and colleagues (2011) and Norton and colleagues (2019). Some narrowly constructed decision projects take scenario planning ideas to an extreme, involving minimal discussion of more abstract, qualitative issues. In this respect, the exploratory projects described in this chapter do almost the opposite. Often eschewing technical analysis, these projects focus almost exclusively on qualitative analysis and discussion.

Conclusion

This chapter describes how urban planners have adapted scenario planning ideas developed primarily in the private sector to the unique challenge of creating urban scenarios. These practices draw on the approaches described in chapter 3, but they make important modifications. Although those creating urban scenarios accept the importance of rigorous analysis to forecast plausible futures, they reject the flawed notion that planning requires predicting a single future. Similarly, while accepting the importance of stakeholder involvement, scenario creators retain the unique long-term focus of planning beyond the disputes of today. At the heart of the scenario method is a careful consideration not only of a community's desires (the focus of visioning) but also of the potential influence of external factors outside the community's control (a key concern of strategic planning).

Of course, pulling off an effective scenario planning project requires more than adopting an alternative theoretical paradigm. If quantitative analysis is desired, it might require using digital tools to create, visualize, and analyze urban scenarios. Therefore, the adoption of scenarios in urban planning has often been closely related to the adoption of tools that facilitate such scenario-building activities. Furthermore, differences between scenario planning and older forms of practice mean that even projects relying on long-standing tools must use them in new ways and be mindful of important limitations.

The next chapter discusses digital tools, especially those strongly associated with scenario planning.

Chapter Summary

- Scenarios are most appropriate in urban planning contexts in which some or all of the likely futures, key issues, and problems are unknown.
- Urban scenario planning projects all combine technical analysis of key issues and trends with discussion about values and goals.
- A typology of the interrelated components of urban scenario planning projects divides them into context, project, process, and outcome categories.

- There are two general categories of scenario planning projects: normative and exploratory.
- Normative projects aim to produce a single scenario that describes a community's preferred vision.
- Exploratory projects explore multiple possible futures, either to learn what could be or to inform plans or other specific decisions.

5 Digital Scenario Tools

The appropriate tools to use for scenario planning depend on the style of planning conducted, the project's substantive focus, the stakeholder communication and collaboration required, and practical considerations such as budget size. Some projects rely on complex sets of integrated models to design, analyze, and visualize urban scenarios. These projects use digital tools, or computer models, databases, and software programs. Some scenario projects are entirely qualitative and use digital tools sparely, such as an agency website to disseminate a report.

This chapter discusses digital tools and makes some mention of related issues, including qualitative methods and their incorporation in planning processes. The term *planning support systems* (PSS) describes technologies used for information gathering and storage, visualization, communication, analysis, and modeling in planning (Geertman 2006; Klosterman 1997; Vonk, Geertman, and Schot 2007). Since many PSS provide "methods to produce, transform, or transmit knowledge" (Gudmundsson 2011, 145), they fall into the further category of *knowledge technologies*, vehicles for the introduction, application, and creation of knowledge.

This chapter cannot provide a comprehensive overview of the many tools available or go into great technical detail about them. It instead describes the main categories of digital tools most strongly associated with scenario planning practice, discussing their conceptual approaches and commenting on their strengths and weaknesses. Because each project is unique, with local contextual factors and its own goals and values, practitioners must tailor tools to a project's needs. Successful scenario planning also requires participant learning, so project participants must understand results of knowledge technologies. Chapter 6 addresses how to effectively implement digital tools in practice.

If we compare the digital tools used in a scenario-based project with those used in other forms of planning, we find the greatest differences among knowledge technologies—the tools for modeling and analysis. This is partly due to scenario planning's systems perspective, which considers multiple issues outside of any single sector. Modeling and analysis tools for scenario planning must allow users to change variables and assumptions and create and analyze scenarios. In contrast, in a more conventional planning project, variables are often fixed because they are based on forecasts or assumptions. This chapter discusses four knowledge technologies used in scenario planning practice.

The first is generic systems modeling, a set of techniques for developing a shared abstract representation of a system and analyzing how it functions. Although the focus of this chapter is quantitative tools, the section on generic systems modeling also describes some qualitative techniques. Box 3 describes serious games, which are also often used to foster systems thinking. Demographic and economic models, the second knowledge technology, are well-established quantitative modeling approaches that can be applied to scenario projects. The third, place-type development and analysis, is a family of digital tools that facilitate creating and analyzing alternative land use scenarios. The fourth, urban systems models, captures complex interactions between subsystems by applying theories from the real estate, transportation, and housing sectors. To achieve their aims, scenario projects are often more participatory and collaborative than other forms of planning practice, and they can therefore involve distinctive tools in that area. The section on participation, communication, and visualization tools highlights a small subset of digital tools in these areas whose use is most associated with scenario planning practice.

Generic Systems Modeling

Scenario planning is at root a method for planning *systems*, and practitioners often draw on the large collection of methods developed by the field of systems analysis. When a clear understanding of a problem does not exist,

BOX 3 Serious Games as a Scenario Tool

Scenario planning and simulations and gaming have a long association because of the systems perspective common to both. Indeed, as described in chapter 2, the pioneering Cold War strategist Herman Kahn presented scenarios and role-playing simulations as preparation for possible nuclear conflict. The field of serious games, also called policy games, develops novel learning experiences for individuals and groups (Mayer 2009; Mayer et al. 2014; Wouters et al. 2013). The field of serious games has become large, with its own professional societies, conferences, and publications, and is discussed here only in brief.

Serious games were popular in the 1950s and 1960s in urban planning. Urban planning scholars such as Richard D. Duke (Duke 2011; Duke and Geurts 2004) and Allan Feldt created multiplayer games simulating urban planning decisions (Light 2008). A new generation of scholars continues to explore the value of games, especially digital ones, for planning education (Gaber 2007) and public participation in planning (Poplin 2012).

Although scenario planning and serious games share strong theoretical linkages and both are potentially powerful educational and planning tools, each is typically used in a separate professional practice. Unlike serious games, which are set in imaginary places and use fictional player roles, scenario planning applies to a real place and to the real identities of participants. Instead of involving scenario planning project participants in a full-blown serious game, practitioners are more likely to create game-like activities or interfaces to generate and explore scenarios. These can be interactive activities involving stickers to show land use types (chapter 4) or toy blocks to build regional growth maps (chapter 6). Or practitioners provide digital scenario tools for participants to input assumptions into quantitative analyses.

or when there are different perspectives on a problem, diagramming elements and how they relate to one another is useful. One such approach involves creating fuzzy cognitive maps, which show a set of concepts and their relationships (Kosko 1986), which have been used for many purposes, such as working with scenario project participants to create shared conceptual models of the solar energy sector (Jetter and Schweinfort 2011) and Europe's freshwater system (Van Vliet, Kok, and Veldkamp 2010).

To specify more precise, quantitative relationships, causal loop diagrams, the basis of systems dynamics, are used (for an overview of systems dynamics methods applied to business, see Sterman 2000). A causal loop diagram includes variables and their quantitative relationships. Causal loop diagrams reveal positive feedback loops, or relationships that tend to make a system shift toward a new state, and negative feedback loops, or relationships that tend to stabilize a system. In some cases, a model can represent a specific quantity of a resource, such as money or materials, and then test how different conditions will affect that resource. One benefit of systems dynamics is that it can be used to understand the behavior of complex systems over time.

The best-known application of systems dynamics to urban planning was by Jay Forrester, a founder of the field of systems dynamics, who published *Urban Dynamics* in 1969. The extremely complex quantitative model did not encompass qualitative considerations; furthermore, how Forrester's model accommodated well-developed theories of aspects of cities, such as urban economics, transportation research, or sociology, was unclear. A prominent critic was Douglass Lee, who in "Requiem for Large-Scale Models" (1973) charged that Forrester's model could include only one viewpoint. For these reasons, urban systems models today are mostly projects that use relatively simple models to explore a focused issue—such as the model described by Lee himself (1994)—and larger projects that use them to show the interrelation of issues that are typically considered separately.

Although systems dynamics models are not widely used in urban planning practice, two examples illustrate how they can facilitate the development of urban scenarios. A multifaceted research project of the Transportation Research Board's National Cooperative Highway Research Program resulted in the NCHRP Report 750 series *Strategic Issues Facing Transportation*. These reports address transportation-related topics such as freight movement, climate change, technology, sustainability, energy, and sociodemographics. To explore key uncertainties facing the transportation sector, this project created four alternative-future scenarios: Momentum, Technology Triumphs, Global Chaos, and Gentle Footprint. Volume 1 of the series describes the scenarios in qualitative narratives about how trends may unfold (Caplice et al. 2013). The volume 6 research team, for sociodemographics, created a systems dynamics–based model called Impacts 2050 to explore the relationships between changes in land use, employment, transportation infrastructure, and sociodemographics (Zmud et al. 2014). As a systems dynamics model, it is not spatial and facilitates an analysis of these issues only at the aggregate level for an entire city. Still, it explores how transportation-related variables may change because of changes in the sociodemographic, land use, or employment sectors (figure 16).

Another application of systems dynamics is the Environmental Protection Agency's Sustainable and Healthy Communities Research Program, which conducted a prototype analysis of the Durham-Orange Light Rail Project in North Carolina as a case study (Araujo et al. 2016). The analysis began with a conceptual model of the project, developed with extensive input from a diverse array of stakeholders. The study included the land around the proposed stations for the light rail line. The researchers translated the conceptual model into a quantitative systems dynamics model to evaluate three primary policy scenarios: a business-as-usual scenario, a light rail scenario, and a light rail and redevelopment scenario. The model explored 17 additional scenarios of combinations of policy interventions, demographic and market shifts, and technology changes. As figure 17 shows, the causal loop diagram for this model encompasses variables for transportation as well as land use, water, economy, health, energy, and social equity. The analysis led to the conclusion that, although the light rail would result in more positive environmental and health outcomes, it might increase traffic congestion by stimulating real estate development in the station areas, and not all the occupants of the new buildings would necessarily use light rail.

Figure 16 IMPACTS 2050 System Dynamics Model Structure

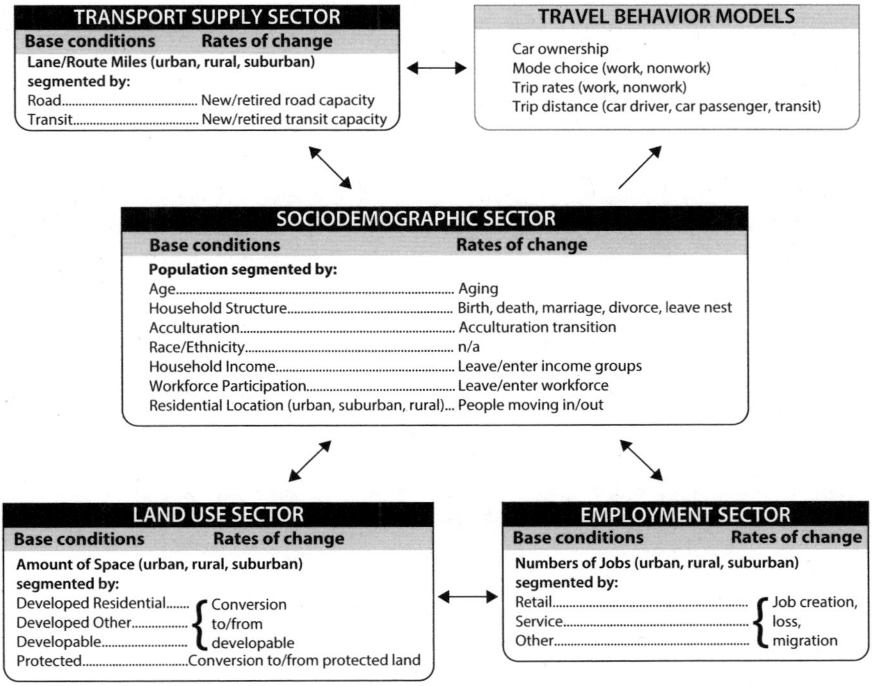

Zmud et al. (2014). Transportation Research Board via Copyright Clearance Center, Inc.

Generic systems modeling techniques have several benefits. Typically, they start without a defined model structure and are readily customized to suit the project context. They can also build a common conceptual model of the problem for stakeholders that crosses typical disciplinary boundaries. Projects that take the further step of developing a quantitative model can use it to explore the sometimes-counterintuitive relationships between variables. These techniques also have costs, however. Starting from scratch and building a conceptual model that bypasses analytic approaches often means that results from generic systems models are difficult to explain and compare. Projects that create quantitative generic systems models may inadvertently marginalize qualitative issues. Systems dynamics models also often do not represent the spatial character of urban phenomena. Moreover, the uncertainty associated with inputs or parameters can undermine

Figure 17 Causal Loop Diagram for Durham-Orange Light Rail Systems Dynamics Model

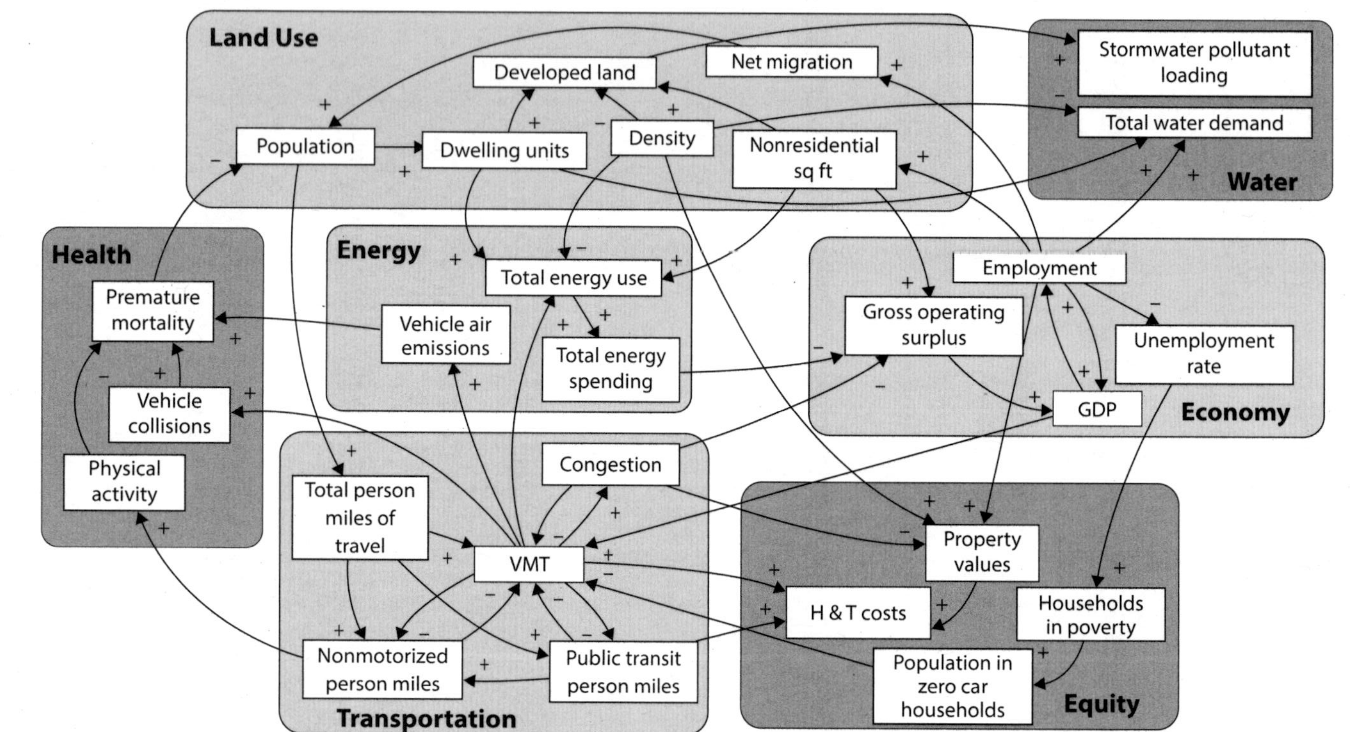

Based on Araujo et al. (2016, fig. ES-2).

confidence in the results. Finally, as the examples illustrate, these models can quickly become very complex and require significant technical expertise to construct, calibrate, and operate. Because of these limitations, systems dynamics seems to work best when a small group of people is developing a high-level understanding of a single problem, as in the cases of environmental policy making described by Van den Belt (2004).

Economic and Demographic Models

Whereas generic systems modeling stresses the uniqueness of each problem context, two modeling traditions apply systems modeling approaches to economics and demographics in standard ways. I describe them only briefly here. These are well-established models that are documented elsewhere. In particular, Klosterman's *Community Analysis and Planning Techniques* (1990), revised and reissued with coauthors as *Planning Support Methods* (2018), describes common analysis and projection techniques for creating scenarios, including methods for projecting populations, analyzing economic bases, and projecting changes to employment.

In economic theory, it is possible to analyze the effects of changes in employment on particular sectors. For example, growth in a technology sector may benefit other sectors, such as services and retailers that serve the new employees and companies that provide supplies. Models that estimate these relationships are known as input-output economic models, since they quantify the material and financial inputs and outputs for the city, state, or nation being analyzed (Isard 1998; Miller and Blair 2009). This type of modeling explores future conditions and is typically conducted at the national or regional scale. Although it is sometimes used to create forecasts, that requires many input assumptions; therefore, it is more often used in scenario planning to analyze the economic impacts of trends specified by previously developed scenarios.

Demographic analysis is often used by planners, most commonly the cohort-component method, which forecasts future population for an area by applying assumptions for migration, mortality, and fertility to the existing population (Klosterman et al. 2018; Smith, Tayman, and Swanson 2013). Isserman (1984) reminds us that such forecasts are simply a mechanical projection showing the results that logically emerge from the inputs provided. Planners should, he argues, use them to create and explore alternative scenarios to "learn how the world can work," rather than using them uncritically (Isserman 2007, 175). This perspective is reiterated in the final pages of *Planning Support Methods*: "Scenario planning that uses the methods described in this book can encourage the people in a community to co-write a compelling story about their past and present that motivates them to work together to create a better future" (Klosterman et al. 2018, 260).

Place-Type Development and Analysis

Generic systems modeling is nonspatial; another family of tools takes a different approach. Place-type development and analysis tools describe a desired future land use pattern as well as other scenarios, such as one showing plausible consequences of current trends. This section provides a conceptual description of these tools, and box 4 lists some currently available to planners. Among urban planning's many topical domains and subspecialties, land use planning receives particular professional focus. One reason is that most local jurisdictions have strong legal powers to regulate land development and are mandated to prepare plans to explain and justify regulations like zoning. Tools for place-type development and analysis break from historical land use planning by considering multiple scenarios and by rethinking the basic conceptual categories of land use planning.

Since the mid-20th century, rising rates of auto ownership and use have led to the expansion of highways and roadways, and land has been developed into large, single-use tracts accessible most easily by automobiles: residential subdivisions, shopping plazas and malls, and office and industrial parks. This pattern of much of the developed world has been widely criticized: low-density development consumes sensitive habitat, automobile domination congests traffic and makes places difficult to access by pedestrians and bicyclists, and vast parking lots and energy consumption lead to polluting runoff and climate change (Duany, Plater-Zyberk, and Speck 2000). Much land use and transportation planning still encourages this form of development, and two are especially problematic. Single-use land use plans and zoning often segregate people by income and race, and they

BOX 4 Tools for Place-Type Development and Analysis

The use of place types has become widespread in planning because it provides a powerful framework for creating and analyzing alternative land use patterns. The following lists leading digital tools that provide this functionality, although, as noted, they often combine it with others.

CommunityViz. A long-standing planning tool, CommunityViz (https://communityviz.city-explained.com/communityviz/index .html) is commercially available as licensed software from the consultant City Explained. Because it is an extension of ArcGIS, however, it requires access to and knowledge of that software. CommunityViz creates and analyzes place types, and it contains a wide range of additional functions that can be flexibly combined, which makes it more akin to a digital planning toolbox. CommunityViz includes sketch tools, a build-out wizard, suitability analysis, and 2-D and 3-D visualization functions. The tool's functionality and applications are described in *The Planners Guide to CommunityViz* (Walker and Daniels 2011).

Envision Tomorrow. Developed by the planning consulting firm Fregonese Associates, the firm improved Envision Tomorrow with funding from a U.S. Department of Housing and Urban Development Sustainable Communities Regional Planning grant and in collaboration with researchers at the University of Utah's Metropolitan Research Center. The tool suite is free and available online (www.envisiontomorrow.org). Core elements (building prototypes, scenario spreadsheets, and an ArcGIS extension) define place types, construct alternative land use patterns, and conduct basic analysis. Envision Tomorrow includes models for analyzing location efficiency, balanced housing, regional- and district-level travel, redevelopment feasibility, health impacts, affordable housing, and fiscal impacts.

SPARC with INDEX Online. A cloud-based service for organizing GIS data and creating and analyzing land use scenarios, SPARC

Box 4 *Cont'd*

with INDEX Online (www.crit.com/sparc) is offered by the consulting firm Criterion Planners. SPARC is a long-standing tool for creating neighborhood-scale land use scenarios (Allen 2001; 2008).

UrbanFootprint. The web-based planning tool UrbanFootprint (https://urbanfootprint.com) was developed by Calthorpe Analytics and is available either by purchasing a monthly subscription or through more specialized consulting arrangements. The core functionality constructs place types and analyzes them along multiple dimensions, including land consumption, infrastructure costs, energy and water use, distance traveled, travel time, fiscal impacts, health impacts, and greenhouse gas emissions. Furthermore, a Risk and Resiliency Module analyzes either current conditions or scenarios for flooding, sea-level rise, and fire risks (see figure 18).

Figure 18 The planning support system UrbanFootprint has functionality contained in many place-type development and analysis tools, including the ability to paint development types, view related spatial data, and analyze and compare scenario performance.

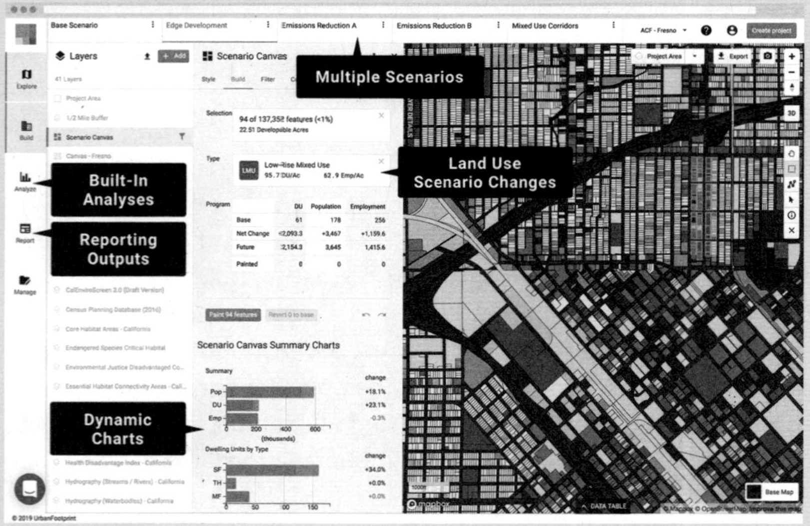

© 2019 UrbanFootprint, https://urbanfootprint.com.

separate residential land use from other land uses (Rothwell and Massey 2009). In transportation planning, widespread use of travel forecasting models has allowed planners to improve mobility—but not travelers' ability to reach their destination (Levine, Grengs, and Merlin 2019). Such models contain many deep-seated biases in favor of high-income automobile drivers (Nostikasari 2015) (see box 5). Contemporary transportation–land use planning seeks to break from this tradition by deliberately planning for mixed land uses and adopting different transportation analysis methods.

Development type is the building block for scenario construction and analysis that does not favor single-use development. In this type of planning, *prototype buildings* are the basic ingredient to construct land use scenarios. These buildings are both generic and specific. They are generic in the sense of not being designed for specific lots or locations, and they are specific in that they are more than a physical description of building size and activities in them, also describing assumptions about attributes like financial characteristics, parking, energy use, and landscaping (Fregonese Associates 2012a). With this detailed analysis, planners can consider whether desired buildings are economically feasible and analyze how the neighborhood as a whole will perform. Once defined, prototype buildings are used to define development types (Fregonese Associates 2012b). A development type might contain only one kind of prototype building or may integrate multiple kinds. A development type contains neighborhood-level assumptions, such as the characteristics of streets and the amount of land reserved for parks, schools, and other public facilities.

A set of development types can be a palette for constructing scenarios, as in figure 19, and these scenarios can continue current patterns or illustrate alternatives of greater density, mixed-use buildings, and walkability. Although development types may be sufficient for comparing land use alternatives for a small area, researchers have found that travel patterns depend not only on neighborhood design factors but also on each neighborhood's broader regional context, including accessibility to jobs and other destinations, access to transit service, and existing walkability.

Therefore, some practitioners take the additional step of combining a development type with an *area type*, or the regional location. For example, the Oregon Department of Transportation (2017b) defines area types according

BOX 5 Transportation Demand Modeling for Scenario Planning

One well-developed area of urban modeling is transportation demand modeling (or travel forecasting). Partly because of long-standing federal funding mandates, most U.S. states and regions have transportation demand models institutionalized within metropolitan planning organizations. The models are routinely used to evaluate proposed transportation infrastructure changes and prepare long-term transportation plans (Transportation Research Board 2007). As a result, transportation demand models are often part of regional-scale scenario construction. A conflict between scenario planning and transportation models is that the latter typically assumes that only a single land use pattern merits prior planning. In contrast, the systems perspective of planning views transportation, land use, and other issues as interconnected: instead of one inevitable future, planning explores plausible alternative configurations to decide which are desirable. Even when transportation modeling explores configurations, it has limitations practitioners should be aware of.

Mobility Versus Accessibility. A growing chorus in the transportation field has criticized its facilitation of *mobility* (the rapid movement of people across space) rather than *accessibility* (the ability of people to reach the destinations they care about). The issue is discussed in depth in *From Mobility to Accessibility* (Levine, Grengs, and Merlin 2019), which argues that even a city with high mobility, where vehicles flow very quickly, can still have low accessibility if destinations are far apart, necessitating long and costly commutes. In Levine, Grengs, and Merlin's view, routine traffic analysis and transportation demand models to reduce congestion mistake a means for an end. In place of measuring congestion, they urge the adoption of accessibility metrics and describe how planners can use them to measure the transportation benefits of local land use proposals.

Assumptions Perpetuate Inequality. Lower-income and minority populations in U.S. cities do not have the mobility of other groups, and Nostikasari (2015) investigates how the travel models typically used by MPOs perpetuate mobility inequality. She compares the assumptions made by the transportation model of the North Central Texas Council of Governments—an example of the widely used four-step transportation model—with the everyday experiences of 15 residents in the Dallas–Fort Worth area. Her findings raise serious concerns about conventional travel modeling practices:

- Household income is one of the transportation model's main variables for predicting the number of trips for each area, and she shows how the model has a built-in tendency to strengthen mobility for residents of high-income areas. In the Dallas model, a high-income four-person household is predicted to make about four times more trips per day than a four-person household in the lowest income category. However, the travel diaries she collected show that, on average, people in lower-income households had to travel farther and longer to reach their destinations.
- The transportation model's mode-choice step assumes that all modes are available to all travelers and even that members of households without a car can travel by car anyway. In contrast, the qualitative data from the travel diaries show that low-income residents had limited access to cars, and even when they did own one, it was not always reliable or available.
- The transportation model's mode-choice step also neglects to account for lack of public safety and residents' physical limitations (such as from old age and disabilities), which make walking and riding public transit difficult for some.

Smart Growth Sensitivity. Most four-step transportation demand models use relatively large zones as their unit of spatial analysis, and they incorporate only a few rough measures of urban form when estimating travelers' decisions. They thus tend to underestimate the changes to travel behavior actually observed when smart growth land use and transportation strategies are implemented,

> **Box 5** *Cont'd*
>
> such as increasing walkability, adding mixed uses, and enhancing transit service. One study in California concludes that many local models have "very little sensitivity" to smart growth, and its authors advocate the use of tools that employ "4D elasticities" to analyze travel as a function of density, diversity, design, and destinations (California Department of Transportation 2007, 4)—the methodology primarily used by the place-type development and analysis tools described earlier. Although proponents of transportation models and urban systems models sometimes argue that their more analytically complex models are superior to place-type development and analysis tools, this discussion shows that simpler models sometimes provide more accurate results.
>
> Many regions have well-developed transportation models, and some regions have made great strides in adapting them to address contemporary questions. However, their roots lie in postwar planning that built freeways for suburban commuters. Therefore, they are often poorly suited to breaking trends and boosting transit, addressing equity, or achieving sustainability.

to their level of destination accessibility, density, and walkable street design: regional center, close-in community, suburban and town, and low-density and rural. Combining an area type with a development type results in a *place type*—an overall characterization of a place. *Place types* allow contextual analysis of anticipated travel patterns of development types, taking into account their relative location in the region.

Planners can then conduct several forms of analysis on these scenarios within and beyond the place-type tools, as shown in figure 20. First, because scenarios constructed from place or development types are extremely detailed, a wide range of descriptive statistics can be calculated from the simple summaries of quantitative attributes associated with prototype buildings and development types. Indicators such as the area of surfaces impervious to rainwater or the amount of land required to accommodate population growth at various densities are often surprising to project participants. Second, indicators can be calculated by combining

Figure 19 The Structure of Place-Type Development and Analysis Tool, Envision Tomorrow

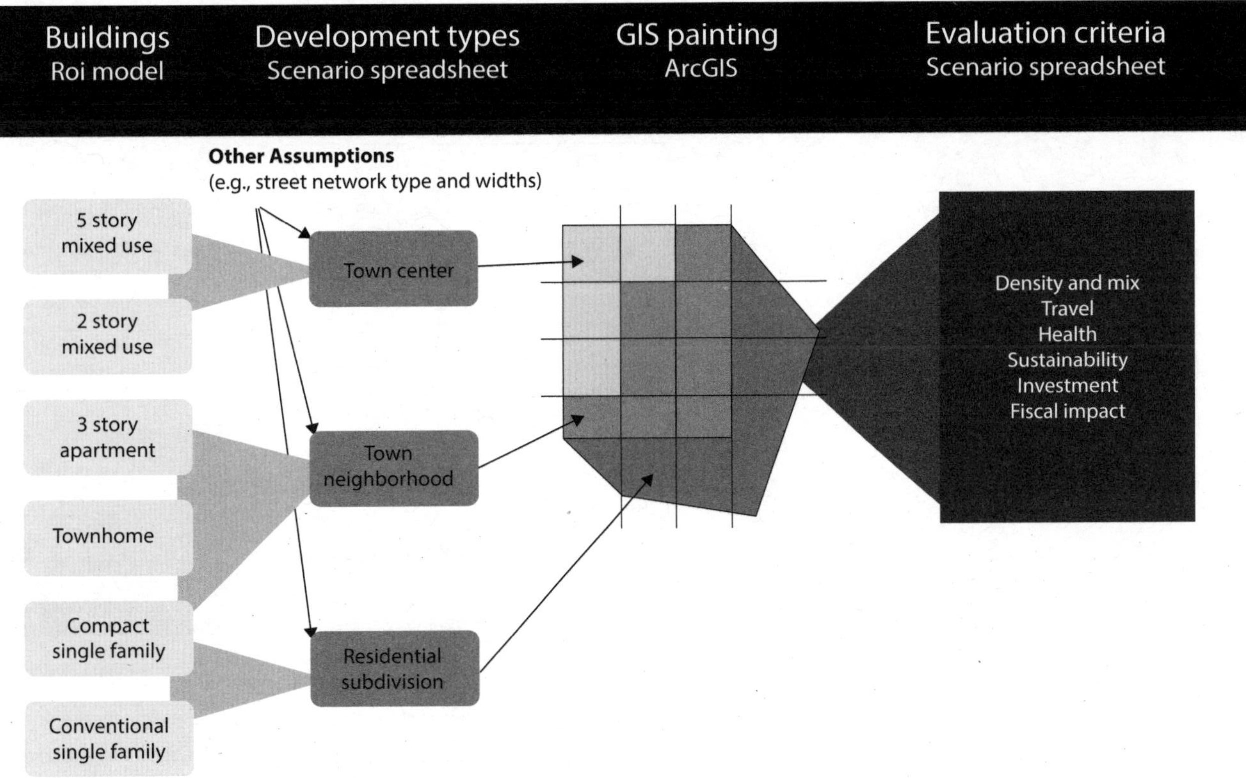

Fregonese Associates, Inc.

Figure 20 Place-Type Development and Analysis Tools Calculate Evaluation Indicators, Converting a Conceptual Development Type into a Quantitative Representation

Development Types

Town center

- Compact and walkable
- Streetfront retail
- Residential, office, and service uses
- Community gathering places
- Mostly 2–3 floors
- One acre contains 32 jobs and 24 households

Quantitative Representation

Building: Infill residential

Lot coverage (%)	68%
Parking coverage (%)	22%
Building size	73,455 SF
Avg. rent	$1,225/month
SF per use	70% residential, 20% retail

Neighborhood: Mixed use

Block size	400 ft
Lanes	4
Lane width	11
Bike lanes	Y
Sidewalk width	12
% Cul-de-sacs	0%
Intersection density	127 / mi^2
Street miles / Acre	0.12
% Land for streets, civic uses, parks	27%

Assumptions and empirical studies

Evaluation Indicators

Population density
Housing unit mix
Land use mix
Developed acres
Housing cost
Housing unit size
Parking spaces

} Descriptive

Energy use
Water use
CO_2 emissions
Vehicle miles traveled
Mode choice

} Predictive

the scenario attributes with outside assumptions, such as estimates of a scenario's fiscal impact on municipalities (based on tax rates) or carbon dioxide emissions per household (based on types of energy available regionally). Third, empirical research findings can be applied to scenario measures to estimate future performance, such as travel behaviors like mode choice (see box 5) and health outcomes like obesity. Fourth, the outputs of place-type tools can be fed to other digital tools; possibilities range from geographic information systems (GIS) to compute spatial measures (such as the proportion of residents near key community facilities in each scenario) to external transportation demand models.

As this section has outlined, place-type development and analysis tools allow planners to create more sustainable land use patterns, and they accommodate many types of indicators. When place-type development and analysis tools create scenarios through open-ended sketching on paper or computer tablet, however, they rely on planners' judgment or external analyses to ensure plausible amounts, types, and locations of development. To further ensure the feasibility of scenarios, some place-type tools include basic financial analyses for each building based on local inputs. There are also limitations to the place-based approach to computing indicators; for example, tools can predict travel patterns for neighborhoods but require other tools to determine where to add public transit lines or which roads will see congestion.

Urban Systems Models

Couclelis (2005) observes that land use models rely on myriad assumptions based on current conditions; they can be useful for analyzing present but not necessarily future conditions. This observation likely also applies to the urban systems models (sometimes called large-scale models) that practitioners and researchers have created to understand cities. Proponents of these models criticize place-type development and analysis for inadequately understanding the interplay among city systems. For example, place-type analysis estimates travel mode choice, but it cannot design a transportation system or illustrate how new transportation infrastructure will stimulate new development. As a consequence, urban scenarios created by place-type development alone may have implausible futures or be based on a poor understanding of the magnitude and nature of changes required to achieve them. Accurately representing city system dynamics requires incorporating many complexities and associated assumptions, typically determined from historical trends or current conditions, neither of which may hold true in the future. The uncertainty around these assumptions makes the resulting models tricky to use in scenario planning, which explicitly considers how present relationships and processes might change. Therefore, using urban systems models in scenario planning involves an important trade-off: the potential of generating insights that simpler models may overlook versus the risk of embedding a hidden conservatism in future scenarios because of their many assumptions.

At a technical level, urban systems models combine generic systems modeling's ability to represent dynamic systems with the spatial specificity of place-type development and analysis models. In fact, as noted earlier, place-type development and analysis models are sometimes used together within a broader set of models to understand connections between proposed land use patterns and other issues, such as impact on transportation patterns. Urban systems models generally represent a city's pattern of land uses, but they differ in how, in what other aspects of cities they include, and in the exact methods used to predict changes. Even more than other types of tools, urban systems models are highly varied and idiosyncratic because of the unique structure of each city and the many types of analysis they perform.

Urban systems models therefore have no one-size-fits-all form but rather are developed by agencies or researchers with specific motivations and perspectives. Consequently, reviews of the literature reveal dozens of different models in practice—as well as discussions that assume a technically sophisticated audience (Hunt, Kriger, and Miller 2005; Schwarz, Haase, and Seppelt 2010; Silva and Wu 2012). Furthermore, a full appreciation of a model's strengths and weaknesses requires detailed investigation, meaning that most reviews can capture only the basic structure and approach of a model.

This section provides a high-level, conceptual overview of four urban systems modeling approaches: cellular-automata-based models, statistical models of land use change, spatial interaction models, and agent-based models. These four categories are inspired by the organization of Landis's (2011) accessible overview of the field and are presented in increasing order of analytic complexity. The descriptions include references to specific models that are freely or commercially available.

Cellular-Automata-Based Models

In extremely simple terms, a city is an area of urbanized land surrounded by nonurban land. Viewed from afar, in satellite images or from an airplane at night, cities look as if they expand organically. Generally, urban growth occurs at the fringes of an existing city, around existing settlements and transportation corridors, and it avoids steep slopes or areas where development is actively prohibited.

Cellular-automata-based models adapt methods of a branch of mathematics known as cellular automata (CA) to describe urban growth, using a regular pattern of spatial units, called grid cells (for an introduction, see Batty 2007). Probably the best known of these models is SLEUTH, created by the geographer Keith Clarke and his colleagues S. Hoppen and Leonard Gaydos (1997). In the SLEUTH model, growth occurs by spreading from existing urbanized areas, near transportation networks, through spontaneous development anywhere, or from outward growth of any cell. Growth of all types is influenced by slope of the ground and areas excluded from development. The model name is an acronym of inputs this model requires: slope, land cover, exclusion, urbanization, transportation, and hill shade (a visualization of slope). Applying the model requires calibration using historical data, but its basic inputs and logic make it appealing for a wide variety of applications and customizations (Jantz, Goetz, and Shelley 2004; Silva and Clarke 2005).

Although the basic SLEUTH model does not consider potential for redevelopment, other scholars have created CA models that more fully account for it (Li and Yeh 2000). More recent work has also incorporated additional complexities, such as variable cell sizes and multiple categories of urbanized land (White et al. 2015). The merit of the more complex models lies in being able to explore, with limited input data, how cities might grow, to produce future growth scenarios. Therefore, these models are well suited for fast-growing places with relatively loose development rules, where the resulting maps of these patterns can describe and analyze future urbanization scenarios. They are less suited for places where governance structure means that specific decisions and rules are more important in understanding potential growth patterns than historical trends.

Statistical Models of Land Use Change

The ability of CA to represent the organic qualities of land use change also inspired statistical land use change models, but these models combine CA with more realistic representations of both land use and the factors that influence changes in it. Conceptually, the boundary between cellular-automata-based models and statistical land use change models is blurry; however, the models are presented separately because of how the two types have evolved.

An example of a statistical land use change model is the California Urban Futures model, which was designed by John Landis along with several related subsequent models. These models also represent cities with grid cells, but they assign each cell to one of several categories instead of identifying only urban and nonurban land. Whether a cell changed categories was determined by statistical relationships among historical changes and by change drivers like local site characteristics and broader neighborhood characteristics (Landis 1994; 1995; 2011; Landis and Zhang 1998a; 1998b). Another mature example of this approach is the Land-use Evolution and Impact Assessment Model (LEAM), created by Brian Deal, Varkki Pallathucheril, and collaborators at the University of Illinois at Urbana–Champaign (Deal and Pallathucheril 2008; Sun, Deal, and Pallathucheril 2009). Provided a specific number of households and jobs, LEAM generates a future land use pattern on the basis of the abstract logic of CA and spatially detailed drivers, such as accessibility or geographic considerations. Over time, the model has grown more complex, and its creators have used it for projects in which they allow some growth drivers, such as transportation congestion, to be updated after each simulated year (Deal and Pallathucheril 2008).

Statistical models of land use change retain CA models' often-useful focus on spatial patterns while adding an empirically based estimation of development probability and taking advantage of the rich GIS data available to planners. However, the models' professional appeal remains limited because of their simple taxonomy of possible land uses, limited ability to analyze transportation infrastructure, and mixed success in forecasting land use. Another limiting factor is their weak theoretical basis: although statistical relationships can be found among historical variables, correlation is not causation. Instead of representing cities as quasi-organic entities influenced by many factors, other urban modelers have focused on cities as being shaped by the locations of jobs, households, and transportation networks and on social science theories that describe how these elements are related.

Spatial Interaction Models

Spatial interaction models emerged from the fields of geography and urban economics and often focus on cities' economic dimensions. With the underlying perspective that commuting times and options are the primary influences on where households choose to live, spatial interaction models examine how companies' locations account for proximity to workers, markets, and real estate costs. Analysts divide cities into zones and mathematically estimate the number of people living in a zone who need to travel to other zones (e.g., for employment), resulting in an origin-destination matrix. Assigning these trips to a transportation network yields estimates of travel demand.

The central role of the transportation system in influencing urban form has made this framework popular in transportation planning, where it underpins the four-step travel model used to forecast demand for transportation infrastructure and evaluate changes to transportation networks (Rodrigue 2017). Future land use patterns are fixed in many transportation applications, however, and not allowed to evolve along with the transportation network. This restriction has inspired tailoring models to answer various questions. A spatial interaction model used to evaluate both land use and transportation decisions is the MetroScope model of Portland, Oregon, described by Moore (2008).

Spatial interaction models have analytic limitations, however; because they lump together people and jobs in zones, they do a poor job of linking zone-based estimates with careful analyses of specific development activities at the sites and scale needed to accommodate different numbers of people or jobs for each zone. Similarly, because they use aggregate data to estimate travel behavior, these models are not well suited for fine-grained analysis of subgroups. They also generally assume that cities are in economic equilibrium instead of ongoing evolution.

Agent-Based Models

Agent-based models seek to make up for other models' weaknesses, but do so at the cost of great additional complexity. Agent-based models are similar to spatial interaction models but avoid the limitations of more aggregate spatial interaction models by introducing agents representing individual people, firms, and developers as the units of simulation.

Paul Waddell's UrbanSim, perhaps the most widely known example of this category, includes representative sets of households, employers, and developers (Waddell 2002). During each imaginary year, imaginary people and jobs are created or lost, some households and workplaces decide to move and select new locations, and real estate development creates space in places where it is economical to build. This requires calibrating many formulas from extensive reference data. Although Landis's review of urban growth models makes clear his belief that UrbanSim is the most potentially powerful, he also notes, "Pulling together and organizing the many data layers needed to calibrate and run UrbanSim can take months of full-time work" (2011, 136). Containing dozens of quantitative models fitted with historical data, UrbanSim unsurprisingly often produces results that strongly resemble the past. Moreover, like many of the models discussed here, UrbanSim does not provide quantitative measures of error. In an article presenting the model, Waddell compares a prediction by the model against real-world change and observes that the model could not foresee "isolated events" such as the downsizing of a major paper plant or the opening of a new mall, two events that could be easily anticipated—and analyzed—from a scenario point of view. Although he argues that his model should "come out of the 'black box'" and be used to support dialogue among participants (2002, 312), its complexity and rigidity present obstacles to using it in this way.

In sum, although many urban systems models have been created, they all have caveats and trade-offs. Practitioners must reflect carefully on the models' suitability for their project. Regardless of which model is chosen, the development of scenarios commonly requires practitioners to engage in participation, communication, and visualization. The next section addresses the use of digital tools for these important activities.

Tools for Participation, Communication, and Visualization

Most tools in the participation, communication, and visualization category are not specific to scenario planning per se; rather, they are part of the planning and design field's broader toolkit. This section first reviews researchers' conclusions about the visualization tools scenario planning often incorporates, such as GIS maps and visual simulations. It then discusses in greater detail two digital tools used to facilitate participation in scenario planning.

Empirical research on visualization mediums within planning practice highlights some considerations about digital tools for participation, communication, and visualization use. Al-Kodmany (1999) argues that sketches and GIS maps are most effective at the early stages of a planning project, and photorealistic renderings prove more useful later, when specific ideas are under consideration. Kwartler and Longo (2008) describe many examples of successfully incorporating different forms of visualizations into planning. Some practitioners have also explored technologies for creating more immersive and vivid experiences, such as overlaying digital data on physical models (Ben-Joseph et al. 2001) or placing participants in decision theaters where visual information is displayed on multiple large screens (Salter et al. 2009). Although there may be settings where such devices are useful, a mismatch is possible between these highly specific visualizations and the abstract issues that are planning's focus. For this reason, as well as these technologies' cost and effort required, many projects instead combine paper maps with static images projected onto screens to inform a discussion about more generic urban scenarios.

The use of visualizations is not without drawbacks, though. Using detailed empirical research from planning workshops in Antwerp, Belgium, Van Herzele and Van Woerkum (2008) argue that GIS maps disconnect people from local knowledge because local knowledge often concerns topics that cannot easily be placed on a map. Similarly, participants' perspectives or frames about how to use maps—for example, for analysis, design, or negotiation—can result in miscommunication or conflict (Carton and Thissen 2009). Such frames can also explain why different participants sometimes interpret the same maps differently.

A study evaluated the effects of six visualization mediums—a community voices film, a policy film, a physical model, a 3-D digital model, an analytic energy consumption model, and a digital summary with visual renderings of proposed developments—used in debates about increasing neighborhood density in Vancouver (Senbel and Church 2011). Researchers held a participatory workshop in a neighborhood undergoing transformation after the opening of a new transit station, and participants provided feedback through surveys and interviews. The researchers considered each visualization medium's potential to facilitate six outcomes of design empowerment: information, inspiration, ideation, inclusion, integration, and independence. The community voices film, energy consumption model, and digital summary all had strong or medium relationships with the information, inspiration, and ideation outcomes. The physical model, 3-D digital model, and energy consumption model led to strong empowerment for the inclusion, integration, and independence outcomes. Although limited by the unique study context and difficulty of measuring these outcomes, this study's findings support the broader conclusion that different mediums serve different participation goals and therefore should be thoughtfully incorporated to achieve project-specific aims.

The mediums just discussed are broadly used in planning practice, and generic tools can be used in the early stages of a scenario project, but two tools have been developed specifically to facilitate online participation in scenario projects. Once key issues and options have been developed, more specialized tools are often useful.

Scenario planning projects often help participants understand how multiple priorities and policies interact. Sasaki Associates developed and used CrowdGauge (http://crowdgauge.org) as part of its Tomorrow Plan, a regional plan for sustainable development in central Iowa. Now available as an open-source tool, CrowdGauge gets the focused feedback needed to develop specific scenarios from a broad audience. Participants using CrowdGauge select and rank priorities from a long list. Next, they are shown how different planning policies and decisions would affect their selected priorities. Finally, they allocate a fixed number of digital tokens to different actions, and an illustration shows how well their funding choices would serve their priorities. A similar tool, Choices & Voices, was created in 2013 by the Delaware Valley Regional Planning Commission as part of its Connections 2040 Plan for Greater Philadelphia. The tool allows participants to select preferred transportation projects and growth pattern for the region and to compare their answers with those submitted by other participants (DVRPC 2014a). Although they in some ways resemble surveys, these tools are unique in that they allow participants to connect their priorities with specific actions a plan could include and to consider how to allocate limited resources. This helpfully sets the stage for more in-depth discussions to refine the plan's final scenarios.

Yet another tool in this category, MetroQuest, allows professionals to communicate scenarios online to participants beyond those able to participate in the in-person engagement activities. It can be used at a kiosk, on a personal computer, in presentations, or in workshops and can be customized. Participants create scenarios by selecting from MetroQuest's library of precalculated scenarios. They compare them against those under consideration, explore relationships between policy choices and specific outcomes, and provide feedback for their refinement to planners (Haas Lyons et al. 2013; Walsh and Burch 2012).

Conclusion

This chapter provides an introductory overview of the wide range of digital tools used to create and analyze urban scenarios. How they are incorporated most effectively into a project is addressed in chapter 6, which rounds out the presentation of urban scenario planning practice.

Chapter Summary

- Urban scenario planning projects use a wide range of digital tools to design, analyze, and visualize urban scenarios.
- To create multiple scenarios, projects use modeling tools in different ways, and practitioners should be attuned to those tools' biases and limitations.
- Scenario projects may use generic systems modeling, demographic and economic models, place-type development and analysis, and urban systems models.
- Digital tools can support participation, communication, and visualization. Those most associated with urban scenario planning allow participants to understand and compare scenarios through websites or interactive multimedia visualizations.

6   Effective Scenario Practice

As with any complex form of professional practice, use of scenarios requires a good deal of judgment and craft, difficult or even impossible to teach. Some practitioners have resisted codifying their approaches beyond a certain point because they believe scenario planning involves more art than science—a stance reflected in the title of Peter Schwartz's classic book *The Art of the Long View* (1991). However, planning methods advance not only through professional innovation but also through research. This chapter describes the goals, structure, and limitations of this type of research in order to provide the context for the discussion of research studies about different aspects of scenario planning practice. It also includes some related scholarly theory, arguments, and perspectives about scenario planning that may be useful for practitioners.

Researchers in several applied fields have argued that research that aims to improve professional tools and practices should be called *design science*, since it differs from conventional scientific research, which primarily aims to describe, explain, or predict the world but not change it. In contrast, the primary result of design science research is design propositions, which inform specific practices, artifacts, or tools. Straatemeier and colleagues (2010) argue planning should also make use of design science to answer "Through which mechanism does a certain intervention impact on a certain context to determine a certain outcome?" (579).

The development of specific design propositions for how to conduct scenario planning in effective ways remains in its infancy. Scenario planning projects can differ in many ways, making it difficult to compare projects or generalize about the relative importance of their elements. Furthermore, most scenario planning design propositions have not been formalized and rigorously tested by practitioners or researchers. Scenario projects also differ in which goals are prioritized, which in turn influences the methods chosen. Yet, despite these obstacles, nothing prevents a deeper understanding of scenario planning from emerging over time, and its growing body of published literature may one day culminate in a complex and robust understanding of what Xiang and Clarke suggest calling "scenariology" (2003).

This chapter discusses four elements of urban scenario planning that apply to the projects described in previous chapters: the qualities of effective scenarios, participation and collaboration in the planning process, indicators to compare scenarios, and digital tool use. Academic evaluations are addressed in chapter 8.

Qualities of Effective Scenarios

Although the practice models described in earlier chapters often provide guidance, professionals have a great deal of latitude in determining the number and type of scenarios to create. Xiang and Clarke (2003) point out that scenarios have a dual nature: Scenarios are methods for organizing complex information about urban places, which they call modeling, but scenarios also serve a bridging function, connecting modeling with planning activities, such as developing goals, strategies, plans, and policies. The authors argue, using insights from psychology, that scenarios support modeling by *chunking*, or organizing information into fewer, more abstract categories. Scenarios also encourage *stretching*, or broadening perspectives to overcome well-documented biases of reasoning that affect decision making (see figure 21). For example, people tend to draw on easily available information, known as the availability heuristic. Xiang and Clarke's account strongly resembles Chermack's (2004) argument that scenario planning mitigates well-known decision-making biases, such as the tendency to use established mental models to think about issues, even if the models are no longer relevant. Xiang and Clarke argue that "a scenario set may be considered good only when it performs both the bridging func-

Figure 21 Schematic of Xiang and Clarke's Hypothesis about the Psychological Benefits of Scenarios to Improve Land Use Planning Decision Making

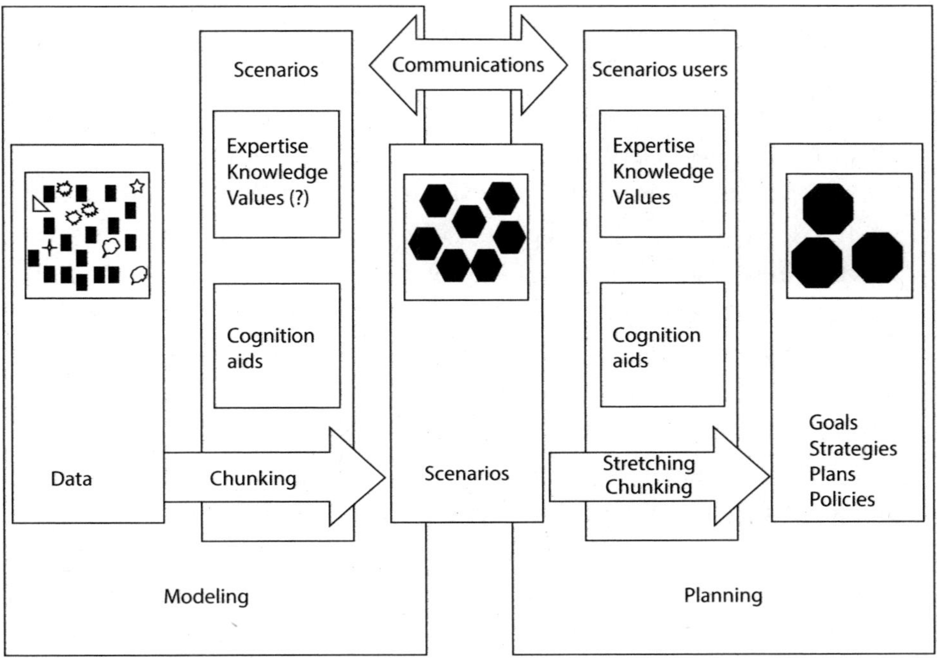

Xiang and Clarke (2003). © SAGE Publications, Ltd.

tion and the stretching function well and contributes to an effective decision making process" (2003, 890). On the basis of this assumption, as well as extensive reading on the use of scenarios, Xiang and Clarke propose qualities for good scenarios: ergonomic design, informational vividness, and plausible and surprising futures.

Ergonomic design refers to decisions resulting in creative scenarios that are both intellectually challenging yet easy to understand and therefore can stretch thinking. Xiang and Clarke propose three ways to stretch thinking: the number of scenarios, themes explored, and time horizon. Although the second and third are usually specified by the type of scenario planning practice selected, all the models discussed in previous chapters leave some ambiguity as to how many scenarios a project should use. Practitioners generally advise creating more than three scenarios but fewer than seven. With at least three, scenarios can be viewed along a spectrum; using too many scenarios runs the risk of confusing participants. Xiang and Clarke set an upper limit of seven on the basis of chunking theory, which holds that most people can keep no more than about seven ideas in mind at once. They also point out that some argue against odd numbers of scenarios altogether, because participants tend to assume one represents a compromise. Especially when scenarios are quantitative, it is possible to create many, but Xiang and Clarke believe this reduces their utility for decision making. In fact, some analysts outside of planning create large numbers of quantitative scenarios (Lempert, Popper, and Bankes 2003), but that practice more closely resembles work done in the field of decision analysis than scenario planning as defined in this book.

Informational vividness of a scenario comprises emotional interest, imaginability, and proximity and directness. These qualities ultimately rely on the artistic quality of scenario narratives and visualizations, but most teams use the simple technique of creating pithy, memorable names for each scenario to help people remember and discuss them. Scenario projects also typically include visual representations—including comparison tables, maps, and renderings—that further help audiences understand the scenarios. Creating person-oriented narratives, or personas, presents abstract issues in an engaging way (Metrolinx 2017; Zapata 2007). Such narratives take the viewpoint of an imaginary person living the scenario, allowing the reader to understand it through effects on daily life.

Finally, the most important element of Xiang and Clarke's scenarios is offering plausible and surprising futures—believable unexpectedness, diversity of perspectives, inconsistency, and comprehensiveness—which highlight lesser-known perspectives or implications of new uncertainties. This quality is subjective, given its dependence on scenario creators' skills and knowledge, and scenarios are thus embedded in the broader context of how a community thinks at a particular moment about the future (Urry 2016). Nostalgia for a time in the past may also be an obstacle to planning, and Baum (1999) describes engaging with and moving beyond such memories to make planning possible.

Participation and Collaboration

Many actors shape cities—municipalities, transportation providers, real estate developers, firms, households, and more—and their engagement informs the goals, values, and priorities of a scenario planning project. Practitioners find scenarios extremely effective in sparking conversations about planning among these actors, because they convey complex information in an understandable way, highlight connections among issues, and clarify the importance of present-day choices.

Virtually all applications of scenarios in urban planning involve two groups of participants: stakeholders and citizens. Stakeholders are representatives of organizations, interests, or communities. Citizens are individuals, typically residents of the study area, who will be affected by decisions. In practice, the two groups do not have sharp boundaries. I briefly discuss here the relationship between the broader collaborative perspective on planning and well-known participation frameworks, then I describe the workshops of a planning project that used toy blocks to create regional growth maps, a participatory method specific to scenario planning to illustrate these ideas in practice.

Well-known theories of public participation may cause practitioners seeking collaboration to miss opportunities to collect necessary knowledge or to foster productive deliberation because of their more narrow focus. In her well-known article "A Ladder of Citizen Participation," Sherry R. Arnstein (1969) proposes an eight-rung ladder for public participation activities, ranked by the degree of power delegated to citizens: manipulation, therapy, informing, consulting, placation, partnership, delegated power, and citizen control. She calls the first two nonparticipation, the next three degrees of tokenism, and the last three degrees of citizen power. Her ladder has proved extremely popular, since it focuses on power and criticizes so-called participatory activities that are actually undertaken in bad faith and may even harm participants.

Democratic theorist Archon Fung argues that Arnstein's ladder provides a "useful corrective to naive and untempered enthusiasm for public participation" but that she assumes power delegation is always desirable (2006, 67). He proposes a broader view of the benefits and forms of participation in an alternative typology with three dimensions: degree of inclusiveness of participants, degrees of intensity of mode of communication and of decision making, and degrees of authority and power. This typology of participatory activities may involve deliberation to clarify preferences or to generate new ideas. In his view, gaining participation may justifiably require limiting power delegation, but participation's ability to improve the legitimacy, justice, and effectiveness of public decisions can make it worthwhile regardless. The International Association of Public Participation also considers the influence of participants on decisions and emphasizes the importance of collecting from them five types of input along a spectrum: inform, consult, involve, collaborate, and empower (IAP2, n.d.).

These ideas and collaborative planning theory have similarities, but their differences are also important. Theories of participation like Arnstein's and Fung's often conceptualize participation as interactions between many participants and a convening organization that is presumed to hold power. Collaborative planning emphasizes the distributed nature of power and the collective nature of planning activities. Organizations acting in accordance with collaborative planning theory would know that, even if they had substantial legal authority, their ability to implement a preferred strategy almost always requires cooperation and support of others.

Collaboration provides a road map for everyone seeking broader support for their priorities. Powerful interests and privileged individuals too often dominate public participation, perpetuating existing social hierarchies (e.g., McCullum et al. 2004). Practitioners frustrated by powerful stakeholders' use of participation to further their own agendas can use collaborative planning to level the playing field. Indeed, theorists such as Forester (1989) provide advice about how to inclusively facilitate and mediate disputes. Most importantly, organizations and individuals—even those with power—may feel frustrated by the status quo, and through collaboration can generate new, creative ideas.

Scenario practitioners have a wide repertoire of participatory activities to choose from in a planning process. One mainstay is the public meeting, which typically involves formal presentations, a period for questions and answers, and sometimes opportunities to provide ideas or vote on proposals. Although useful for exchanging information, this format clearly reflects conventional assumptions about participation. A novel participatory technique, Reality Check, features collaborative ideas (Chakraborty 2011). Planning projects in the Washington, D.C., region used this technique in workshops with stakeholders, who placed toy blocks representing the jobs and housing units forecast for the region, which faced rapid urban growth, on maps to create a spatially explicit growth scenario. The objective of the meeting was not to create a regional growth scenario but instead to foster dialogue about how the region should accommodate growth among the invited developers, elected officials, and community representatives. The blocks and maps focused the discussion on a common problem, but wide-ranging conversation by stakeholders was also welcome. Such a short event cannot generate the creativity and consensus that emerge from long-term deliberations, but it nonetheless successfully adopted the collaborative perspective that participation is as much about obtaining valuable input for the meeting hosts—the real estate organization the Urban Land Institute—as it is about fostering deliberation on a shared problem among diverse stakeholders.

Collaborative ideas do not exclude more narrow forms of participation, such as surveys and open houses. They remind planners of the importance of allowing deliberation and influence among groups to achieve a shared future.

Indicators to Compare Scenarios

The use of indicators in decision making, as in participation, is a topic that extends far beyond scenario planning. This section briefly introduces them and the specific ways they are used in scenario planning.

An indicator is a quantitative measurement of some real-world phenomenon of interest. It incorporates both a conceptual definition and a technical method of calculation (Perdicoulis and Glasson 2011; Wong 2006). Innes argues that, to be influential, an indicator's definition must be accepted by the audience, and a definition can require a lengthy development process to design (Innes 1990; Innes and Booher 2000). An indicator thus refers simultaneously to technical methods of operationalization and measurement and to a social and political process of deciding which measures are most useful in understanding the world.

Innes and Booher propose three general types of indicators in the context of urban planning that embrace the complex systems view of cities. *System performance indicators* provide a high-level "shared sense of direction for the community" (2000, 180). These might include concrete measures like vehicle miles traveled and total waste produced or subjective ones such as quality-of-life ratings from a survey. The key is that system performance indicators relate to basic issues of broad concern and can inform ongoing planning and decision making. The *policy and program indicator* focuses on a particular issue, one useful to the ongoing management and implementation of policies and programs. Because this indicator refers to existing policies, it does not require consensus to be meaningful, and it can be levels of satisfaction, cost effectiveness, or usage of services. Finally, *rapid feedback indicators*, such as traffic reports and utility usage, inform the day-to-day decisions of individuals and organizations.

Scenario plans with quantitative elements typically use system performance indicators to compare alternative scenarios, although the precise terminology can vary: Avin (2007) calls them *evaluation criteria*, Hickman and Banister (2014) describe *sustainable impact*, and the *Futures 2040* plan of New Mexico, discussed in chapter 4, uses the term *performance measures*. However, unlike the system performance indicators for urban planning described by Innes and Booher, those used in scenario projects are projected into the future according to scenario assumptions and analysis methods; they do not describe the city as it is today. Suitable indicators for comparing plans may already exist, whether they are mandated, suggested by external parties, or already in use by the local governments and organizations involved in indicator programs (Phillips 2005; Sawicki and Flynn 1996).

Most scenarios have a qualitative dimension, which complements the picture painted by the comparison indicators. When a plan involves new issues for which there are no existing measures, planners should take the necessary time to ensure that audiences understand and accept the indicators used. For example, several alternative scenarios may meet sustainability indicators equally well, but the community may nonetheless have strong feelings about which scenario it prefers because of the alternatives' qualitative characteristics, such as their urban design qualities or their preservation of important places. Therefore, even projects relying on extensive quantitative analysis should include photos, maps, visualizations, and illustrations that convey the qualitative content of the scenarios.

Digital Tool Use

The nature of cities—and planning activities—makes the scenario-creation and analysis tools described in chapter 5 much more difficult to use than simply running an app. With that in mind, this section returns to the two types of theory—complexity and collaboration—described in chapter 1 to lay out some of the practical and theoretical challenges surrounding the use of digital tools for urban scenario planning. It then discusses available empirical evidence for effective use of digital tools at three scales of analysis: engagement, process, and information infrastructure.

When Jane Jacobs writes about cities, she does not consider them in abstract, statistical terms. Instead, she describes their intricate, place-specific qualities—although physical attributes like buildings, streets, and parks are important, she explains, understanding their role requires examining the unique social and cultural qualities of different neighborhoods (1961). Jacobs's perspective is consistent with viewing a city as a complex system, and it calls attention to the unique qualities of different cities. Cities exist in biophysical contexts quite different from one another; they also contain place-specific infrastructures, policies, and histories. Practitioners must therefore carefully examine any digital tool used to describe an urban place to ensure that its underlying assumptions and logic apply to the specific characteristics and factors at work. This involves much more than simply tuning a model for local climate and land use; it often requires planners to make nuanced assumptions—for instance, about which existing regulations are sacrosanct and which are likely to change or whether deep-seated ideas about neighborhoods and their associations constrain change or make it possible. In short, fitting a digital tool to a place is not merely a technical exercise; rather, it requires input from project stakeholders. Otherwise, the analysis may be so flawed that it can be useless.

Digital tools have been relatively neglected in collaborative planning theory. But, in fact, collaborative planning theory provides additional arguments in favor of digital tool use in a planning project and highlights potentially harmful consequences of applying them rigidly and unthinkingly. One of the important claims made by collaborative theorists is that group deliberation can result in new ideas, which in turn can shape the institutional environment. This perspective is based in part on the philosophy of Jürgen Habermas (1987, 120–126), who distinguishes between the subjective lifeworld (the shared perspective or understanding possible among a group) and the system (the broader abstract social systems like the law and science that transcend everyday discussions), in which technical rationality tends to dominate. I propose (Goodspeed 2016b) that planning theorists have too often accepted Habermas's view that technology is primarily associated with technical rather than moral rationality, which leads them to overlook technology's potential normative dimension. As we have seen, even choosing a digital tool requires making value-laden judgments about what issues matter enough to be analyzed. Because digital tools typically inherit the worldviews and assumptions of their creators, even well-meaning applications of them can inhibit potentially valuable new ideas or critical perspectives. Inspired by the philosopher John Dewey's (1922) concept of a planning (versus planned) society, which makes intelligent decisions today for the future, I propose the term *tool of inquiry* to describe an ideal in which tools are continually shaped, used, and tested by public users (Goodspeed 2016b, 584–587). This section draws on my theoretical argument, which the theorists Innes and Booher have incorporated in their book (2018, 161).

Translating these theoretical aspirations into professional practice is easier said than done, however. Urban planning projects grapple with constrained budgets, fixed timelines, and stakeholders with often-conflicting worldviews that may make some of these suggestions seem difficult (see box 6). Furthermore, readers may be wondering whether empirical evidence exists for digital tools' efficacy along these lines, especially because theoretical ideals may seem out of reach in practice.

In the following, I discuss research and practice of using digital tools in collaborative planning at three scales: engagement, process, and information

BOX 6 Is Scenario Planning More Expensive?

One common question practitioners ask about scenario planning is whether it is more expensive than traditional forms of urban planning practice. As we have seen, many notable applications of scenario planning in urban settings have been complex, regional-scale projects or have received supplementary grant funding. Examples of smaller-budget scenario projects are harder to find. Although there is no definitive answer to the question of expense, this box discusses reasons for scenario planning differing in cost from other methods and provides some limited empirical evidence about the costs of scenario projects.

As the many types of projects discussed thus far have shown, scenario planning methods are flexible and can be used in various ways. Therefore, it may seem that scenario methods could be scaled to fit any budget. Indeed, small-budget projects exist and can simply feature a smaller number of meetings, fewer outside experts, and limited analysis and topics. At the extreme, exploratory scenario projects may even involve nothing more than a few in-person meetings and exclusively qualitative analysis. But this speculation may be too simple.

Unlike some planning traditions, such as those based in forecasting, scenario planning invites consideration of a wider array of topics and greater attention to the complex external environment. Scenario methods may thus result in more intensive research and require more complex digital tools than the traditional approaches. In addition, achieving some of the benefits of these methods may require a minimum degree of sophistication—for example, quantitatively modeled scenarios may be needed to persuade stakeholders who do not find qualitative analyses credible. On top of these substantive considerations, practitioners adopting new methods and tools face one-time costs to build their capacity for understanding and using the scenario approach effectively.

A short report published by the U.S. Department of Transportation's Federal Highway Administration provides the only empirical research on this topic (U.S. Department of Transportation

Box 6 *Cont'd*

Federal Highway Administration 2018). The report focuses exclusively on metropolitan planning organizations (MPOs), which receive federal funding for transportation planning activities under federal law. On the basis of survey data collected from MPOs and detailed case studies created of nine MPOs, the report concludes that scenario planning does often result in additional costs—at least for MPOs—but in most cases these costs are modest and easily met through available resources. In the survey, responding MPOs reported that adopting scenario planning had increased the cost for recent long-range transportation plans by about 19 percent, but this increased cost represented only 2–10 percent of the overall funds for planning they were provided (since smaller regions are provided less funds), meaning most agencies could meet the additional costs relatively easily through reallocation of internal funds and altering the project to fit the funds available. These responses raise the possibility that, although scenario planning proved more expensive in most cases, practitioners perceived it to be more effective than alternative approaches and thus well worth the cost. Because the survey had a modest response rate (about 64 percent) the results cannot be generalized.

Study of the nine detailed cases also identifies four specific benefits of scenario planning in exchange for the costs: it leads to investment decisions that align with regional goals, integrates regional transportation and local land use planning, improves public and stakeholder involvement, and broadens agency and public understanding of future challenges and opportunities.

Practitioners in certain settings, such as MPOs and some big-city planning departments, can make a case for using existing planning resources for scenario projects, perhaps through temporarily reducing other activities. Other planners must proactively make the case for one-time expenditures, which typically must be done for occasional plans anyway. In some settings, funding from the private sector, charitable foundations, or government grants may be available. Though scenario planning can incur more expense than traditional approaches, it often carries benefits that offset costs, which is why further discussion of evaluation is key.

infrastructure. I draw on the interdisciplinary field of planning support systems (PSS), in which scholars develop and study digital tools for planning.

Engagement

A primary implication of collaborative planning theory is that digital tools must be used in a participatory way in order to benefit the project. As a result, the PSS literature in the last two decades bolsters interest in organizing and studying engagement opportunities. PSS workshops, which Peter Pelzer and I define as a "sociotechnical setting where a PSS is used within the broader context of planning practice," help practitioners use engagement opportunities effectively (Goodspeed and Pelzer 2020). These workshops share digital tools among participants via laptops, projections, or other interactive devices like touch-sensitive screens and often involve meeting facilitators and operators for the digital tools. In PSS workshops, a group performs a planning task, typically modeling, information gathering and storage, visualization, communicating, or analysis (Vonk, Geertman, and Schot 2007).

Pelzer and I found 25 empirical evaluations of such workshops, but their contexts, measures, and outcomes are so varied that they cannot be compared through a formal synthesis. They nonetheless contain a rich trove of insights for practitioners, and some studies examine the outcomes obtained from workshops that use different types of digital tools by evaluating the decisions, plans, or ideas produced, often through experimental designs, by the groups. These evaluations document the potential impact of PSS. For example, Eikelboom and Janssen (2017) find that the substantive decisions made by groups varied depending on how the PSS presented results. They note, however, that some evaluations suggest the use of a PSS may hinder creativity (Te Brömmelstroet 2015). In another study, a comparison of tablet computers and group map tables shows that the users of tablets generated more ideas (Champlin, Te Brömmelstroet, and Pelzer 2018).

A related, larger group of studies defines PSS success in terms of process outcomes, such as individual and group learning. These studies use surveys, interviews, observation, and other methods to measure process outcomes, and some find evidence of participant learning at PSS workshops using digital tools that enabled participants to see rapid feedback (Goodspeed 2013; Slotterback et al. 2016). One case illustrates the subtle interplay between the use of a digital tool and the overall workshop structure. McEvoy and colleagues (2018) investigated four separate treatments tested by fourteen groups of six or eight students: minimal instructions and no PSS, a map-based touch-table PSS, a procedural protocol without a PSS, and a group model-building exercise without a PSS. Using observations and surveys, the researchers evaluated the performance of each group in four areas: learning effects, development of shared understanding, resulting products, and nature of participation. Unsurprisingly, the groups that received no suggested procedure or PSS struggled the most and achieved the worst outcomes. The groups assigned to use the PSS said they learned from its information and appreciated the ability to visualize information on a map, but students with engineering backgrounds sometimes dominated the urban planning students in the discussion, because the PSS contained only quantitative indicators primarily aligned the engineering students' priorities and no indicators addressing the design quality concerns of many planning students. The group model-building exercise—a qualitative method of analyzing a system that did not use a digital tool—achieved the greatest convergence of topics and developed a shared language.

In sum, empirical evidence suggests that planning can benefit from a PSS; however, it also documents the potential for negative influence of digital tools on discussion. Thus, it supports the theories described earlier and provides pragmatic ideas for practice.

Processes

Of course, planning projects consist of more than a single workshop, and scenario projects can easily extend to myriad meetings, discussions, and events. How, then, should digital tools be integrated into a project? The issues are complex, collecting data from real-world planning projects is difficult, and there is relatively little empirical research on this topic. That said, the few studies that do exist fortunately contain intriguing findings that support the value of participatory design and the use of digital tools throughout a project's life cycle.

I made a brief case study of the Boston Metropolitan Area Planning Council, which highly customized a CommunityViz model as part of its MetroFuture Regional Plan from 2005 to 2008, and found evidence of the potential benefit of a PSS created with extensive stakeholder involvement (Goodspeed 2016b). The project was designed with extensive input from an interissue task force of stakeholders, and another study of the project concludes that "stakeholder engagement in group model building of comprehensive rule-based models is achievable and desirable" and can "open up the 'black box'" of PSS (Paul 2010, 81).

Two additional, more rigorous studies have built on the encouraging but empirically limited case. Focusing on how to improve PSS functionality and usability, Vonk and Ligtenberg (2010) compare PSS created in two ways. The first was the "traditional" approach, involving a small group of researchers, developers, and geographic information systems specialists from a government agency. The second PSS was designed through a sociotechnical development process, with iterative and close collaboration among technical experts, landscape architects, and planning practitioners—the intended users. Whereas the traditional approach resulted in a PSS that planners rejected almost immediately, the second resulted in a PSS with a wider variety of functionalities, organized and aligned with planning tasks. This study focuses on aspects of the interface—and not, for example, on the substantive scope of the underlying data or indicators—but it nonetheless suggests the importance of involving users in designing digital tools. Other researchers have also argued that PSS should be created in similar participatory ways (Te Brömmelstroet and Schrijnen 2010).

Two cases presented by Ulibarri (2018) are noteworthy for results similar to Vonk and Ligtenberg's, although they originated in the realm of environmental management, not planning. She describes two licensing negotiations in which stakeholders debated how to manage large hydropower facilities to meet conflicting energy-generation, water-supply, flood-control, environmental, and recreational needs. Both projects created computer models, had similar sets of stakeholders, and addressed similar policy questions. The project that embodied what Ulibarri termed the consultative approach was led by an engineering consultant. It featured fewer meetings and little deliberation among participants; as a result, the participants roundly ignored the model that was created by the consultant. The other project used what she describes as the collaborative approach and developed a model through intense collaboration among stakeholders. It became "the central hub for negotiating potential management regimes" (Ulibarri 2018, 138) because it was tailored to address the project participants' specific questions and concerns. Ulibarri argues that the active stakeholder participation resulted in a model that was generally trusted, which facilitated greater analysis to support decisions. Although the model was intertwined with many other aspects of the project, making it hard to isolate benefits of collaborating, it nonetheless demonstrates the importance of ongoing deliberation about digital tools used in collaborative settings.

Information Infrastructure

Proponents of digital planning tools have long dreamed of a world where planners in different places had a shared collection of digital tools and information. In a classic article proposing his PSS concept, Klosterman (1997) called for an *information infrastructure* that continuously processes information collection, design, and analysis among planning stakeholders. Building on his ideas, Hackel and I propose a PSS infrastructure to be "the set of organizational practices, technical infrastructure, and social norms that collectively support planning tasks by diverse users on an ongoing basis" (Goodspeed and Hackel 2017, 778).

This vision is understandable in a world with prolific private websites containing vast repositories of maps, information about transit systems, and real estate transactions, and where many governments have created spatial data infrastructures, too. Creating infrastructures specifically for planning has run into many challenges; as I have observed throughout, cities and their forms of planning are highly diverse, even within a single metropolitan region. Furthermore, the inconsistent funding and political support for planning in many places adds to the difficulty.

As a result of these difficulties, most scenario projects create and use digital tools independently of any shared infrastructure—but this may be changing. Hackel and I took advantage of a project by the Southern California Association of Governments (SCAG) to create a PSS infrastructure, the Scenario Planning Model, as an opportunity to research the real-world challenges such projects face (Goodspeed and Hackel 2017). Drawing on in-depth interviews with nine stakeholders who collaborated with SCAG to create this tool, Hackel and I propose seven lessons for creating PSS infrastructures: use participatory design, support a variety of planning practices, address indirect costs to users, encourage collaboration among users within each organization, give stakeholders appropriate access, be mindful of tool framing, and embrace technology's transformative potential. The model tailored software provided by the consulting firm Calthorpe Analytics to SCAG's region. This company recently launched UrbanFootprint, a web-based place-type development tool for customers across the United States (see box 4 in chapter 5). How this and other emerging PSS infrastructures evolve in coming years will be an exciting area for planning research and professional practice.

Chapter Summary

- Although scenario planning is both an art and a science, as are all complex forms of professional practice, evidence and research from professional and scholarly sources on conducting urban scenario planning grows.
- Projects should generally have four or six scenarios, each with a memorable title, and they should be plausible.
- Urban scenario planning projects combine *collaboration*, in which individuals represent interests or an organization, with *participation*, in which individuals speak for themselves as citizens.
- Most urban scenario planning projects use accepted, validated indicators to rigorously compare the performance of alternative scenarios.
- Digital tools should be tailored to the project and used to further collaboration among project participants.

PART 3

PROJECT OUTCOMES AND EVALUATION

7 Defining Scenario Project Outcomes

What makes a scenario planning project successful? To answer requires navigating a thicket of competing ideas about the nature and purpose of planning, as well as defining the specific value of scenario planning—a method used in many settings to achieve many goals. A small number of scholars, with diverse theoretical perspectives, have sought to answer this question through evaluation research on scenario planning projects. Evaluation in urban planning has often led to overly narrow, quantitative exercises that neglect important qualitative outcomes. This neglect is remedied by proposed evaluation approaches for analyzing planning processes and their resulting plans found by Oliveira and Pinho (2010) in a thoughtful literature review. While recognizing the many types of planning projects and the difficulty and complexity in their evaluation, they persuasively argue that evaluation is necessary to provide legitimacy and improve practices. Although evaluation of urban scenario planning is currently the domain of academic research and relatively immature, I share Oliveira and Pinho's belief that it is crucial for improving practice, and I therefore address it in this book.

This chapter begins with the theoretical underpinnings of project evaluation of urban scenario planning. It discusses how urban scenario planning should be evaluated not only on the basis of planning theory but also scenario planning theory. In chapters 8 and 9, I review existing scholarly research featuring empirical evaluations of scenario planning projects, and I propose an evaluation framework. This chapter argues that, as a strategic planning method, scenario planning should be evaluated by the performance principle, which holds that planning processes and resulting plans should be judged primarily on how they affect future decisions.

The value of scenario planning therefore lies mainly in individual and group learning that reinforces individual and collective decisions. Those decisions, in turn, shape institutions and ultimately the functioning of urban systems. Relatively strong empirical evidence suggests individual participants in scenario planning projects experience learning and social outcomes; however, few of these studies probe the strengths of scenario planning compared with other planning approaches. The few existing studies provide some support for theoretical arguments that scenario planning improves individual learning by reducing well-known psychological biases.

Powerless Planning?

Can scenario-based plans change the physical form of cities? On one hand, practitioners can cite many cases in which scenarios seem to have shaped urban outcomes. Envision Utah used scenarios in a multifaceted effort in which Salt Lake City growth patterns moved from low-density sprawl and toward development along a new regional transit system (Matheson 2011; Scheer 2012). In Oregon, the LUTRAQ study played a role in stopping the proposed Westside Bypass highway outside Portland through its use of alternative land use scenarios (Oregon 2012). Less intense urban scenario planning projects in exurban Austin, Texas, seem to have resulted in smaller, yet concrete outcomes, such as convincing residents of suburban subdivisions of the need for a proposed street connecting their neighborhood to a historic downtown, as exploratory research details in chapter 9. On the other hand, the limited academic research on the topic finds more mixed results, such as only partial implementation of the much-heralded Sacramento Region Blueprint plan (Allred and Chakraborty 2015). Even for the success stories here, it is hard to separate scenario methods from other factors to know how they contributed to the positive outcomes. For many more scenario projects, resulting physical changes were seemingly absent.

Thomas Campanella sums up a common U.S. planning perspective in a provocative book chapter, "Jane Jacobs and the Death and Life of American Planning." The discipline has "been largely unsuccessful over the last half century at its own game: bringing about more just, sustainable, healthful, efficient, and beautiful cities and urban regions," and U.S. planners "lack the agency and authority to turn their idealism into reality" (2011, 142). Campanella traces the origins of this failure to the crisis of confidence within planning that followed the publication of Jacobs's book, arguing that planning practice has lost its ability to effect change in the ensuing years. After writing admiringly of China's vast national infrastructure projects, he contrasts them with a seven-year process to construct a footbridge and lengthy environmental reviews for a local rail project in his home state of North Carolina, suggesting that the "United States needs more of that very effective Chinese sledgehammer" (2011, 155). Of course, he omits that the United States is a democracy and China a one-party state. Campanella argues for greater visionary planning by professionals in the U.S. political context and writes approvingly of Vishaan Chakrabarti's (2009) proposal for the United States to sweep aside local land use regulations, streamline environmental laws, and pour billions into new rail infrastructure. From this perspective, almost all U.S. planning processes and their plans are lacking, because they often fail to dramatically advance sustainability goals and are rarely implemented with the alacrity and decisiveness desired. Consequently, many planners who share Campanella's frustrations turn to alternative ways of achieving their goals, such as cultivating powerful politicians who will back more rapid change (Sadik-Khan and Solomonow 2016) or resorting to "tactical urbanism," which involves flexible action such as creating temporary parks and is thought to be capable of stimulating more change than traditional plans (Lydon and Garcia 2015).

I am sympathetic to Campanella's frustration and sense of urgency in achieving changes. Professional criticism and innovation are needed across the field. Certainly, planning is only one means for social or urban change, and politics and advocacy have important roles to play. Indeed, in complexity theory—which lay at the heart of Jacobs's worldview—the city is deeply intertwined with many aspects of society, but most of those aspects are beyond the direct control of any one actor in a democratic, capitalist society with deliberately distributed political power. Legendary planner Edmund Bacon presciently highlights the conceptual flaw of Campanella's view: in the gendered language typical of that era, he observes, "The building of cities is one of man's greatest achievements," and "the form of his city always has been and always will be a pitiless indicator of the state of his civilization" (1967, 13). Campanella's yearning for a more assertive form of planning is actually a desire for a different, more centralized society, which he only partly concedes.

Good planning practitioners understand that their task is to navigate the world while shaping it into a better one. Dewey (1922) famously distinguishes between a *planned* society, which subordinates the present in pursuit of a rigid planned future, and a *planning* society, which is intellectually preoccupied by the future but knows that only the present—and not the future—can be controlled. Good planning should ultimately be judged by the quality of the decisions made, not only the amount of concrete poured.

Even Campanella's example of China is illustrative: although the country's rail infrastructure has many undeniable benefits over the United States' system of highways and roads, many other aspects of Chinese urban planning are cause for concern—not envy. With its growth slowing and society aging, China may have urbanized too rapidly and at too high an environmental and social cost to sustain. Poorly coordinated urbanization has led to many, wide-spread housing vacancies, monotonous development that fails to support community, razing of historic buildings, ruthless displacement, and a legacy of pollution and environmental destruction that will linger for generations.

That said, U.S. planning is hardly ideal, either, and this book aims to shake up stale practices and institutions. Planning in a pluralistic society like the United States—characterized by its long history of systemic racism, sexism, xenophobia, myopic individualism, environmental disregard, rapacious capitalist enterprise, and much more—will always be difficult. But in the past few decades, many U.S. cities have demonstrated what is possible through planning with expanded transit systems, revitalized downtowns, improved air and water quality, and new public amenities. The solution lies not in the armchair wish that the United States return to another time but rather in a method for progressive practice that catalyzes change among those who individually and collectively shape its cities. With the drawbacks of a centralized planning system increasingly visible, some

Chinese cities are today beginning more strategic forms of planning, some of which even incorporate scenarios (Wu and Zhang 2007).

An intensified program of research into and methodological development of scenario planning evaluation is needed to spark the next wave of progressive planning that U.S. cities so urgently require. The next section considers how scenario planning should be evaluated from the perspectives of both planning theorists and scenario planning practitioners. This sets the stage for further discussion in following chapters of evaluating scenario planning.

Plan Performance

How planning practices should be evaluated is the subject of a large and varied literature (Oliveira and Pinho 2010), and this section describes some of the insights from this literature that are relevant to urban scenario planning practice.

Mastop and Faludi (1997) propose that there are two types of plans, project and strategic, which should be evaluated quite differently from each other. Presenting them as ideal types, they define a *project* plan as one that "provides blueprints of the intended end-state of the physical environment, including the measures necessary to achieve that state" (819). Project plans are thus most appropriately evaluated through the conformance of the plan with what actually occurs (Laurian et al. 2004; Talen 1997). In contrast, Mastop and Faludi (1997) argue, a *strategic* plan serves as a "frame of reference" for future decision making, with stated intentions, coordination of diverse actors, and some conjecture because it relies on uncertain information and incomplete knowledge. To evaluate strategic plans, Mastop and Faludi propose the *performance principle*: "a strategic plan is performing well, that is, serving its function, if and only if it plays a tangible role in the choices of the actors to whom it is addressed" (822). Clearly, urban scenario plans more strongly resemble strategic plans than project plans.

This theoretical perspective merits some modifications before it can usefully evaluate scenario planning. Although Mastop and Faludi espouse what they call a social-interaction perspective, which values input from all stakeholders, they argue that plan performance should be evaluated by investigating the decisions of those "to whom . . . [the] plan is addressed" (Mastop and Faludi 1997, 820)—that is, decisions by government. Empirical studies generally examine public sector decisions (e.g., Faludi 2000; Van Damme et al. 1997). Other planning theorists, however, such as Booher and Innes (2002), highlight the importance of coordinating multiple actors and argue that planning must move beyond government actors to influence the decisions of many participants.

A narrow focus on public sector decisions may also obscure other ways plans can influence outcomes, such as by changing stakeholder preferences or changing the ways problems are understood. The collaborative planning literature especially emphasizes these influences; for example, in Booher and Innes's (2002) DIAD model, interdependent participants can come to share identities, meaning, and heuristics and can produce innovations through deliberation. Similarly, Deyle and Wiedenman (2014) propose that collaborative dialogue results in quality plans, organization satisfaction, and successful implementation. Although effective plans directly influence participants, these theories suggest that the plans may not be explicitly cited during decision making if the ideas they contain become deeply internalized and are subsequently taken for granted. Elaborating on their DIAD model in *Planning with Complexity*, Innes and Booher propose that successful collaboration can result not only in specific intended outcomes but also in second- and third-order effects, which they call "system adaptations" (2018, 37). These adaptations point to the importance of investigating broader shifts in thinking sparked by planning activities and looking for evidence that participants explicitly use the plans in formal decision making.

Scholars outside the collaborative tradition have proposed similar ideas. In a paper considering the ways climate action planning may affect legislation, regulations, and system outcomes, Millard-Ball (2012) lays out five causal pathways: (1) coordinating interdependent decisions; (2) generating knowledge; (3) shaping preferences; (4) aggregating preferences (agenda-setting); and (5) imposing reputational costs for violating plans. Of these, (2), (3), and (4) apply to strategic planning and plans, and (1) and (5) better describe policy plans with specific proposals. Although Millard-Ball does not address the more fundamental forms of learning hypothesized by collaborative planning, he nevertheless sees multiple pathways of influence that should be examined in an empirical evaluation.

To summarize, because scenario methods are typically used to create strategic plans, they should be evaluated primarily on the basis of the *performance principle*. Performance evaluation traditionally focused on the narrow question of whether or how government decision makers referred to plan documents, but newer perspectives suggest that the impact of planning may occur through learning or changed decisions by a broader set of stakeholders. Plan evaluation should consider not only project outcomes like concrete decisions, legislation, regulation, or policies but also less tangible changes like the emergence of new ideas. The limited empirical studies on plan performance do not adequately address this expanded scope of outcomes and participants, however. The next section turns to the broader literature on scenario planning and finds that the method can improve decisions in these ways.

Improving Decisions

The discussion thus far has not addressed the unique qualities of scenario-based plans. However, as chapter 3 discusses, there are many ways to conduct planning. Scenarios often perform better than alternatives in encouraging general learning, but that is not the goal of most practitioners. Instead, their scenarios are meant to result in specific forms of learning that are either not the focus of or absent from other planning approaches. To clarify what these precise forms of learning are, this section considers the scenario literature to understand the full scope of what practitioners call *strategic insights*—and learning specific to scenarios—both of which are theoretically linked to improved decision making.

Scenario planning stems from management literature, so a useful place to start is to consider how scenario planning is connected to business. In that literature, the value of scenario planning methods lies primarily in aiding decisions that allow a firm to survive and prosper given an uncertain future (e.g., Schwartz 1991). Management theorists claim this occurs in diffuse and indirect ways and argue that individual participants in scenario creation experience a perspective shift that affects their subsequent actions within the organization (Van der Heijden 2005).

Scenario practitioners, however, often wish to make the link between scenarios and specific decisions more concrete. Van der Heijden (2005) describes one way: the first use of a scenario developed by a firm is to evaluate its current business idea. That idea, to Van der Heijden, is the "rational explanation of why the organization has been successful in the past, and how it will be successful in the future" (63) and underlies the company's business model. This leads to internal conclusions about the nature of the firm itself and external conclusions about how the organization may need to change in reaction to external changes. Regardless of the specific conclusions, however, the next step is generating, refining, and evaluating a set of internal and external strategic options for the organization. Decision makers consider strategic options in light of scenarios to decide how the company can maximize financial return while minimizing financial risks.

These basic ideas parallel the use of scenarios in urban planning, but they require important modifications because of the differences in context. Xiang and Clarke's (2003) description of land use scenarios points out scenarios' dual nature, and they describe how both natures work together to improve decision making through modeling systems, bridging between topics and ways of thinking, and planning activities to develop goals, strategies, and policies (see figure 21 in chapter 6).

This framework highlights only some ways using scenarios can improve planning, but it also organizes some of the specific benefits of scenarios in producing strategic insights, as discussed by scenario practitioners (Quay 2018). I argue that the specific value to planning of creating multiple scenarios arises in three areas: modeling, bridging, and planning:

Modeling
- System structure
- System dynamics
- System evolution

Bridging
- Integration of values and analysis
- Detailed, rigorous scenarios

Planning
- Strategy generation
- Strategy prioritization and implementation analysis
- Strategy evaluation
- Relationships among multiple strategies

First, scenario development can result in insights about the city system being conceptually modeled. These include understanding how elements connect and interact more deeply (system structure and dynamics) and the range of possible futures. When modeling involves an analysis of how events unfold over time (system evolution), insights may include *trigger points*, events that define the scope of future options and can be anticipated, or *key interventions*, events that would make current goals very difficult or impossible. Although these insights are potentially quite important, they are not the typical justification for using scenario methodology, because there are multiple ways to build this type of system understanding. In particular, collaborative model building can yield system insights without creating a set of scenarios (e.g., Ulibarri 2018; Van den Belt 2004).

Second, developing scenarios results in value through *bridging*, enabling constructive communication among modeling experts, who bring analysis, and planning stakeholders, who define values. For scenario projects aimed at creating a vision, scenario methodology's primary benefit is bridging, because it may lead to a shared vision based on more careful analysis and because it is more rigorous and detailed than qualitative visioning alone allows. The use of scenarios can also integrate values and analysis in a way that is difficult or impossible for other planning approaches.

The benefit of scenario planning becomes even more apparent with the insights it enables during action planning. Whereas Van der Heijden discusses option planning, I use *strategies* for the specific actions. Strategies encompass building infrastructure, adopting a policy, implementing a plan, and more, but continuing current policies is a form of action in its own right. Once scenarios have been created, they can be used to generate, understand, and select strategies. Strategy generation includes surfacing strategies that already exist but the scenarios clarify as important. Strategy analysis involves developing a deeper understanding of particular strategies. For example, an insight might clarify which strategies are higher or lower priority, which are flexible, and which can be implemented by mainstreaming existing strategies as opposed to effecting institutional transformation.

Scenarios can be used to assess the value of strategies today in light of plausible futures. A robust strategy is one that performs well across a wide range of possible futures, whereas a contingency strategy makes sense only for specific futures (Chakraborty et al. 2011). Strategies that may perform well in only some scenarios while still retaining positive benefits under all scenarios are called no-regrets strategies. Strategies that prevent or minimize undesirable characteristics of a worst-case future are known as hedging strategies. Finally, considering multiple strategies can sometimes uncover important trade-offs or synergies among possible strategies, or it can identify strategies that create options for the future. For well-structured decision contexts, such as water planning, theorists have proposed detailed methodologies to organize actions by type and across time. In these decision contexts, elaborate plans with decision pathways, as determined by the scenarios and previous decisions, delineate all options decision makers could face in the future (Haasnoot et al. 2013). However, analyzing decision pathways requires a planning context with a finite set of variables and a fixed set of discrete decisions, neither of which are always present in planning situations.

To begin the discussion of how to define and evaluate scenario success, this section considers ideas from planning theory and scenario theory. The field of planning evaluation offers key insights: strategic plans should be evaluated according to their usefulness for decision making because they do not provide a simple blueprint for implementation. Furthermore, effective planning may not always occur through formal government decision-making processes, which historically have been the focus of performance studies. Evaluation schemes, then, must account for the broader set of participants and pathways between planning and impact. Scenario planning theorists and practitioners have elaborated on some of the types of insights scenarios are said to produce; they suggest specific mechanisms by which scenarios improve decisions. However, the discussion has been largely limited to hypotheses thus far.

So what empirical evidence is there for scenarios' performance? That is the focus of the following chapters in part 3, in which I review the empirical literature on evaluating scenario planning in several fields.

Chapter Summary

- Because scenario methods are typically used to create strategic plans, they should be evaluated primarily according to the performance principle, or whether they influence decision making, not only whether their ideas are implemented.
- Practitioners have suggested scenarios can improve decision making by generating strategic insights—that is, relevant lessons about the nature of a system or specific strategies for a situation.

8 Scenario Outcomes Research

This chapter presents a literature review of empirical studies published in English that investigate the effects of scenario planning methods. The studies come from the urban planning, business management, and environmental management literatures and include studies using qualitative and quantitative methods, field studies, and laboratory experiments. Using a category Xiao and Watson (2017) propose for literature reviews, this chapter presents a *scoping review*, or a snapshot of the field. My review uses textual narrative synthesis to make comparisons across studies. Textual narrative synthesis is suitable for synthesizing quantitative and qualitative research and for reviews in which a quantitative metastudy is not possible because their measures and methods are too different (Lucas et al. 2007).

I began the review by searching for the phrases "scenario planning evaluation" and "scenario planning outcomes" in Google Scholar (https://scholar.google.com) and Web of Science (https://clarivate.com /webofsciencegroup/solutions/web-of-science/), two large databases of research publication and citation data. To these search results, I added the works cited by the initial articles. For all resulting articles, I used Google Scholar's "cited by" functionality to search forward and backward in time. The search discovered only one study from before 2000, so older scholarship not being included in online databases is not a likely limitation of this review. I screened the articles by their titles and then abstracts, including only studies published in peer-reviewed journals, except for one peer-reviewed project report published by a reputable think tank. Given the diversity of the studies and the aims of the review, I applied no further quality criteria.

This search gleaned 56 articles. I then removed many that did not present systematic evaluation outcomes but instead discussed scenario methods and theory. I also removed studies on narrow aspects of scenario planning methods that did not contain information allowing the overall projects to be evaluated (Bradfield 2008; Goodier et al. 2010; Roubelat 2000). I also excluded experimental studies that tested the interpretation of forecasts after subjects had read scenario narratives, because this chapter's review focuses on projects testing the effects of participating in the creation and use of scenarios, not merely of reading them (Kuhn and Sniezek 1996; Önkal et al. 2017). However, I included studies in which participants had no input into the scenarios but participated in intense workshops where they learned about them (Bowman et al. 2013; Groves et al. 2008; Phadnis et al. 2015). From the remaining 21 studies, I extracted the following: study context, project form, specific outcomes, evaluation method, evaluation design, and findings. This information is summarized in tables 11, 12, and 13.

Urban Planning

Table 11 shows five studies from the urban planning field. Most use the intuitive logics method (see chapter 4). One examines the effects of scenario projects to create land use and transportation plans, and the rest examine the effects of exploratory scenario projects. Allred and Chakraborty (2015) evaluate the implementation of the Sacramento Region Blueprint plan for land use and transportation and investigate whether building permit applications after the plan's adoption are occurring in places it recommends and whether the plan is being incorporated into local jurisdictions' general plans. They find that growth is occurring in recommended places only in some jurisdictions, and only some general plans refer to the Blueprint. Pointing to this partial success, they conclude that the project illustrates the limits of scenario-based voluntary regional planning. They do not, however, examine whether all growth, irrespective of location, is improving in the region according to plan criteria—that is, whether the region as a whole is performing better according to the plan's goals.

Zapata (2013) performed a qualitative evaluation concerning individual and organizational outcomes of the Valley Futures Project in California.

An exploratory project described in chapter 4, this project convened a stakeholder group that constructed exploratory narrative scenarios for California's Central Valley (Cummings 2007). Zapata concludes that, although individual transformative learning occurred, few long-term changes to professional practices or within organizations resulted from the project. Bowman and colleagues (2013) similarly focus on long-term organizational outcomes in a case study of a Scottish local authority's use of scenario planning over nine years. Two projects in the case study used different study methods. The first project, which created qualitative exploratory scenarios as narratives, had qualitative outcomes such as fostering strategic thinking. The second project, in which a focus on the scenario narratives was lost and the focus was on detailed discussions of policies, was not successful.

Finally, two projects tested short-term changes among participants in transportation scenario projects by using surveys before and after workshops. In part because of a small sample size, Zegras and Rayle (2012) find only modest changes to actor networks and inconclusive evidence for changes in perceptions of the problem and project. Phadnis and colleagues' (2015) survey finds only modest changes to professionals' judgments about investment decisions after exposure to scenarios during workshops about the future of freight transportation.

Environment

Although scenario planning has been widely used in the environmental field (Peterson, Cumming, and Carpenter 2003), its applications have not been widely evaluated. Hulme and Dessai (2008) propose evaluating national climate scenarios by their predictive success, decision success, and learning success, but they acknowledge that no metric for scenarios is easy to define, and scenarios should be evaluated relative to project-specific goals. A review by Oteros-Rozas et al. (2015) of 23 case studies of participatory scenario planning in place-based socio-ecological research finds that 15 studies conducted some form of evaluation, such as surveys, interviews, or observation, primarily to assess participants' learning. Leaders of nine projects said there was strong evidence of short-term (less than

Table 11 Scenario Project Evaluations in Urban Planning

Source	Study Context	Project Form	Specific Outcome Types Evaluated	Evaluation Method	Evaluation Design	Findings
Allred and Chakraborty (2015)	Sacramento, California, region	Regional blueprint	System: identify preferred institutional housing unit types	GIS analysis and manual plan review	Post hoc, $N = 28$ cities	Postplan development in highly rated neighborhoods not more prevalent
Bowman et al. (2013)	Scottish intraorganizational partnership	Intuitive logics and scenario refinement	Psychological: improve long-term strategic thinking and planning	Interviews	Nine-year longitudinal case research, 24 interviews	Qualitative benefits
Phadnis et al. (2015)	Transportation stakeholders	Exposure to existing intuitive logics	Psychological: expert judgments for transportation infrastructure investments	Judgment survey	Pre- and postworkshop surveys, $N = 100$ (estimated)	Changes in expert judgments were generally not significant
Zapata (2013)	California's Central Valley	Intuitive logics	Psychological: transform learning and behavior	Interviews	Post hoc (five years later), $N = 13$	Some individual transformative learning and actions but limited organizational outcomes
Zegras and Rayle (2012)	Portuguese transportation planning	Intuitive logics (three scenarios)	Psychological: update social networks, change related perceptions (collaboration, common goals, problem relevance, shared definition)	Survey	Pre- and postworkshop surveys, $N = 22$, 17, respectively	Modest changes to networks and collaboration but inconclusive effects on views and understanding

one year) and long-term (more than one year) outcomes and impacts, but only two conducted formal long-term evaluations. All projects that conducted formal short- and long-term evaluations found strong evidence of impact, and the review authors speculate that more rigorous evaluations of the other cases could discover additional evidence of their effects.

Another five studies in my review came from scholarly journals broadly related to the environment, as table 12 shows. Two separately published articles discuss the methods and results of the two formal evaluations included in the Oteros-Rozas et al. (2015) review. These projects used similar methods, shared the same international-group facilitation team, and used adaptive comanagement, a natural resources management approach for improving ecological, livelihood, and community outcomes (Butler, Young, et al. 2015; Plummer and Armitage 2007). The projects were in the Nusa Tenggara Barat Province of Indonesia and in the West New Britain Province of Papua New Guinea. The projects and their scenarios are presented in Butler, Bohensky, and colleagues (2016). The projects had three phases: preparing stakeholders for action (including creating scenarios), developing policies and programs, and implementing adaptation. Before and after surveys at workshops found that the primary outcome of the workshops was innovative ideas; less than 20 percent of respondents reported gaining new contacts, new information, or new sources of funds. However, many also reported that they identified potential new partners at the workshops (Butler, Wise, et al. 2015). A separate evaluation of the project interviewed 17 project participants after the project was completed (Butler, Suadnya, et al. 2016). The interviews used survey questions to gauge learning, trust, new institutional arrangements, and management plans and agreements. This evaluation is notable for including the implementation phase and for providing a methodological model to collect information about perceived institutional changes through structured interviews. Its drawback is a lack of in-depth case information needed for validation and for deeper understanding of the stated results.

The remaining environmental studies in table 12 are either for water management or for U.S. National Parks. Groves and colleagues (2008) report changes in water managers' attitudes regarding uncertainties, modeling, and risk after the managers were exposed to three types of scenarios developed by RAND Corporation researchers. The study does not find statistically significant results for most changes in attitudes, perhaps because of the small sample size; however, the managers' reported perceptions of climate change did shift somewhat. Two papers evaluate the effects of scenario projects in the U.S. National Park Service: Knapp, Fresco, and Krutikov (2017) find evidence of individual learning in post hoc interviews among 30 participants in a scenario project for the Alaska National Parks, but evidence in organizational outcomes for learning was limited, due to a lack of project follow-up. Cobb and Thompson (2012) describe scenario projects conducted for the Assateague Island National Seashore off the coasts of Maryland and Virginia and Wind Cave National Park in South Dakota and conclude that the project was useful in challenging participant assumptions, downscaling climate change science to local contexts, and negotiating scientific uncertainty.

Management

As table 13 shows, the largest collection of empirical scenario planning evaluations comes from business management literature, in which eleven studies analyzed scenario planning applications for strategic planning in corporations or other large organizations. Of these studies, seven involve consultant and researcher Thomas Chermack as an author or coauthor—that is, most studies in this field are largely due to the efforts of one scholar.

One of the best-known evaluations of scenario planning applied to corporate strategic planning is that of Phelps, Chan, and Kapsalis (2001), who report on the performance of water and information technology industries. The study considers subjective and objective performance measures, including financial performance and measures of service quality. For water industry companies, the study finds some evidence that scenario use correlated with greater financial performance and worsened customer service levels, but neither relationship has strong statistical significance. For information technology consulting firms, the authors find a relationship between scenario planning and improved financial performance, and they note a weak relationship between scenario planning and client growth, a

Table 12 Scenario Evaluations in Environmental Research

Source	Study Context	Project Form	Specific Outcome Types Evaluated	Evaluation Method	Evaluation Design	Findings
Butler, Bohensky, et al. (2016)	Indonesia and Papua New Guinea	Exploratory, with normative backcasting, as described in Butler, Bohensky, et al. (2016)	Psychological: livelihood challenges, strategy priorities, social learning, knowledge exchange, empowerment, and bridging social networks	Survey	Pre- and postworkshop surveys (questions varied), $N = 141$	Innovative ideas but less empowerment
Butler, Suadnya, et al. (2016)	Indonesia	Exploratory, with normative backcasting, as described in Butler, Bohensky, et al. (2016)	Change indicators: leaders, trust, empowerment, networks, solutions, partnerships, and others	Structured interviews	Postworkshop survey, $N = 17$	Changes to trust, leaders, social networks, and, implementation actions more limited
Cobb and Thompson (2012)	Assateague Island National Seashore and Wind Cave National Park	Intuitive logics	Institutional: organizational resiliency and systems innovation	Participant observation	Participant observation	Scenario methods useful for challenging assumptions, downscaling science, and negotiating scientific certainty

| Groves et al. (2008) | Water managers | Intuitive logics, probabilistic forecasts, and policy-relevant scenarios (participants reviewed but did not create the scenarios) | Change indicators: attitudes regarding climate change uncertainties, long-term planning, modeling, actions, and managing risk | Survey | Pre- and postworkshop surveys at three workshops, $N = 31, 23, 14$, respectively | Some changes to climate change attitudes but no changes to action preferences |
| Knapp, Fresco, and Krutikov (2017) | Alaska National Parks | Intuitive logics | Educational: knowledge of climate change, uncertainty, and relational outcomes | Interviews | Post hoc, $N = 30$ | Individual learning outcomes recorded but organizational outcomes more limited |

Table 13 Scenario Planning Evaluations in Management

Source	Study Context	Project Form	Specific Outcome Types Evaluated	Evaluation Method	Evaluation Design	Findings
Chermack et al. (2015)	Four organizations	Intuitive logics (five workshops)	• Learning • Perceptions of organizational climate	• Dimensions of Situational Outlook Questionnaire	Pre- and postworkshop surveys, treatment and control groups, $N = 100$	Improvement in most organizational climate survey dimensions
Chermack, Lynham, and van der Merwe (2006)	Educational institute in southeastern United States	Intuitive logics	• Learning • Organizational learning	• Dimensions of Learning Organizations Questionnaire	Pre- and postworkshop surveys, $N = 9$	Improvement in organizational learning
Chermack, van der Merwe, and Lynham (2007)	Educational institution in southeastern United States	Intuitive logics	• Learning • Strategic conversation quality	• Conversation Quality and Engagement Checklist (CQEC)	Pre- and postworkshop surveys, $N = 9, 10$, respectively	Null findings
Chermack and Nimon (2008)	U.S. technology firm	Intuitive logics	• Learning • Decision-making style	• General Decision-Making Style Survey	Pre- and postworkshop surveys, treatment and control groups, $N = 84$	Significant changes to reported decision-making style
Glick et al. (2012)	Ten U.S. organizations	Intuitive logics (five workshops)	• Institutional change • Mental model style	• Mental model styles	Pre- and postworkshop surveys, $N = 129$	Scenario planning promotes efficiency, social, and systems mental model style
Lang and Ramírez (2017)	Two universities	Intuitive logics	• Learning, institutional change • Social capital changes	• Mixed methods (e.g., semistructured interviews, descriptive surveys, and document analysis)	Post hoc, 70 interviews	Scenario planning results primarily in cognitive capital

Meissner and Wulf (2013)	Management	Intuitive logics, compared with workshops using other planning techniques	• Learning • Framing bias and decision quality	• Framing bias questionnaire	Pre- and postworkshop surveys, partial control group, $N = 252$	Scenario planning reduces framing bias and improves decision quality more than other strategic planning methods
Phelps, Chan, and Kapsalis (2001)	Water and IT firms	Intuitive logics	• System change • Financial performance, client growth, service quality	• Data analysis and survey	Post hoc, each category $N = 28$	Some support for improved financial performance
Schoemaker (1993)	Business management students	Intuitive logics	• Psychological • Confidence ranges for key uncertainties	• Attitude survey	Pre- and postworkshop surveys, $N = 130$ (scenario creators vs. readers), experiment control group, $N = 75$	Scenario planning results in greater subjective confidence ranges
Veliquette et al. (2012)	Ten U.S. business organizations	Intuitive logics	• Learning • Strategic conversation quality skills	• Conversation Quality and Engagement Checklist (CQEC)	Pre- and postworkshop surveys, $N = 137$	Scenario planning related to increases in conversation and engagement skills
Visser and Chermack (2009)	Nine big firms	Unspecified	• Learning, institutional change • Firm performance	• Key informant interviews	Post hoc, firms $N = 9$	Scenario planning results in qualitative benefits for decision making

proxy for service quality. Harries (2003) presents four criticisms of the study: its definition of scenario planning differs from the standard, it does not examine other firm characteristics that might explain both performance and scenario use, firms may differ in their organizational goals, and the most appropriate objective measure for strategic planning may not be average financial performance but rather financial performance during rare events, such as industry crises or industry recessions. Another study of overall firm performance that complements the Phelps, Chan, and Kapsalis study is Visser and Chermack (2009), which reports the results of a qualitative study of multinational firms using scenario planning methods. Interviewees reported that scenario planning was useful to explore the business environment and risks, isolate trends, understand interdependent forces, and consider the implications of decisions. The authors do not propose how to measure these outcomes quantitatively.

The remaining empirical studies focus on individual-level outcomes, and they use before and after surveys of participants at workshops. Two examine whether participation in scenario planning changes participants' self-reported conversation and engagement skills using the Conversation Quality and Engagement Checklist. The first study, of nine participants, was inconclusive (Chermack, Van der Merwe, and Lynham 2007). A study with a similar design but a much larger sample finds that participants in scenario planning reported statistically significant increases in these skills (Veliquette et al. 2012).

Other studies investigate organizational outcomes: Chermack, Lynham, and Van der Merwe (2006) find evidence that participation in scenario planning improved perceptions that organizational learning occurred, but the study is limited by a small sample size. A study of participants in a scenario planning project in a U.S. technology firm concludes that the project resulted in a more intuitive decision-making style, as measured by the General Decision-Making Style Survey (Chermack and Nimon 2008). Glick and colleagues (2012) investigate whether scenario planning encouraged a particular mental model style. Their survey included five styles—political, financial, efficiency, social, and system—and they conclude that participants in scenario planning shifted toward the latter three styles. Finally, Chermack and colleagues (2015) test the effects of scenario planning on perceptions of creative organizational climate and report that participating in scenario workshops changed how participants perceived their organization's climate for creativity. Although two of the Chermack-involved studies include control groups, most are survey-based field studies of participants in real-world projects on which he formally consulted. In addition to lacking control groups, this raises questions about researcher objectivity.

Complementing these studies are two papers that describe laboratory experiments that used control groups to test hypotheses. In the first paper, an experiment with business students compared changes in framing bias and decision quality among four groups: a control group, a strategic planning group, a full scenario process group, and a partial scenario analysis group. Participants in the full scenario process group reported the highest decision quality and greatest reduction in framing bias (Meissner and Wulf 2013). In the second paper, Schoemaker (1993) presents the results of four experiments, two of which investigate the effects of using scenario planning on students' subjective confidence ranges for particular events. Of the two experiments, one found that, after a scenario construction exercise, the range of expected values for outcome variables increased substantially. The second of the two experiments, however, found that exposure to extreme scenarios reduced the uncertainty perception in some cases. Basing his conclusions on these experiments, Schoemaker determines that scenario methods improve decision making by countering one set of biases (such as overconfidence) through the exploitation of others (such as the conjunction fallacy, wherein multiple events presented together are seen as more likely).

In summary, the business management field contains the largest body of scenario evaluation research. In my review, several studies feature control groups and two describe experimental research. A large proportion of these studies, however, involve one scholar, Thomas Chermack, who as a scenario consultant may have a vested interest in positive results. Other limitations are that the Chermack studies provide little information about the cases from which their data are drawn, give few details about the scenario methods, and generally report aggregate effects among all participants. Some of Chermack's articles do not include the length or number of workshops, but those that do suggest that they all followed a similar format; for example, the Glick and colleagues (2012) study, for which Chermack is the second author, includes participants in five workshops. Chermack describes his approach in a book (2011) and explains that this limited contextual information is due to client confidentiality. Most of the Chermack-related studies also use existing survey instruments from the management field, which may not align with outcomes of interest to other fields. In the management studies, as in the other fields I reviewed, just one study measures objective outcomes (Phelps, Chan, and Kapsalis 2001).

Chapter Summary

- A systematic literature review identified 21 studies evaluating the effectiveness of scenario planning in the urban planning, business management, and environmental management fields.
- Although differences in projects and research approaches make generalization difficult, there is relatively strong evidence that individual participants of scenario planning projects experience outcomes such as learning, making new connections, and viewing problems in new ways.
- Evidence for longer-term effects of scenario planning is more mixed and remains limited by the few studies that evaluate long-term outcomes.

9 Urban Scenario Outcomes Evaluation Framework

Previous chapters outline how scenarios might be evaluated in theory and how researchers have empirically evaluated scenario planning. The result, however, is a long list of outcomes, hypotheses, and research designs using diverse measurements. The evaluation of urban scenario planning is in a nascent stage. This chapter advances it by proposing a conceptual framework organizing the ideas for evaluation presented so far. A conceptual framework is "primarily a conception or model of what is out there that you plan to study, and of what is going on with those things and why—a tentative theory of the phenomena that you are investigating" to inform more specific research design (Maxwell 2013, 39). Frameworks are particularly useful for topics that can be investigated from multiple perspectives, such as urban scenario planning, and they facilitate comparison of scenario planning with alternative methods to understand their relative strengths and weaknesses, leading to better decisions.

I developed an urban scenario outcomes evaluation framework in several steps. First, the framework begins with the concepts presented in chapter 7 from the literature on the performance of plans in urban planning and of scenario planning in business management. Next, as described in chapter 8, I reviewed the literature on outcomes and evaluation. Then, I drew on the theoretical concepts and existing evaluation literature to construct the framework. Finally, to preliminarily evaluate the draft framework, I interviewed practitioners who had been involved in recent urban scenario planning projects to test whether the framework categories aligned with their experiences. Two of these projects, part of the Austin Sustainable Places Project, used normative transportation–land use planning for demonstration sites, and the Denveright project used exploratory scenario planning. On the basis of the interviews and my review of methods used in research, I discuss how my framework applies to urban scenario planning and propose evaluation instruments to measure outcomes uniformly.

Introducing the Urban Scenario Outcomes Evaluation Framework

Business management literature provides a useful starting point for a framework that incorporates the broader influences of scenario planning on participants. Chermack (2003) argues that corporate performance can be measured at the three levels Rummler and Brache (1995) propose: the organization, the business process, and the job or performer. Chermack proposes that performance at each level can then be evaluated from one of three theoretical perspectives proposed by Swanson (1995) in the context of human resources development: economic, psychological, and systemic (i.e., systems thinking and modeling, such as the ideas discussed in Senge [1990]). To evaluate scenario planning as a corporate strategic planning method, Chermack combined these three levels and three perspectives into a blank three-by-three framework to fill in (table 14). As described in chapter 8, Chermack, together with other researchers, carried out a theoretical and empirical research program explicitly organized according to this framework.

Table 14 Chermack's Scenario Planning Evaluation Framework

Level of Performance	Theoretical Foundation		
	Economic	Psychological	Systemic
Job/performer			
Process			
Organization			

Chermack (2003).

The only other evaluation framework for scenario planning in management is by Harries (2003), and Harries's considers whether the assessment is subjective or objective, whether the decision maker's or the technique's goals are the evaluation focus, and what evaluation method to use (theoretical analysis, simulations, experiments, or real-world decision making). Harries's framework is too broad for my aims, because it includes purely subjective outcomes, which I exclude, and nonempirical evaluation methods such as theoretical analysis and simulation to determine the technical quality of scenarios. Nonempirical evaluation of plan contents is what Baer (1997) calls plan assessment in urban planning. In scenario planning, too, plan assessments have documented the diverse substantive contents of transportation–land use scenarios (Bartholomew 2007; Bartholomew and Ewing 2008). Thus, plan assessment has a role in scenario planning—for example, in checking the accuracy of scenario models—but it is not the type of evaluation I aim to develop since its focus is too narrow. Chermack's framework provides the most suitable starting point for urban scenario planning evaluation—albeit with several modifications.

The first group of changes to Chermack's framework concerns performance levels: I renamed the job performance level *individual* and the organization performance level *organizational*, and I added *city* (used to indicate project geographic unit regardless of size) as a level, given that urban plans aim to achieve outcomes throughout a particular place. The inverted order of levels indicates the primacy of the city performance level, and I removed the process level because improving participants' specific practices (by which Chermack means business processes) is not a central aim of urban scenario planning.

The second group of changes concerns the evaluation dimensions. I renamed theoretical foundations *outcome categories*, because each already contains many theories, some of which overlap. I removed the economic theoretical foundation because public sector plans are typically created as a public good—benefits accrue to many parties and are often difficult to appraise—and economic outcomes are considered for the city as a whole, rather than one firm. I renamed the psychological theoretical foundation *learning*, which more specifically describes what scenario practitioners hope to achieve.

Researchers in several fields have concluded that individual-level theories alone are inadequate to explain system outcomes in cities, such as economic performance or natural resources protection. I have thus also added a complementary category to individual performance level. *System change* focuses on social-environmental-physical systems. Institutions—made up of rules, norms, and shared mental models (Mantzavinos, North, and Shariq 2004)—are durable aspects of society that powerfully shape individual behavior and therefore help explain differences in outcomes between places (for a review of institutions in planning, see Kim [2011]). Institutions might therefore be particularly important to planning for two main reasons: First, many planning problems can be described as collective action problems, and according to Ostrom (1990), they can be addressed through institutions. Second, achieving goals typically requires creating policies, programs, and practices, so generating consensus about strategic questions of community goals or vision is therefore insufficient. To achieve these system outcomes, planning must also stimulate *institutional change*, the third outcome.

The Evaluation Framework

This section presents the full urban scenario outcomes evaluation framework (table 15) of three outcome categories at the individual, organizational, and city performance levels.

As previously discussed, the primary goal of scenario planning is improved decision making, as described in the literature. This is, in turn, defined more specifically according to the context—for example, in business it is avoiding biased thinking (Chermack 2004); in exploratory scenario planning, identifying robust strategies that work across multiple decisions (Chakraborty et al. 2011); or in normative scenario planning, deciding on a preferred scenario after careful consideration of the alternatives (Oregon Department of Transportation 2017a). It may be possible to evaluate these specific outcomes, but I instead describe more abstract outcomes that can be applied practically to scenario planning projects.

Table 15 Urban Scenario Planning Outcomes Evaluation Framework

Level of Performance	Outcome Category		
	Learning	Institutional Change	System Change
City	Community learning	Community capacity	Goal performance
Organizational	Group learning	Policies, programs, and practices	General plan, laws, regulations, and implementation decisions
Individual	Conceptual, normative, and relational learning	Shared mental models	Behavior change

Learning

The relationship between the scenario planning method and learning outcomes is the best-developed area of evaluation research. At the individual performance level, following Haug, Huitema, and Wenzler (2011), I propose that learning outcomes can be conceptual, normative, or relational learning. I further subdivide these: Conceptual learning is single- or double-loop learning. Single-loop learning involves changing our actions in response to results; double-loop, or transformative, learning reconsiders basic assumptions (Argyris and Schön 1996). Normative learning refers to shifts in preferences, values, and attitudes, such as the changes in professional judgments examined by Groves and colleagues (2008) and Phadnis and colleagues (2015). Relational learning involves changes to relationships with others, such as new contacts or connections (Butler, Bohensky, et al. 2016; Rayle 2010), changes to trust (Butler, Suadnya, et al. 2016), and improvements to engagement skills (Veliquette et al. 2012).

At the organizational level, group learning refers to changes in an organizational climate or environment that correspond to greater interest from members in developing shared knowledge. Two studies apply the Dimensions of the Learning Organization Questionnaire, and another investigates whether scenario planning improves perceived creativity of an organization. Bowman and colleagues (2013) present a qualitative analysis of the impact of scenarios on a local government. Finally, at the city level, community learning refers to shifts in shared knowledge, or public opinion.

Institutional Change

The institutional change category describes outcomes that—though related to learning outcomes—are characteristics of the durable social structure of a place, which may be confined within a formal organization or shared among organizations. Institutional theory explains the persistence of institutions through individual-level shared mental models; therefore, shared mental models from scenario planning fit here. In addition, other outcomes within an individual institution could include practice change and decision-making style. At the organizational level, institutional change refers to changes to policies, programs, and practices, which Butler, Suadnya, and colleagues (2016) and Zapata (2013) each investigate. Finally, at the city level, outcomes include changes to the broad institutional environment. Healey (1998) conceptualizes institutional capital of a place as part of planning, whereas Butler, Suadnya, and colleagues (2016) provide an unusual approach to empirical measurement of institutional outcomes, investigating changes to institutions and community capacity.

System Change

The system change category relates to changes to a city system's physical and social elements. At the individual level, the relevant outcome is behavior changes in daily life, such as changing one's usual transportation mode. System changes at the organizational level affect general plans, laws, regulations, and implementation decisions. Some theorists consider these institutional outcomes, but I place them in the system change category because they have a concrete effect on decisions and the administration of material resources. This outcome thus includes direct-implementation activities, such as government-led infrastructure construction. Finally, city-level system change is goal performance. In keeping with the collaborative perspective of this entire book, however, my framework does not suggest that we evaluate scenario-based plans against a single universal set of indicators, as Ingram (2009) does to evaluate smart growth policies.

Applying the Framework to Existing Evaluation Studies

Chapter 8 reviews 21 empirical studies from the urban planning, business management, and environmental management literatures. Table 16 organizes them according to my proposed framework. If a study considered multiple outcome types, it is counted in multiple categories. Most studies focus on learning outcomes at the individual or organizational performance levels, and the most common study design uses surveys of participants in scenario planning workshops conducted before and after either individual workshops or the project itself. These studies directly investigate the psychological outcomes that theorists posit are a primary benefit of scenario planning. Only a few studies investigate possible institutional changes, though—Allred and Chakraborty (2015); Butler, Suadnya, and colleagues (2016); and Zapata (2013). Only two studies investigate the relationship between practices and system outcomes. Despite its weaknesses, Phelps, Chan, and Kapsalis's (2001) study stands alone in the management literature as establishing a correlation between strategic planning methods and firm-level outcomes. Similarly, Allred and Chakraborty (2015) present a unique evaluation of system-level outcomes (in this case, the location

Table 16 Scenario Planning Evaluation Studies by Level of Performance and Outcome Category

Level of Performance	Outcome Category		
	Learning	Institutional Change	System Change
City	0	1	2
Organizational	8	3	2
Individual	15	4	1

Note: Total is greater than 21 because studies are counted for all outcomes they include. See chapter 8 for descriptions of the studies.

of housing construction) after a regional scenario planning project. Investigating scenario planning's effects at the organizational and city performance levels would require controlling for factors outside the scenario process, and I am not aware of a study that has attempted it.

Empirical Evaluation

I conducted a preliminary empirical validation of the framework with three cases of urban scenario planning, selected to contain examples of two contrasting approaches: inductive analysis and visioning. For the first, I analyze the Denveright XSP Demonstration Project, an Exploratory Scenario Planning (XSP) case (Roberts 2014). XSP, developed by the Lincoln Institute of Land Policy and Sonoran Institute, adopts the inductive method described in chapter 4 to analyze driving forces and uses a matrix to consider interactions of driving forces. The resulting scenarios undergo a qualitative analysis.

The other approach, vision projects, uses methods pioneered for planning projects such as Envision Utah and the Sacramento Region Blueprint to create land use scenarios. Vision projects define a set of possible future development patterns and describe them qualitatively and quantitatively. Stakeholders develop transportation and land use scenarios for the study area that fit the patterns and then typically select a preferred scenario. These techniques usually involve planning support systems (PSS; see discussion in chapter 5) to calculate the indicators for comparing scenarios, sometimes while the scenarios are being created (Holway et al. 2012). I selected two vision projects, both part of the Austin Sustainable Places Project, introduced in chapter 4. The projects were completed in Hutto and Lockhart, two Texas cities in the exurbs of Austin, and both communities used similar techniques with locally tailored demonstration site boundaries and topical focus.

My key-informant interviews in the three cases asked questions that probed the preliminary framework categories. I reviewed the project reports and the community master plans, which in the Texas communities had been updated since the project's completion. Since I spoke to just one or two people involved in each project, these findings are necessarily tentative and may not capture outcomes unknown to the professional staff, such as stakeholder learning or decision making. To obtain the most accurate information, I provided all interviewees with anonymity.

Denveright

The Denveright XSP Demonstration Project was conducted in the spring and summer of 2016 by the staff of Western Lands and Communities, a joint program of the Lincoln Institute of Land Policy and the Sonoran Institute. The project involved interviews and two workshops. The participants were members of the Blueprint Denver Working Group, a group of city staff and consultants involved in the Blueprint Denver project to create an integrated land use and transportation plan for the city. The project's focal question was, "As Denver continues to change and evolve over the next 25 years, how can the city provide greater access to opportunities, services and amenities for current and future residents?" (Stapleton 2017, 3). Critical uncertainties included the level of economic growth, the extent of mode shift away from automobile travel, political will to make changes, and net migration of millennials. All scenarios assumed several certainties, such as an aging population and more frequent extreme weather events caused by climate change. The project resulted in four scenarios— Denver Today, Boom!, Brown Cloud, and Denverisco—which participants used to analyze strategies such as improving alternative transportation modes, articulating the value of planning, and improving affordable-housing policies.

I interviewed two city staff members who participated in the workshops, and they reported a limited amount of individual and collective learning and some changes in how the project subsequently conducted outreach. The project had only a modest effect, which they attributed to its short duration and the limited diversity of participants, but they nonetheless found it useful. The first interviewee believed the project facilitated an "honest" internal discussion about the city's future, creating a venue where staff felt comfortable, she said, "talking about our hopes and dreams for the city, and an opportunity for us to share the things that were keeping us up at night." Discussion included excitement about the benefits of the city's recent and future growth but also concerns about affordability and whether the desired transportation mode shifts would occur. Such conversation was not an anticipated benefit of the project, but it helped the participants recognize their common goals and define the focus of the project.

The scenario exercise also generated ideas about how to conduct public outreach as part of the planning project. This first interviewee reported that the project helped participants remember to talk about urban development in a way that would make sense to the public. For example, they talked about tangible improvements to daily life instead of abstract density numbers. Both interviewees believed the project did not succeed in developing shared understanding or transformative learning, however, because it was such a short process—and the second interviewee noted that "everybody goes back to their jobs and they have to face the realities of current policies and current regulations." She agreed that the primary benefit of the project was enabling participants to step back and have a broader conversation about the plan, fostering cross-departmental collaboration within the city. She thought it also contributed to a mental shift among city staff from creating static plans in the past to creating more adaptable and resilient plans in the future.

Austin Sustainable Places Project: Hutto, Texas

The Austin Sustainable Places Project scenario explorations all used a similar methodology, the same group of consultants, and a visioning meeting featuring a general discussion about demonstration site issues and vision for it. At a charette, local stakeholders in a participatory exercise created draft land use and transportation scenarios, which consultants then refined for presentation at a final public meeting. Each project's final report presented the scenarios used and specific implementation recommendations, such as changes to zoning and other local ordinances.

In Hutto, I interviewed two staff members involved in the project. They believed the project had helped generate community support for certain elements of the plan, such as developing a bicycle network and improving walkability. However, one thought the short duration of the project meant that it did not result in major changes to the participants' perspectives. For example, the plan had suggested building a road to connect newer subdivisions with Hutto's older existing downtown, leading the city to reserve land for the road within a new development. She said that the project consultant did a "great job" of showing how the street could create a useful connection and be designed to ensure slow traffic speeds, to ease community concerns about traffic the street might create. But the new road was never built; neither were changes made to a state route managed by the Texas Department of Transportation nor was redevelopment of a city-owned property done. The staff reported, however, that these ideas were incorporated into a revised comprehensive plan and related plans that the community compiled after the project's completion. In my cursory review of the city's comprehensive plan, I found it does mention the Austin Sustainable Places Project by name as one component of the public involvement used to develop its contents, and the future land use map contains some mixed-use residential areas that are consistent with the project's concept.

The interviewees said learning about the specific planning method was one goal of the project, but that did not occur. One recalled attending a training session at which computer problems occurred, and both pointed out that staff turnover had limited institutional memory. Overall, the project seems to have reinforced community consensus on a set of planning priorities while generating some specific ideas that have, at least partially, been incorporated into subsequent decision making and formal planning documents. According to the interviewees, the primary weakness of the project was a lack of support from external stakeholders such as the Texas Department of Transportation and, to a certain extent, within the city government.

Austin Sustainable Places Project: Lockhart, Texas

A similar planning process was conducted in Lockhart, Texas. Like Hutto, Lockhart has a population of around 15,000 people, but as the county seat, it has a larger traditional downtown centered on a courthouse. The resulting plan focused on that downtown and on land near a newly constructed toll highway on the outskirts of town. The project plan proposed revitalizing downtown by redesigning the streets around the courthouse and

Figure 22 A suggestion from a scenario project in Lockhart, Texas, was to redesign the streets surrounding a downtown courthouse to be more pedestrian friendly, seen here before implementation of the project.

developing vibrant street life to attract visitors (figure 22). The plan also proposed creating parks along creeks, creating a gateway to the community near the toll exit, and developing mixed-use housing.

The local planner involved in the project said the project was "very educational and useful" and gave residents an opportunity to discuss how to encourage compact housing and whether to preserve a local creek, which had not been the subject of detailed discussions in the past. The plan contains a proposal to reconfigure streets in the downtown square, and he reported that the city is working with the Texas Department of Transportation and with city staff to implement this proposal. In addition, he reported that the city's newly hired economic development director has been using the plan as a guide for his activities. Use of the plan by nongovernmental stakeholders has been limited, but at least one property owner pursued developing a new mixed-use building after learning that the plan designated the site for mixed use. The land use plan has not been amended to reflect the project's ideas, but the interviewee reported this was on his personal to-do list. The widening and reconstruction of a major street to accommodate bike lanes and sidewalks—a plan that predated the project but was incorporated into it—is now underway.

Relative to the framework, the interviewee said the project resulted in some modest individual and collective learning. Although its land use recommendations have not yet been incorporated into city plans and regulations, he thought they would be included in future zoning code revisions. Downtown streetscape improvements have not been constructed, but he reported extensive implementation discussions with stakeholders like the city engineer and the Texas Department of Transportation and believed that improvements probably would occur in the near future. Therefore, there is evidence that the plan's recommendations for the design of this part of Lockhart are influencing decision making.

Discussion

The interviewees' comments broadly confirm the relevance of the framework's dimensions, and they highlight the challenges facing any scenario planning evaluation. First, interviewees agreed that important learning occurred in all the projects, even if they thought transformative learning did not take place, owing to project limitations. Of the three levels of performance, community learning received the fewest comments; however, this may be due to these projects' not engaging in extensive public outreach. Still, the Lockhart interviewee said that memory of the project seems to have faded already, "except for the downtown people, who keep asking . . . , 'When are we gonna do that?'"

The interviewees' feedback suggests that the project did result in some degree of community learning. Regarding institutional outcomes, although interviewees hesitated to conclude that shared mental models had been built, they believed the projects played a role in developing community consensus about local issues or specific proposals, and such consensus implies that some degree of change to mental models occurred. Similarly, the interviewees provided specific examples of changes in policies, programs, and practices, but the effect was modest. No one I interviewed thought the projects had resulted in changes to community capacity, but that may be due to the projects' small scale. Finally, regarding system outcomes, interviewees could not comment on potential behavior or performance changes, although they did give examples of general plans, laws, regulations, and other implementation activities for how the plan was being used in decision making and to some extent being incorporated into other planning documents.

Applying the Evaluation Framework

Any evaluation needs to consider which outcomes to prioritize for measurement and recognize that outcomes may be interrelated. In general, these relationships move to the left or upward in the framework—that is, from specifics to generalities (see table 15). For example, individual-level behavior changes arise from revised mental models, which relate to conceptual, normative, or relational learning. Similarly, individual-level categories are often related to organizational-level categories, which are related to city-level categories. These are not necessarily related, however, and many factors beyond the framework probably explain each outcome. For example, behavior change can occur without learning if an outside force affects the choices available to urban residents (e.g., mortgage credit becomes more difficult to obtain). Zapata (2013) highlights a cautionary case in which a project seemed to result in individual transformative learning but that learning did not translate into organizational- or city-level outcomes.

Another consideration is that outcomes differ in their importance, because they depend on a project's goals, and are harder or easier to measure. Measurements for five outcomes are detailed in this section. Four outcomes are either difficult to measure or relatively less important from a theoretical perspective: behavior change and shared mental models at the individual level, and community learning and community capacity at the city level.

At the individual level, behavior change is typically relatively easy to measure, but it is less important to evaluating scenario planning for theoretical reasons. Motivating individual behavior change is not usually a primary objective in urban planning, which typically aims to affect collective decision making; in addition, as previously noted, behavior has many influencers, and it may be difficult to link a behavioral shift to involvement in a scenario planning project, even when behavior is measured.

Also at the individual level, the outcome of shared mental models is difficult to measure, and therefore many practical applications omit it, but it is of interest to scholars (Mohammed, Klimoski, and Rentsch 2000). Shifts in mental models among project participants have been documented using interviews (Otto-Banaszak et al. 2011), questionnaires (Stone-Jovicich et al. 2011), textual analysis (Carley 1997), and other methods (Langan-Fox, Code, and Langfield-Smith 2000). In systems analysis, causal loop system diagrams created by participants before and after an intervention can be rigorously compared (Schaffernicht and Groesser 2011), but most planning projects do not create such diagrams. Therefore, testing shifts in mental models may not be feasible for most scenario project evaluations.

At the city level, community learning could be measured through public opinion surveys conducted before and after a project or through extensive case research such as that conducted by Holden (2008) in her study of sustainable development practices in Seattle. Also at the city level, community capacity is important to know. Healey (1998) proposes the related concept of institutional capital, which she defines as the knowledge resources, relational resources, and capacity for mobilization of a place. Stone (2001) relies on extensive case research to propose civic capacity as explaining cities' abilities to mount reforms to their educational systems. Although new methods like network analysis may be useful for operationalizing civic capacity (Weir, Rongerude, and Ansell 2009), assessing community learning and capacity requires detailed surveying, which is logistically difficult and can be expensive.

After deciding which outcomes are important and measurable, evaluators must choose a unit of analysis and time frame, and the literature offers no firm guidance for this. Units of analysis should probably increase with levels of performance, going from the individuals who participate in a scenario planning project to organizations that are formally involved to potentially all organizations and individuals in the geographic area. In practice, however, each unit must be defined more precisely, but residents and organizations come and go. At the individual level, choices must be made about whom to include: all participants from all phases of the project or only those from specific meetings. The same considerations apply to organizations, which also have gradations of involvement. At the city level, evaluators must define spatial boundaries of their study (a particular jurisdiction or a larger region).

Measurement of outcome categories may provide more valuable results if the time frame for analysis is longer rather than shorter. Learning outcomes are typically measured before and after individual workshops. Meissner and Wulf's (2013) experiment indicates, however, that some of scenario planning's benefits may appear only after a complete application of the method, such as at the conclusion of the project when the plan is finalized. Therefore, the most appropriate way to measure institutional changes may be to document changes in a group of people at the beginning and end of a project, rather than a workshop, which introduces additional administrative challenges since it requires returning to the same participants months or even years after the initial survey. Institutional and system changes are measured through post hoc analysis. How much time should pass before conducting an evaluation has no consensus. Allred and Chakraborty (2015) investigated the Sacramento Region Blueprint seven years after its 2004 adoption, and they found that only 14 of 29 jurisdictions had updated their general plans. Institutional outcomes, such as development of new policies or programs, may occur more quickly than system outcomes, but both are subject to unpredictable external influences, such as political priorities and economic cycles. Policies may take several years to develop but can still have a large impact if they remain in place for many years. Measuring institutional changes over time also allows evaluators to assess their decisions' durability—a valuable secondary outcome that shows a consensus has been created and revisiting issues is unnecessary. I do not present durability as an outcome here, however, because conditions change and durability may not be desired.

How Should Scenario Projects Be Evaluated?

This chapter opens with the assertion that scenario planning is fundamentally about making better decisions, but the ensuing discussion has muddled what a better decision looks like. Even management theory has no consensus on how a firm's objective should be measured—whether in terms of profits, customer growth, or simple longevity and ability to withstand shocks. Scenario theorists and evaluation researchers alike seem most comfortable basing evaluations in the realm of psychology, in which a good decision is one that minimizes an individual's biases and maximizes relevant information and insights—which scenario planning can readily do. This perspective contrasts with the common view in urban planning that good decisions are those that implement specific normative agendas, such as smart growth, new urbanism, strong towns, or the just city.

Such a mind-set is problematic, because it not only presumes to know what is best for society but also neglects the possibility of rapidly unfolding events. Instead, the goal should be a progressive practice in which the general direction may be roughly known but the exact path or goal is not. Our cities face multiple crises. Albrechts makes a passionate argument for the planning field to break free of the traps of extrapolating from the past to understand the future and of being "mesmerized" by the myth of control through regulations. He calls for transformative practices that involve thinking beyond "customary job descriptions, conventional knowledge, and traditional government structures in order to address the problems in new ways and to accept that the past is no blueprint for how to go forward" (2010, 1123). He calls for planners to embrace visioning to create spatial plans that pursue transformation through long-term visions and short-term actions and strategies, citing scenario planning literature approvingly, if indirectly.

Transformation is the fundamental goal of planning practice, as this chapter has shown. An evaluation of transformation—with its wide range of effects on people, organizations, and places—is theoretically and methodologically tricky, but it is ultimately necessary to understand whether—and how—our practices live up to our aspirations.

Chapter Summary

- Scenario planning can be evaluated in many ways. This chapter presents an urban scenario outcomes evaluation framework to organize outcomes.
- I group scenario planning outcomes into three categories: learning, institutional change, and system change. Each of these categories is measured at individual, organizational, and city performance levels.
- The most measurable and professionally relevant outcomes in the evaluation framework are individual and collective learning; institutional changes to policies, programs, and practices; system changes like laws, regulations, and implementation decisions; and system performance.
- I interviewed five practitioners involved in three scenario projects. They agreed on the framework's categories, and specific evidence from their projects fit within the framework categories.
- To apply this evaluation framework to scenario planning projects, researchers and practitioners must consider the types of outcomes that are most important to a project, where and how change should be measured, and the timing of the evaluation.

PART 4

TRANSFORMATION AND CONCLUSIONS

10 Toward Transformative Scenario Practice

Stakeholders' and citizens' engagement and participation distinguish scenario projects in urban planning. Their inclusion is consistent with collaborative planning theory and the importance of deliberation in achieving new, potentially emancipatory forms of knowledge. Most people are never asked for their views about the future of their neighborhood, city, or region—if anything, they are typically asked to weigh in on discrete decisions, not to help craft a cohesive vision. Creating a long-range plan requires participants to conceptualize the future in representations that are abstract and not always related to everyday life. Can we realistically expect scenarios, even collaboratively created ones, to describe progressive futures that drive social change, or do scenarios necessarily continue current arrangements into the future?

I argue that certain intrinsic characteristics of scenario methods yield more progressive results than other forms of long-range planning. That potential is not always realized in practice, however, so this chapter discusses how scenario planning can be used to intentionally pursue more transformative planning. Specifically, considerations of race—arguably most responsible for forming social institutions that lead to urban inequality in U.S. cities—can and should enter into scenario planning. Transformative planning can manifest in many different ways: as an empirical phenomenon for mapping and analysis, in collaborative and participatory activities, as a lens through which to evaluate planning proposals, and as the subject of scenario-building exercises itself.

Colonizing and Emancipatory Futures

Because collaborative planning theorists have not yet addressed colonization and emancipation of the future in detail, this discussion draws on the insightful work of Sandberg (1976), whose analysis of planning from the perspective of critical theory anticipated collaborative ideas. Sandberg argues that the mid-20th-century advent of planning by corporations and government administration was problematic because it was another power resource, like the other "political, economic, intellectual and ideological resources" wielded by powerful contemporary social actors (21). Consequently, urban planning should not be limited to the discussion of technical methods; it should extend to the question of who has authority to determine the terms and assumptions behind planning decisions. After a detailed examination of how planning operates from a critical perspective, Sandberg concludes that planning methods can serve two functions: On one hand, they can colonize the future, so that "today's powerful interests, organized in established institutions, prolong the prevailing situation into the future by anticipating and counteracting crises and threats, accomplishing this *inter alia* through futures studies and planning" (257). Planners presuppose a harmony among interests, and planning therefore tends to become a self-fulfilling prophecy, "one of numerous possible future developments . . . presented as the probable future, entrenched behind a wall of calculations and scientificness" (257).

On the other hand, Sandberg asserts that planning could also foster emancipation, because "good futures research does not present any self-fulfilling prophecies. Conditional prognoses and conditional plans oppose reification of developments, and demonstrate alternatives and possibilities for change through active measures" (1976, 257). In his view, the publication of trends and prophecies can be the first step toward criticizing and breaking them: "In this manner they can become self-destroying by goading people into preventing an undesirable development" (259). In response to the criticism that alternatives are often a narrow range of options, Sandberg argues that projects involving real alternatives typically require the participation of organizations and individuals with diverse interests. If alternatives are presented in political terms, plans could activate the democratic process: "Instead of creating harmony and making compromises legitimate, good planning helps to reveal real conflicts, both by pointing to alternatives that are based upon different fundamental assumptions, and by promoting different interests" (257). More recently, planning scholar Miraftab Faranak makes a similar argument for what she calls the "decolonization of future(s)," concluding that the "politicization of imagination and the future as a terrain of struggle for justice is key if we are to plan for a world more just, and an urbanism more humane" (2017, 285).

This raises a key question: To what extent does scenario planning colonize or emancipate the future? To answer, we must consider intrinsic characteristics of scenario methods and how they are applied in urban planning. Several aspects of scenario planning suggest that it may hold greater potential for emancipation than the approaches described in chapter 3. Forecasting projects are oriented toward a single possible future. In contrast, presenting multiple scenarios may encourage debate about the likelihood and desirability of possible futures. Conversations about them often have explicitly political dimensions. In one intriguing case (see box 7), for instance, equity activists in San Francisco used legal and political leverage to force professional planners to consider an alternative scenario of their own design.

Visioning projects can also gloss over some interests about the future and obscure how present practices may make achieving a vision difficult. Scenarios, in contrast, can highlight differences in preferences for the future, and their focus on plausibility encourages detailed analyses of the changes necessary to achieve goals. Avin and Dembner explain that, although most scenario projects lead to shifts in beliefs, the exploration of alternatives highlights differences in values and "almost always clarifies choices, allowing a coalition of interest groups to move forward," even in the absence of consensus (2001, 26).

By placing uncertainties at the center of planning discussions, scenario methods further invite debate about which aspects of the present are desirable for the future and which should be changed. The emancipatory potential of scenario planning is largely conjecture, however, and many projects' scenarios vary along only narrowly prescribed dimensions. Zapata

BOX 7 Challenging Official Futures with an Equity, Environment, and Jobs Scenario in San Francisco

Metropolitan transportation planning is one of the most technically complex and influential forms of planning. Long-range transportation plans guide billions of dollars of transportation investments. The formal planning process is dominated by highly complex modeling, overseen by metropolitan planning organizations (MPOs) whose boards are overwhelmingly white (Sanchez and Wolf 2005) and organized in most places in ways that give disproportionate influence to suburban and exurban jurisdictions (Lewis 1998). Activists seeking transportation improvements for low-income communities of color have struggled to make inroads in the planning process. A notable success is the advocacy work of the San Francisco Bay Area's 6 Wins for Social Equity Network, a coalition of more than 20 social justice, faith, public health, and environmental organizations (Urban Habitat 2018).

California's pioneering climate change legislation, the Sustainable Communities and Climate Protection Act of 2008 (SB 375) mandates that California MPOs incorporate scenarios into regular long-range transportation plans, including land use and transportation scenarios that show how the region will meet its assigned greenhouse gas reduction targets. In 2010, the Metropolitan Transportation Commission (the San Francisco region's MPO) and the Association of Bay Area Governments began to prepare scenarios for their first plan under the new law. Contemporaneously, 6 Wins was formed to advocate for six key policy goals: improved bus service, affordable housing, investment without displacement, quality jobs, healthy and safe communities, and community power.

Frustrated by the limited ambitions for these goals in the official scenarios from the professional planners and elected officials, 6 Wins took the unusual step of creating its own: the Equity, Environment and Jobs (EEJ) scenario. The EEJ scenario combined investments in local public transit with land use proposals to create affordable housing near jobs in high-opportunity suburbs; it further required jurisdictions to implement novel antidisplacement mea-

Figure 23 Supporters of the 6 Wins for Social Equity Network Attending a San Francisco Metropolitan Transportation Commission Meeting to Advocate for the Equity, Environment and Jobs Scenario

Courtesy of Paloma Pavel/2012 Breakthrough Communities.

sures. The coalition, pictured at a meeting in figure 23, successfully lobbied the MPO to have its scenario analyzed as part of the plan's environmental impact report. To the MPO's surprise, its technical analysis revealed that, of all the scenarios considered, the EEJ scenario would result in the greatest greenhouse gas reductions, the lowest housing and transportation costs, and the greatest mode shift toward public transit (Association of Bay Area Governments and Metropolitan Transportation Commission 2013).

Although the Metropolitan Transportation Commission and the Association of Bay Area Governments did not adopt the EEJ scenario as its official selection, their 2013 plan did include three amendments inspired by the EEJ scenario: build more transit operations,

> Box 7 *Cont'd*
>
> direct cap-and-trade revenues to disadvantaged communities, and pursue antidisplacement measures. In 2016, 6 Wins also successfully advocated for an EEJ 2.0 scenario as part of the region's subsequent plan, which resulted in further policy changes that directed millions of dollars to affordable housing and antidisplacement.
>
> Although the activists fell short of fundamentally reshaping the official plans, this case illustrates Sandberg's (1976) contention that discussions of alternative futures can activate constructive democratic debates by clarifying conflicts, identifying alternatives, and promoting different interests. The EEJ scenarios revealed how regional transportation planning choices prioritized certain goals and communities over others, and the coalition leaders believed that "the introduction of a community-developed scenario immediately sparked intense debate at the agencies, bringing the needs of disadvantaged communities to the fore in a planning process that had mostly sidelined them" (Marcantonio and Karner 2014, 7). The EEJ scenarios had institutional and technical constraints, however, and, as in many areas of planning, regional transportation planning remains a clash of priorities and interests. Still, the scenarios led the Metropolitan Transportation Commission to give more consideration to a community that typically struggled to be heard.

and Kaza (2015) criticize the diversity and depth of stakeholder involvement in four high-profile scenario projects in urban planning, and they track the effects of the resulting lack of intellectual diversity among the scenarios. Although the logic of the scenario method makes transformation possible, realizing this potential depends on the choices made by professionals and participants.

Racial Inequality and Empowerment in Planning

One of the most striking characteristics of many U.S. cities is their strong spatial pattern of racial segregation. In many northeastern and midwestern cities, race strongly divides the central city and its suburbs, especially between African American and white communities. In many southern cities, racial segregation continues along historical dividing lines. As I discuss in more detail later, racial segregation and metropolitan built environments play important roles in perpetuating socioeconomic inequality. Even where residential segregation is less stark, such as in the fast-growing cities of the Sunbelt, race plays both subtle and overt roles in influencing urban development. Often, white opponents improving public transportation or new housing construction stoke fear of "those people" coming into "our" community. With the election of President Donald Trump, America entered a new phase of race relations, resulting in changes to laws, policies, and practices that have worsened racial segregation and spatial inequality. One planning-related example is the Affirmatively Furthering Fair Housing rule, adopted in 2015 by the U.S. Department of Housing and Urban Development, and its repeal, which removes requirements for recipients of federal funds to consider how their policies reduce inequality.

Yet the role of race has too often been neglected in urban planning practice. The planning historian June Manning Thomas argues that "planners' record concerning minorities, women, and poor people [is] embarrassing" and that planning scholars and professionals must incorporate racial inequality and empowerment as "necessary theoretical constructs" to improve the field's ability to know its past, appreciate the limitations placed on the field by social context, discover fresh insights and perspectives, and draw on history to envision improved futures (Thomas 1998, 198–199). My discussion in this book, too, reflects that bias to a certain extent and has only indirectly referred to racial segregation and inequality. Because I agree with Thomas, though, this section clarifies how race fits within the theory I have outlined thus far. I explain how history provides powerful legal and moral arguments for action and suggest how scenario planning can further address the racial inequality inherent in U.S. society.

Race is a social construction—comprising not only shared beliefs among people but also formal ingredients such as written laws, bureaucratic organizations, and physical artifacts—that influences many aspects of the city system (Kim 2012; Verma 2007). Establishing new legal and economic systems to replace ineffective or oppressive ones requires much more than writing down laws and telling people they can now start businesses; it also requires a broader process of social development, such as that exemplified by the new entrepreneurs studied by Kim (2008) in Vietnam's transition to democracy. Scholars studying nations that have undergone dramatic social and economic changes have highlighted the importance of this more intangible dimension of institutions (Mantzavinos, North, and Shariq 2004), and many institutions of social stratification around the world have persisted despite official efforts to reduce their role in society.

Therefore, abolishing de jure racial discrimination in U.S. law does not abolish racial discrimination, which has existed in this country since before its founding. Because planning often addresses formal institutions—like land use regulations and infrastructure decisions—the legal norm of color blindness somewhat restricts planning's decisions. The residential segregation we see today in metropolitan areas is both the product of private decisions and the legacy of unconstitutional, racially explicit policies and practices at all levels of government over many years (Rothstein 2017). As the legal scholar Richard Rothstein argues, institutionalized discrimination has been most pervasive and harmful in the country's treatment of African Americans, who were systemically targeted by racial zoning, barred from access to government-subsidized mortgages and public housing, and excluded from the housing market by government-enforced racial covenants, among many other policies of the first half of the 20th century. As a consequence, "African Americans were unconstitutionally denied the means and the right to integration in middle-class neighborhoods, and because this denial was state-sponsored, the nation is obligated to remedy it" (Rothstein 2017, xiv).

Urban planning professionals cannot deny their role in this history, given their part in drawing up and enforcing segregationist zoning and land use regulations, planning and implementing urban renewal schemes that devastated African American communities, and routing freeways through minority and low-income neighborhoods, among other measures (Thomas and Ritzdorf 1997). Many planning professionals refused to participate in egregious wrongdoing, though, and some explicitly worked on behalf of African American communities; indeed, Thomas is careful to observe that "the problem of racial prejudice and oppression originated not so much from bureaucratic planners as from the larger society" (1998, 201). No doubt, many professionals today work in, or despite, contexts hostile to fostering racial inclusion and equity or in contexts where their actions are legally constrained. But planners nonetheless wield power that demands they understand and consider the social consequences of their work.

Rothstein discusses possible remedies to historical legal discrimination but admits that some of his ideas would not survive a challenge in court, such as the government purchasing homes in suburban developments that were initially developed as all white and selling them to African Americans at a discount, or denying the mortgage interest tax deduction to suburban homeowners in segregated communities. His discussion of remedies includes many legal and highly feasible changes, however, such as reforming exclusionary zoning, implementing inclusionary zoning ordinances, and encouraging households that receive federal government rent vouchers to live in high-opportunity neighborhoods (Rothstein 2017, 195–213). Racial inequity remains a nuanced, durable part of society—but one that urban planners can tackle in many concrete ways.

Addressing Racial Inequality Through Scenarios

One of the most fundamental steps professionals can take to advance equity has already been addressed in a more general way in earlier chapters: ensure representatives of all affected communities—especially historically disenfranchised groups—have meaningful opportunities to participate in planning. This could include recruiting individuals and organizations to serve on steering committees or making engagement opportunities as inclusive as possible by, for example, providing child care, translation services, and accommodations for those with disabilities. Comparing demographic data of participants with that of the project area can support better understanding of gaps in outreach activities. Fortunately, equity and inclusion are increasingly a focus of public participation, and many resources are available on the topic (e.g., Portland Metro 2016). The remainder of this section addresses less common approaches to incorporate equity considerations into scenario planning projects in more fundamental ways.

The built environment reinforces and worsens social inequality, and a vast library of social science studies documents how urban places shape social outcomes by influencing communities' access to jobs, educational opportunities, safety, clean air and water, and nature. The "geography of opportunity" is now a widely accepted frame for conceptualizing the differences among neighborhoods (Briggs 2005; Squires and Kubrin 2005). Visually representing differences in opportunity across urban space, called opportunity mapping (Reece et al. 2013), overlay indexes of opportunity with demographic data to explore the qualities of neighborhoods inhabited by racial groups. This approach critically highlights how spatial decisions can address social inequality—either by expanding access to exclusive high-opportunity areas or by improving quality of life in low-opportunity areas.

The spatial, quantitative nature of opportunity mapping means that it can be readily combined with spatial forms of scenario planning, and it has proved a powerful discussion starter on issues of racial equity. Opportunity mapping was incorporated in the federal government's now-rescinded Affirmatively Furthering Fair Housing rule, which mandated empirical analysis of local conditions to direct recipients of federal housing funds to "take significant actions to overcome historic patterns of segregation, achieve truly balanced and integrated living patterns, promote fair housing choice, and foster inclusive communities that are free from discrimination" (Notice Withdrawing Deadline Extension for Assessment of Fair Housing, 80 Fed. Reg. 42272 [January 5, 2018]).

Although opportunity mapping is a powerful analytic tool, it typically targets only a relatively meager amount of resources and geographic coverage, and it addresses the role of race only indirectly. Sharon E. Sutton and Susan P. Kemp argue that the urban built environment, even as it perpetuates inequality, can also function as a site of empowerment and transformation for marginalized communities: place-making strategies allow "people of color to join together in collective resistance to the prevailing norms, policies, and practices that relegate them to racialized, underresourced, and politically disenfranchised surroundings" (2011, 113). Sutton and Kemp propose strategies such as housing cooperatives, community gardens, community-university partnerships, and youth leadership initiatives that do not clearly relate to collective, long-term planning, but they also highlight addressing inequality through the lens of spatial interdependence. For example, they suggest equalizing "access to the building blocks of social and racial equality: quality schooling, affordable housing, viable and accessible employment opportunities, and functional transportation systems" through policies such as revenue sharing, transportation investment, inclusionary zoning, and redevelopment of vacant properties (123).

The 6 Wins coalition's EEJ scenario in the San Francisco Bay Area illustrates two important lessons about the relationship between scenarios and addressing regional equity and racial and ethnic inequality. First, it highlights how all forms of regional planning influence regional equity, whether or not they acknowledge it explicitly. Although the 6 Wins EEJ scenario contained some novel affordable housing policies, it generally focused on the equity consequences of existing land use and transportation decisions in all the project's official scenarios, such as where to focus new density and the number and type of transportation investments. Second, the coalition's successes resulted from a major organizing effort by many organizations to develop the EEJ scenario and pressure the MPO to consider it. Equity advocates must weigh planning initiatives against alternative strategies, such as those described by Sutton and Kemp, that more directly address their communities' pressing concerns. U.S. cities and practitioners that do not find equity activists demanding a seat at the planning table should reconsider how their practices and organizations perpetuate racial injustice and inequality through routine, "colorblind" planning decisions.

Additionally, because scenario planning can incorporate any dimension of interest to participants, there is no reason the issue of race in cities cannot be centrally addressed by a scenario, qualitatively or even quantitatively. The Gwinnett County (2009) *2030 Unified Plan* scenarios provide one modest example: Because the county was undergoing rapid demographic transition from a predominantly white population to one with many racial and ethnic groups, planners created an International Gateway scenario. This scenario—which was adopted for implementation by county elected officials—framed the increasing diversity as consistent with the county's economic development goals.

Another notable use of race in scenarios is the Detroit Strategic Planning Project, which used race as a major topical theme, although constructive discussions seem to have had disappointing implementation results (Detroit Strategic Planning Project 1987). The 1992 Mont Fleur Scenario Exercise, conducted by a diverse group in South Africa, also directly addressed racial reconciliation and equity, and it was thought to have contributed to the successful 1994 transition to democracy (Kahane 2012). I am not aware of any scenario planning projects in the 21st century that have broached the question of equity so directly and profoundly, but many examples of constructive and difficult conversations about urban equity, history, and race relations are in other arenas.

Planning that engages explicitly with different communities also needs to reconcile culturally based perspectives on the future. Karen Umemoto documents how an urban planning project conducted in a Native Hawaiian community overcame cultural and linguistic barriers to arrive at a vision statement rooted in Hawaiian culture through use of Hawaiian words and concepts (Umemoto 2001). In a case study of the Foreigners' Assembly in Kawasaki City, Japan, Umemoto and Hiroki Igarashi (2009) explore how deliberative planning can overcome obstacles caused by ethnic diversity.

In the United States, recognition grows of the importance of cultural differences when planners seek to foster discussion of the future. The historian Walter Greason calls attention to the importance of rural African American communities' unique culture and heritage, which a white-dominated process of suburbanization has eclipsed in many places in the late 20th century (Greason 2013). A related trend in popular culture is interest in Afrofuturism, a cultural aesthetic that explores the intersection of African diaspora culture with advanced technology (Dery 1993). Used to describe works by science fiction authors, musicians, and visual artists since the 1950s, the idea reached broad audiences through the popular 2018 film *Black Panther*, which included a vivid depiction of the fictional African nation of Wakanda. The production designer Hannah Beachler created a vibrant and inclusive city that combines futuristic mass transit and other technologies with respect for history and traditions of its society (Flatow 2018). Greason and Julian Chambliss have argued that Afrofuturism provides an impetus for scholars seeking to rethink contemporary metropolitan development (Greason and Chambliss 2018).

Racial and social inequalities are undeniable parts of cities' social institutions, and this section has sought to answer Thomas's (1998) call to place racial inequality firmly at the center of urban planning. If we recognize race as a prominent social institution, it can enter into scenario planning in many ways: as an empirical phenomenon worthy of careful mapping and analysis, as an important consideration for collaborative and participatory activities, as a lens through which to evaluate planning proposals, and as the subject of scenario-building exercises. The challenge of planning for multicultural cities remains partially met at best. I hope this section illustrates how scholars and practitioners can take up the issue and how scenario methods overall hold promise for progressive practice that critically engages with this important dimension of cities.

Chapter Summary

- Although planning may aspire to transformation, its practices can either colonize the future by perpetuating current power relations or foster emancipation by criticizing and disrupting current arrangements.
- The EEJ scenario in the San Francisco Bay Area shows how scenario logic can be used to construct and promote alternatives—yet it required extraordinary organizing and political pressure on conventional planning institutions to achieve, which may be difficult to replicate elsewhere.
- Scenarios can address race—one of the most important facets of urban inequality—through several means: as a consideration in collaborative and participatory activities, through analytic mapping and analysis, as a lens for proposal evaluation, and as the subject of scenario-building exercises.

11 Conclusion

In this chapter, I revisit my goals for the book, briefly touching on the broader perspective I have adopted. Then I discuss the roles for academic research in advancing urban scenario planning. Finally, I offer some thoughts on planning education. I hope this book provokes further discussion and debate about how planning can improve its effectiveness in the face of an urgent need for urban transformation and growing uncertainty about the future.

Revisiting Book Goals

This book has pursued two related goals. The first is to explain scenario planning methods for an audience of urban planning practitioners and scholars. Scenario planning has reached the stage of development in which there is a body of material to draw from but also a need for improved tools and evaluation. I have also sought to elevate the theoretical underpinnings of scenario planning and its relationship to urban planning theories, topics typically neglected in existing professional literature.

The second goal is much less modest. I have explained how scenario planning continues the intellectual revolution in urban planning begun by Jane Jacobs in *The Death and Life of Great American Cities* (1961) and furthered by Horst Rittel and Melvin Webber in their article "Dilemmas in a General Theory of Planning" (1973). Though limited by the state of theory of their respective eras, both works pointed to fundamental flaws in planning practice: Jacobs criticized the design-focused, top-down planning of modernism as being ignorant of the nature of the city, which she described as an example of organized complexity from the nascent field of systems science. Rittel and Webber accepted her systems view in the abstract but further understood that a city's human dimension makes it fundamentally different from systems of other types—meaning a city cannot be effectively analyzed and planned without reference to the perspectives in and about it. In this way, the authors criticized the mainstream systems analysts of the 1960s, who sought to improve urban planning through quantitative models.

I discovered Jane Jacobs's work as an undergraduate while writing a thesis about Detroit's Gratiot Area Redevelopment Project. This urban renewal project, which eventually resulted in the Lafayette Towers housing complex designed by the modern architect Ludwig Mies van der Rohe, exemplified the flaws of the urban renewal era. It forcibly evicted thousands of low-income black residents, destroyed the homes and businesses they occupied, and replaced them with modernist towers (Goodspeed 2004). If this was planning in the 1950s, surely, I thought, planning must be much different today in the 21st century. I explored that basic question during my subsequent master's and doctoral studies, in which I encountered ideas from collaborative planning theory and from Rittel and Webber that reinforced for me the magnitude of the equity problem. I also learned that many scholars view the wicked problems of planning as insurmountable instead of the start of an exciting new chapter.

Planning's crisis of confidence, which coincided with the publication of Rittel and Webber's article, came with the collapse of traditional notions of rationality and comprehensive planning under overwhelming criticism. In response, planners pursued reduced modes of practice such as incremental planning, middle-range planning, advocacy planning, or today's tactical urbanism and placemaking. Collectively, these styles suggest potential for broader transformation through small-scale or short-term planning activities. However useful these more modest approaches may be, though, the need for large-scale, long-range planning has never gone away. Ambitious planning remains indispensable to—and even a legally mandated aspect of—contending with the consequences of large-scale decisions and preparing for uncertain futures.

Scenarios today explore the long-term consequences of decisions and trends, consistent with collaborative theory's view of planning as a process of ongoing learning. In this view, the goal of planning is to make more intelligent decisions today, not to achieve perfect knowledge of the future. As I explain in chapter 1, existing streams of scholarship on urban complexity and on collaborative planning theory lead in fruitful theoretical directions, but neither says much about how to conduct urban scenario planning specifically. The argument of this book is that they can be fused, and concepts from corporate scenario planning can provide the needed substantive structure.

The approach I have taken in this book is to provide advice for practice but not reduce scenario planning to a highly prescriptive formula. First, projects should be tailored to their social contexts; deciding whom to engage in what ways requires project-specific judgment. In addition, the types of expertise and tools required for analysis also depend on local conditions, the particular problems being addressed, the nature of financial resources and information infrastructure, and the context of previous planning and analysis. Our theories can provide suggestions on these issues but ultimately not final answers.

This book's big-tent approach to scenario planning reflects the clear advances that vision projects have made over earlier paradigms—an approach that has proven popular because many diverse stakeholders value its results. Some academics have criticized vision projects, such as those described in chapter 4, for lacking the rich analysis of external uncertainty that characterizes scenario planning in business management. I have tended toward inclusiveness; flawed projects often contain innovative features, and unsuccessful ones provide important learning opportunities. Although many of the projects described in this book simplify scenario ideas, casting a wide net ensures as comprehensive an investigation as possible. It complements discussions through professional networks, such as the Consortium for Scenario Planning (see box 8), in which the methods are debated and advanced.

This book focuses on U.S. case studies, practices, and legal frameworks, but the book has also noted some examples of scenario planning being conducted elsewhere for interested readers. Planners in the Netherlands have created a large number of scenarios for their cities in the 20th century

> ## BOX 8 The Consortium for Scenario Planning: An Emerging Community of Practice
>
> There are growing professional education opportunities to learn more about scenario planning, such as through state- and national-level American Planning Association conferences and educational opportunities. A new community of practice has emerged that complements these resources by allowing for in-depth education and collaboration.
>
> The Consortium for Scenario Planning, an initiative of the Lincoln Institute of Land Policy and established in 2017, fosters growth in the application of scenario planning in urban and rural areas. Sparked by the publication of the Lincoln Institute's 2012 report "Opening Access to Scenario Planning Tools" (Holway et al. 2012), the organization holds an annual conference, hosts webinars, and engages in additional initiatives. Registrants, who pay an annual fee, can participate in collaborative working groups, help guide and expand the field, and access technical assistance, educational resources, and a network of fellow innovators. The consortium may be of interest to professionals who want to dive much deeper into technical details about how to create scenarios, students exploring career opportunities at the cutting edge, scholars conducting related research, and civic leaders interested in exploring ideas to take back to their communities. Learn more or join by visiting the consortium's website at www.scenarioplanning.io.

(Salewski 2012). It is also home to Shell Oil Corporation, a long-standing locus of scenario methods for corporate strategic planning. The Visioning and Backcasting for Transportation (VIBAT) methodology has been implemented in Australia, the United Kingdom, Canada, and India.

Although planning practices must always be adapted to their unique settings, in general I see great opportunities to apply scenario concepts to cities in the global south. With the 2015 adoption of the 2030 Agenda for

Sustainable Development by United Nations member states and the global trend of urbanization, planning to achieve Sustainable Development Goal 11—"make cities and human settlements inclusive, safe, resilient and sustainable" (United Nations 2015, 24)—seems to be a probable international focus in the near future. Because planning is intertwined with broader societal institutions, its practices cannot be easily transferred between places; however, scenario planning is potentially useful in many contexts requiring a framework to analyze uncertainty or coordination across diverse stakeholders.

Research

Many types of academic research inform scenario planning. Empirical research on cities provides a crucial resource for planning; however, in keeping with the collaborative perspective, the relevance of findings to a project's specific times and places must be carefully evaluated. Translational research ensures that empirical findings can be applied to professional practice through the creation of tools, procedures, and models. Planning theories and methods alike benefit from scholarship in philosophy, epistemology, and the humanities. Design research can analyze planning methods and techniques of professional practice—from the nature of the scenarios created to how they are created, to effective tool use—as described in chapter 5. Finally, evaluation research, described in chapter 8, clarifies the benefits and impacts of planning, often through established social science research methods like surveys, case studies, and quantitative analysis.

Translational and design research are relatively new areas for planning research (Goodspeed, Pelzer, and Pettit 2017), although aspects of design research have been present in planning for many years, including reflective practice and research conducted about planning support systems. The core animating ideas for almost all planning lie in the realm of broader scholarship, because the whole field rests on assumptions about the nature of reality and society and the potential for action within them. Academic knowledge may conflict with or be potentially enriched by forms of local and tacit knowledge held by practitioners and communities themselves (Corburn 2003).

Planning Education

The topic of planning education is somewhat more concrete and focused than that of academic research, but it raises equally difficult issues. Professional planning degrees serve a heterogeneous field and span a wide range of specialties and forms of practice: One graduate may conduct quantitative modeling for a Silicon Valley startup, and another may work as a grassroots community organizer—and both may use aspects of their degree and conduct some form of planning. Other programs provide an education in urban studies, which may equip graduates only with knowledge of cities and research methods, not with particular strategies or methods of professional practice. My focus in this book is on planning that informs long-range decisions about the form and function of cities. As cases in preceding chapters show, these projects are often still the province of professional planners employed by public agencies, but participants can include consultants, civic leaders, and even citizens. Therefore, this advice focuses on the master's degree programs in urban planning, which provide the academic credential held by most professional urban planners.

I suggest these programs should contain three general elements: a foundation in systems thinking, training in specific substantive areas and associated methods, and training in different models of professional practice.

First, I advocate adopting the systems thinking perspective described in this book as the overarching intellectual framework for the field. The field's history and theoretical evolution should be covered but not at the expense of adequate coverage of contemporary ideas. As I have argued, city systems cannot be reduced to a quantitative model. This perspective would highlight for students the links between different dimensions of cities, such as housing, economic development, and transportation, strengthening their ability to work across these sectors. National and place-specific planning institutions and planning laws are an important element of the systems context of planning, but they do not define what planning is or should be; redesigning institutions can be part of planning.

Second, professional education should include training in substantive areas and their methods. Some of these are shared among multiple applications, like statistics, modeling, quantitative analysis, or geographic information systems. Others are more specific, such as cohort-component demographic models. Every student should at least be conversant in these areas, both to be able to conduct analyses and to orchestrate broader processes with experts conducting specialized studies. Furthermore, planners' interest in these methods is not only to understand what *is* but also to explore what *could be*, so they must understand their limitations and assumptions.

Finally, a student whose curriculum stopped at this point would be an expert in cities and potentially a skilled analyst but not know how to make an impact. The final ingredient in planning curricula is theories of practice—how to engage the future and make change. Theories of practice are not only scenario planning for long-term systems planning but also for other settings such as consensus building, strategic spatial planning (Albrechts 2004), creative placemaking (Zitcer 2018), and perhaps others. Together, these practice models specify how to organize substantive analysis, collaborative participation, and vision to stimulate change.

In the book, I have argued that the quality of a plan cannot be judged on its face. Rather, it must be judged by the extent to which it reflects the knowledge and perspectives of many participants and the extent to which its creation had reciprocal learning effects among those involved. Furthermore, because no single plan is the last word on the future, many plans should also be judged by their ability to influence decisions and other plans. Conformity between a strategic plan and on-the-ground changes is evidence only of slavish implementation, not necessarily wise decision making, effective problem-solving, or reaching goals. In fact, the history of planning has proved that unthinking implementation can cause more problems than it resolves, and the hallmark of a well-planned city is not only the good ideas that were adopted but also the bad ideas rejected. The successes of planning—such as vibrant downtowns, convenient commutes, protected habitats, high-quality public services, and flood prevention—rarely make news headlines. Since they are the product of collective actions coordinated but not exclusively controlled by planners, the profession lacks the visibility and recognition enjoyed by more individualistic professions such as architecture, entrepreneurship, and invention. Therefore, this book is not so much a reinvention of planning as it is a defense of it. When given the chance, citizens are eager to participate in a process to realize a better future for themselves and their communities, and the fruits of good planning are visible in every city for those who look. Cities exist as they are, not as we wish they were, and scenario planning offers a good way to comprehend and plan them well.

Chapter Summary

- Although this book focuses largely on U.S. professional practice and examples, scenario planning has been and can be implemented in many contexts around the world.
- Areas of academic research that can benefit scenario planning include empirical research on cities, translational research that applies specific findings to professional practice, design research on professional tools and methods, evaluation research of project outcomes, and broader theoretical scholarship.
- Planning curricula should emphasize contemporary theories, knowledge, and methods, including scenario planning.

Acknowledgments

This book is a culmination of years of reflection and work, during which I have incurred many debts. My introduction to the planning field was at the University of Maryland's Master of Community Planning program, where I had the good fortune to learn from the faculty, especially Howie Baum, Sidney Brower, Alex Chen, Jim Cohen, and Qing Shen. I first explored the concept of scenario planning in Boston through both professional and academic settings; as a new planning analyst fresh out of graduate school, I had the good fortune to work at the Metropolitan Area Planning Council for Holly St. Clair, Tim Reardon, and Executive Director Marc Draisen, as well as with Amy Cotter and Jessie Grogan. After I began doctoral studies, MAPC allowed me to continue collaborating on several projects, providing an invaluable learning experience. It has been a pleasure to continue to work with Amy and Jessie in their current capacities at the Lincoln Institute of Land Policy and to have Jessie and Hallah Elbeleidy as managing editors for this book.

At the MIT Department of Urban Studies and Planning (DUSP), I learned about scenario planning methods in the class Simulating Sustainable Futures, offered by Mike Flaxman and Juan Carlos Vargas, both now private consultants in the field. Other DUSP faculty who shaped my thinking include my dissertation committee—Joe Ferreira, Brent Ryan, and Annette Kim—and Amy Glasmeier, Bish Sanyal, Anne Spirn, Larry Vale, and the late JoAnn Carmin. DUSP Ph.D. students Deepak Lamba-Nieves, Lauren Lambie-Hanson, Tijs van Maasakkers, Nick Marantz, Eric Schultheis, Todd Shenk, and Mia White shared academic advice, debated big ideas, or joined me to unwind at the Muddy Charles Pub.

Supportive academic and professional colleagues have been indispensable as I navigated the University of Michigan's tenure track, including Urban and Regional Planning Program colleagues Scott Campbell, Margi Dewar, Harley Etienne, Lesli Hoey, Jonathan Levine, Martin Murray, and Ana Paula Pimentel Walker, who all provided advice and encouragement. Elsewhere, Dick Klosterman and Arnab Chakraborty have been especially supportive, and Arnab was in fact the first person to suggest I write a book on scenario planning. In the world of practice, participants in the Consortium for Scenario Planning (previously the Scenario Planning Apps Network and earlier the Open Scenario Planning Tools Group) have been generous with their time and insights: Janae Futrell read and commented on much of the manuscript. It has also been gratifying to continue to work with Jenni Minner and Bob Paterson in this group, whom I met when they generously allowed me to study their innovative Austin Sustainable Places scenario planning project in Austin, Texas. Ever since providing thoughtful feedback on my first scenario planning class syllabus, Uri Avin has been generous in sharing his wealth of experience in and deep insights into the use of scenarios in urban planning. Jeremy Stapleton shared his experiences and case materials related to the Denveright and Sahuarita cases. Other consortium participants who have supported this project include Frank Lenk, Ted Knowlton, and Ken Snyder. I also wish to thank the Lincoln Institute of Land Policy for providing consistent financial and staff support for these activities, as well as funding several of my research projects on scenario planning.

At the University of Michigan, my colleagues encouraged me to offer a new elective on scenario planning, which eventually led to this book. Many insightful comments by students in my courses have seeped into these pages; at times, I think I learned more from them than they did from the dense assigned readings. In particular, students in my Fall 2018 course read draft chapters of nearly the entire book, providing me valuable insights through our discussions: Rowan Brady, Andong Chen, Tianai Chen, Lu Hao, Jacob Hite, Emily Korman, Ruoshui Liu, Jessica Robbins, Peter Swinton, and Xiaodi Xu. Ph.D. student Xiang Yan created many of the original assignments and served as a course grader. In addition to these, other students who read draft chapters include Yuanqiu Feng, Brett

Fusco, Tom Logan, Anthony Townsend, and Richa Yadav. Our program's indefatigable writing expert, Julie Steiff, edited the entire manuscript. I thank Taubman College of Architecture and Urban Planning for subvention funding. During the publication process, Allison Ehrich Bernstein, Emily McKeigue, Angela Piliouras, and Mary Ann Short edited the manuscript, provided substantive advice, and oversaw the many production details. Any errors that remain are my own.

Through it all, my family made this book possible through their unwavering support. My parents, Greg and Nancy Goodspeed, encouraged me to pursue my interests—even when that led to an unfamiliar field and state. Most of all, I want to thank my spouse, Libby Benton. Since my days as an underemployed waiter, she has offered unconditional love and support as I moved through the academic world, and I am inspired by her fierce determination to help and be a legal advocate for those who are struggling. The arrival of our daughter, Eloise, has led me to see her in a new light as a wonderful mother and has redoubled my commitment to working for a world worth living in: more sustainable, more intelligent, more humane, more fun, and more just.

Glossary

citizen. Individual who has a moral or political right to contribute to decisions made in public participation activities; typically a resident of the study area.

city. An inhabited place, regardless of political boundaries or incorporation, of residences, workplaces, shared infrastructure, and other communal facilities.

collaborative planning. A theory-informed approach to planning practice that uses deliberation and stakeholder engagement to build consensus and to counter power imbalances.

complex system. An organic or inorganic whole composed of multiple interacting parts that exhibits coherent organization, is robust, and adapts to change.

consensus building. A method of dispute resolution that involves deliberation among affected stakeholders.

digital tools. For purposes of this book, computer models, databases, and software programs used to design, analyze, and visualize urban scenarios.

forecasting. Creating quantitative or qualitative predictions about the future.

indicator. A quantitative measurement describing a real-world phenomenon of interest; it is a specific concept derived by a technical method of calculation.

place. The geographic scope of a planning project; it may be a corridor, district, municipality, region, or rural area.

scenario planning. Long-term strategic planning that creates representations of multiple, plausible futures of a system of interest.

stakeholder. Representative of an organization, interest, or community.

strategic planning. Organizational planning that considers internal and external characteristics, such as the organization's strengths, weaknesses, opportunities, and threats.

transformation. A fundamental change to an urban complex system.

uncertainty. Either (1) a general state of not knowing; or (2) an aspect of the future for which different outcomes are possible.

urban scenario planning. The application of scenario planning to the professional practice of urban and regional planning.

visioning. Planning a community through the participatory definition of a shared idea, often described in words and pictures.

wicked problem. An ill-defined, unique public problem that involves normative judgments about values and is addressed through an indefinite list of solutions that cannot be fully tested.

References

Abbott, John. 2005. "Understanding and Managing the Unknown: The Nature of Uncertainty in Planning." *Journal of Planning Education and Research* 24(3): 237–251.

———. 2009. "Planning for Complex Metropolitan Regions: A Better Future or a More Certain One?" *Journal of Planning Education and Research* 28(4): 503–517.

Alberti, Marina. 2016. *Cities That Think like Planets: Complexity, Resilience, and Innovation in Hybrid Ecosystems.* Seattle: University of Washington Press.

Albrechts, Louis. 2004. "Strategic (Spatial) Planning Reexamined." *Environment and Planning B* 31: 743–758.

———. 2010. "More of the Same Is Not Enough! How Could Strategic Spatial Planning Be Instrumental in Dealing with the Challenges Ahead?" *Environment and Planning B: Planning and Design* 37(6): 1115.

Albrechts, Louis, and Alessandro Balducci. 2013. "Practicing Strategic Planning: In Search of Critical Features to Explain the Strategic Character of Plans." *disP: The Planning Review* 49(3): 16–27.

Al-Kodmany, Kheir. 1999. "Using Visualization Techniques for Enhancing Public Participation in Planning and Design: Process, Implementation, and Evaluation." *Landscape and Urban Planning* 45(1): 37–45.

Allen, Eliot. 2001. "INDEX: Software for Community Indicators." In *Planning Support Systems: Integrating Geographic Information Systems, Models, and Visualization Tools*, ed. Richard Brail and Richard Klosterman, 229–261. Redlands, CA: Esri Press.

———. 2008. "Clicking Toward Better Outcomes: Experience with INDEX, 1994–2006." In *Planning Support Systems for Cities and Regions*, ed. Richard K. Brail, 139–166. Cambridge, MA: Lincoln Institute of Land Policy.

Allred, Dustin, and Arnab Chakraborty. 2015. "Do Local Development Outcomes Follow Voluntary Regional Plans? Evidence from Sacramento Region's Blueprint Plan." *Journal of the American Planning Association* 81(2): 104–120.

Ames, Steven C., American Planning Association, and Oregon Visions Project. 1993. *A Guide to Community Visioning: Hands-on Information for Local Communities.* Portland, OR: Oregon Chapter, American Planning Association.

Anderson, Martin. 1964. *The Federal Bulldozer: A Critical Analysis of Urban Renewal, 1949–1962.* Cambridge, MA: MIT Press.

Ange, Katharine, Caroline Dwyer, Kathleen Rooney, and Ed Mierzejewski. 2017. "Next Generation Scenario Planning: A Transportation Practitioner's Guide." U.S.

Department of Transportation Federal Highway Administration, Office of Planning (June).

Araujo, Rochelle, Andrea Bassi, Llael Cox, Nicholas Flanders, Jenna Kolling, Andrew Procter, and Nadav Tanners. 2016. *A System Dynamics Model for Integrated Decision Making: The Durham-Orange Light Rail Project.* Washington, DC: United States Environmental Protection Agency.

Argyris, Chris, and Donald A. Schön. 1996. *Organizational Learning II: Theory, Method, and Practice; Vol. 2: Addison-Wesley OD series.* Reading, MA: Addison-Wesley.

Arnstein, Sherry R. 1969. "A Ladder of Citizen Participation." *Journal of the American Planning Association* 35(4): 216–224.

Assessment, Millennium Ecosystem. 2018. "About." https://www.millenniumas sessment.org/en/About.html.

Association of Bay Area Governments and Metropolitan Transportation Commission. 2013. "Draft Plan Bay Area Environmental Impact Report." In author's possession.

Avin, Uri. 2007. "Using Scenarios to Make Urban Plans." In *Engaging the Future: Forecasts, Scenarios, Plans, and Projects,* ed. Lewis D. Hopkins and Marisa A. Zapata, 103–134. Cambridge, MA: Lincoln Institute of Land Policy.

Avin, Uri P., and Jane L. Dembner. 2001. "Getting Scenario-Building Right." *Planning* 67(11): 22.

Bacon, Edmund N. 1967. *Design of Cities.* New York: Viking Press.

Baer, William C. 1997. "General Plan Evaluation Criteria: An Approach to Making Better Plans." *Journal of the American Planning Association* 63(3): 329–344.

Banister, David, and Robin Hickman. 2013. "Transport Futures: Thinking the Unthinkable." *Transport Policy* 29: 283–293.

Bartholomew, Keith. 2007. "Land Use–Transportation Scenario Planning: Promise and Reality." *Transportation* 34(4): 397–412.

Bartholomew, Keith, and Reid Ewing. 2008. "Land Use–Transportation Scenarios and Future Vehicle Travel and Land Consumption: A Meta-analysis." *Journal of the American Planning Association* 75(1): 13–27.

Batty, Michael. 2007. *Cities and Complexity: Understanding Cities with Cellular Automata, Agent-Based Models, and Fractals.* Cambridge, MA: MIT Press.

Baum, Howell S. 1999. "Forgetting to Plan." *Journal of Planning Education and Research* 19(1): 2–14.

Belt, Marjan van den. 2004. *Mediated Modeling: A System Dynamics Approach to Environmental Consensus Building.* Washington, DC: Island Press.

Ben-Joseph, Eran, Hiroshi Ishii, John Underkoffler, Ben Piper, and Luke Yeung. 2001. "Urban Simulation and the Luminous Planning Table." *Journal of Planning Education and Research* 21(2): 196–203.

Berke, Philip, and Edward J. Kaiser. 2006. *Urban Land Use Planning.* 5th ed. Urbana: University of Illinois Press.

Biggs, Reinette, Ciara Raudsepp-Hearne, Carol Atkinson-Palombo, Erin Bohensky, Emily Boyd, Georgina Cundill, Helen Fox, Scott Ingram, Kasper Kok, and Stephanie Spehar. 2007. "Linking Futures Across Scales: A Dialogue on Multiscale Scenarios." *Ecology and Society* 12(1): 17.

Bishop, Peter, Andy Hines, and Terry Collins. 2007. "The Current State of Scenario Development: An Overview of Techniques." *Foresight: The Journal of Future Studies, Strategic Thinking and Policy* 9(1): 5–25.

Bohensky, Erin L., Belinda Reyers, and Albert S. Van Jaarsveld. 2006. "Future Ecosystem Services in a Southern African River Basin: A Scenario Planning Approach to Uncertainty." *Conservation Biology* 20(4): 1051–1061.

Booher, David E., and Judith E. Innes. 2002. "Network Power in Collaborative Planning." *Journal of Planning Education and Research* 21(3): 221–236.

Börjeson, Lena, Mattias Höjer, Karl-Henrik Dreborg, Tomas Ekvall, and Göran Finnveden. 2006. "Scenario Types and Techniques: Towards a User's Guide." *Futures* 38(7): 723–739.

Boudette, Neal E. 2016. "Autopilot Cited in Death of Chinese Tesla Driver." *New York Times*, September 14, B5.

Bowman, Gary, R. Bradley MacKay, Swapnesh Masrani, and Peter McKiernan. 2013. "Storytelling and the Scenario Process: Understanding Success and Failure." *Technological Forecasting and Social Change* 80(4): 735–748.

Bradfield, Ronald M. 2008. "Cognitive Barriers in the Scenario Development Process." *Advances in Developing Human Resources* 10(2): 198–215.

Bradfield, Ronald M., George Wright, George Burt, George Cairns, and Kees van der Heijden. 2005. "The Origins and Evolution of Scenario Techniques in Long Range Business Planning." *Futures* 37(8): 795–812.

Brail, Richard K. 2008. *Planning Support Systems for Cities and Regions*. Cambridge, MA: Lincoln Institute of Land Policy.

Briggs, Xavier de Souza. 2005. *The Geography of Opportunity: Race and Housing Choice in Metropolitan America*. Washington, DC: Brookings Institution Press.

Brömmelstroet, Marco te. 2015. "A Critical Reflection on the Experimental Method for Planning Research: Testing the Added Value of PSS in a Controlled Environment." *Planning Practice and Research* 30(2): 179–201.

Brömmelstroet, Marco te, and Pieter M. Schrijnen. 2010. "From Planning Support Systems to Mediated Planning Support: A Structured Dialogue to Overcome the Implementation Gap." *Environment and Planning B: Planning and Design* 37(1): 3–20.

Bryson, John M. 2004a. *Strategic Planning for Public and Nonprofit Organizations: A Guide to Strengthening and Sustaining Organizational Achievement*. 3rd ed. San Francisco, CA: Jossey-Bass.

Bryson, John M. 2004b. "What to Do When Stakeholders Matter." *Public Management Review* 6(1): 21–53.

Bryson, John M., and William D. Roering. 1987. "Applying Private-Sector Strategic Planning in the Public Sector." *Journal of the American Planning Association* 53(1): 9–22.

Butler, James R. A., Erin L. Bohensky, I. Wayan Suadnya, Y. Yanuartati, Tarningsih Handayani, Putrawan Habibi, Ketut Puspadi, Timothy D. Skewes, Russell M.

Wise, I. Suharto, Sarah E. Park, and Yusuf Sutaryono. 2016. "Scenario Planning to Leap-Frog the Sustainable Development Goals: An Adaptation Pathways Approach." *Climate Risk Management* 12: 83–99.

Butler, James R. A., I. Wayan Suadnya, Y. Yanuartati, S. Meharg, Russell M. Wise, Yusuf Sutaryono, and K. Duggan. 2016. "Priming Adaptation Pathways Through Adaptive Co-management: Design and Evaluation for Developing Countries." *Climate Risk Management* 12: 1–16.

Butler, James R. A., Russell M. Wise, Timothy D. Skewes, Erin L. Bohensky, N. Peterson, I. Wayan Suadnya, Y. Yanuartati, Tarningsih Handayani, Putrawan Habibi, Ketut Puspadi, N. Bou, D. Vaghelo, and W. Rochester. 2015. "Integrating Top-Down and Bottom-Up Adaptation Planning to Build Adaptive Capacity: A Structured Learning Approach." *Coastal Management* 43(4): 346–364.

Butler, James R. A., Juliette C. Young, Iain A. G. McMyn, Ben Leyshon, Isla M. Graham, Ian Walker, John M. Baxter, Jane Dodd, and Caroline Warburton. 2015. "Evaluating Adaptive Co-management as Conservation Conflict Resolution: Learning from Seals and Salmon." *Journal of Environmental Management* 160: 212–225.

Byrne, David. 2003. "Complexity Theory and Planning Theory: A Necessary Encounter." *Planning Theory* 2(3): 171–178.

California Department of Transportation. 2007. "Assessment of Local Models and Tools for Analyzing Smart-Growth Strategies." https://rosap.ntl.bts.gov/view/dot /27539.

Calthorpe, Peter, and William B. Fulton. 2001. *The Regional City: Planning for the End of Sprawl.* Washington, DC: Island Press.

Campanella, Thomas J. 2011. "Jane Jacobs and the Death and Life of American Planning." In *Reconsidering Jane Jacobs*, ed. Max Page and Timothy Mennel, 141–160. New York: Routledge.

Campbell, Scott. 1996. "Green Cities, Growing Cities, Just Cities? Urban Planning and the Contradictions of Sustainable Development." *Journal of the American Planning Association* 62(3): 296–312.

Caplice, Christopher George, Shardul Sharad Phadnis, National Research Council (U.S.), Transportation Research Board, National Cooperative Highway Research Program, American Association of State Highway and Transportation Officials, and U.S. Federal Highway Administration. 2013. *Strategic Issues Facing Transportation. Volume 1: Scenario Planning for Freight Transportation Infrastructure Investment.* Washington, DC: Transportation Research Board.

Carley, Kathleen M. 1997. "Extracting Team Mental Models Through Textual Analysis." *Journal of Organizational Behavior* 18: 533–558.

Carpenter, Stephen R., and Millennium Ecosystem Assessment Scenarios Working Group. 2005. *Ecosystems and Human Well-Being: Scenarios: Findings of the Scenarios Working Group*, Millennium Ecosystem Assessment, Millennium Ecosystem Assessment series. Washington, DC: Island Press.

Carton, L. J., and W. A. H. Thissen. 2009. "Emerging Conflict in Collaborative Mapping: Towards a Deeper Understanding?" *Journal of Environmental Management* 90(6): 1991–2001.

Chakrabarti, Vishaan. 2009. "Being Dense About Denmark." *Urban Omnibus*. https://urbanomnibus.net/2009/12/being-dense-about-denmark/.

Chakraborty, Arnab. 2011. "Enhancing the Role of Participatory Scenario Planning Processes: Lessons from Reality Check Exercises." *Futures* 43(4): 387–399.

Chakraborty, Arnab, Nikhil Kaza, Gerrit-Jan Knaap, and Brian Deal. 2011. "Robust Plans and Contingent Plans Scenario Planning for an Uncertain World." *Journal of the American Planning Association* 77(3): 251–266.

Chakraborty, Arnab, and Andrew McMillan. 2015. "Scenario Planning for Urban Planners: Toward a Practitioner's Guide." *Journal of the American Planning Association* 81(1): 18–29.

Champlin, Carissa, Marco te Brömmelstroet, and Peter Pelzer. 2018. "Tables, Tablets and Flexibility: Evaluating Planning Support System Performance Under Different Conditions of Use." *Applied Spatial Analysis and Policy* 12(3): 467–491.

Chermack, Thomas J. 2003. "A Methodology for Assessing Performance-Based Scenario Planning." *Journal of Leadership and Organizational Studies* 10(2): 55–63.

———. 2004. "Improving Decision-Making with Scenario Planning." *Futures* 36(3): 295–309.

———. 2011. *Scenario Planning in Organizations: How to Create, Use, and Assess Scenarios*. San Francisco, CA: Berrett-Koehler.

Chermack, Thomas J., Laura M. Coons, Kim Nimon, Peggy Bradley, and Margaret B. Glick. 2015. "The Effects of Scenario Planning on Participant Perceptions of Creative Organizational Climate." *Journal of Leadership and Organizational Studies* 22(3): 355–371.

Chermack, Thomas J., Susan A. Lynham, and Louis van der Merwe. 2006. "Exploring the Relationship Between Scenario Planning and Perceptions of Learning Organization Characteristics." *Futures* 38(7): 767–777.

Chermack, Thomas J., Louis van der Merwe, and Susan A. Lynham. 2007. "Exploring the Relationship Between Scenario Planning and Perceptions of Strategic Conversation Quality." *Technological Forecasting and Social Change* 74(3): 379–390.

Chermack, Thomas J., and Kim Nimon. 2008. "The Effects of Scenario Planning on Participant Decision-Making Style." *Human Resource Development Quarterly* 19(4): 351–372.

Chopra, Kanchan Ratna, and Millennium Ecosystem Assessment Responses Working Group. 2005. *Ecosystems and Human Well-Being: Policy Responses: Findings of the Responses Working Group of the Millennium Ecosystem Assessment*, ed. Kanchan Chopra, Rik Leemans, Pushpam Kumar, and Henk Simons. Washington, DC: Island Press.

Christensen, Karen S. 1985. "Coping with Uncertainty in Planning." *Journal of the American Planning Association* 51(1): 63–73.

Clarke, Keith C., S. Hoppen, and Leonard Gaydos. 1997. "A Self-Modifying Cellular Automaton Model of Historical Urbanization in the San Francisco Bay Area." *Environment and Planning B: Planning and Design* 24(2): 247–261.

Cobb, Ashley Noel, and Jessica Leigh Thompson. 2012. "Climate Change Scenario Planning: A Model for the Integration of Science and Management in Environmental Decision-Making." *Environmental Modelling and Software* 38: 296–305.

Corburn, Jason. 2003. "Bringing Local Knowledge into Environmental Decision Making: Improving Urban Planning for Communities at Risk." *Journal of Planning Education and Research* 22(4): 420–433.

Couclelis, Helen. 2005. "Where Has the Future Gone? Rethinking the Role of Integrated Land-Use Models in Spatial Planning." *Environment and Planning A* 37(8): 1353–1371.

Cummings, Richard. 2007. "Engaging the Public Through Narrative-Based Scenarios." In *Engaging the Future: Forecasts, Scenarios, Plans, and Projects*, ed. Lewis D. Hopkins and Marisa A. Zapata, 243–260. Cambridge, MA: Lincoln Institute of Land Policy.

Damme, L. van, Maaike Galle, M. Pen-Soetermeer, and K. Verdaas. 1997. "Improving the Performance of Local Land-Use Plans." *Environment and Planning B: Planning and Design* 24(6): 833–844.

Daniels, Tom. 2001. "Smart Growth: A New American Approach to Regional Planning." *Planning Practice and Research* 16(3–4): 271–279.

Deal, Brian, and Varkki Pallathucheril. 2008. "Simulating Regional Futures: The Land-use Evolution and Impact Assessment Model (LEAM)." In *Planning Support Systems for Cities and Regions*, ed. Richard K. Brail, 61–84. Cambridge, MA: Lincoln Institute of Land Policy.

Denyer, David, David Tranfield, and Joan Ernst van Aken. 2008. "Developing Design Propositions Through Research Synthesis." *Organization Studies* 29(3): 393–413.

Dery, M. 1993. "Black to the Future: Interviews with Samuel R. Delany, Greg Tate, and Tricia Rose." *South Atlantic Quarterly* 92(4): 735–778.

Detroit Strategic Planning Project. 1987. *The Report of the Detroit Strategic Planning Project, November 1987: ". . . Choosing a Future for Us and for All Our Children."* Detroit, MI: Detroit Strategic Planning Project.

Dewey, John. 1922. *Human Nature and Conduct: An Introduction to Social Psychology.* New York: H. Holt.

Deyle, Robert E., and Carissa S. Slotterback. 2009. "Group Learning in Participatory Planning Processes: An Exploratory Quasiexperimental Analysis of Local Mitigation Planning in Florida." *Journal of Planning Education and Research* 29(1): 23–38.

Deyle, Robert E., and Ryan E. Wiedenman. 2014. "Collaborative Planning by Metropolitan Planning Organizations: A Test of Causal Theory." *Journal of Planning Education and Research* 34(3): 257–275.

Duany, Andres, Elizabeth Plater-Zyberk, and Jeff Speck. 2000. *Suburban Nation: The Rise of Sprawl and the Decline of the American Dream.* New York: North Point Press.

Duke, Richard D. 2011. "Origin and Evolution of Policy Simulation: A Personal Journey." *Simulation and Gaming* 42(3): 342–358.

Duke, Richard D., and Jac Geurts. 2004. *Policy Games for Strategic Management*. Amsterdam: Dutch University Press.

DVRPC. 2014a. "Connections 2040 Choices and Voices." https://dvrpc.org/ChoicesAndVoices/.

———. 2014b. "The Future of Scenario Planning." https://www.dvrpc.org/reports/WP14038.pdf.

———. 2016. *Connections 2045: Greater Philadelphia Future Forces*. Philadelphia, PA: Delaware Valley Regional Planning Commission.

Ehrenhalt, Alan. 2012. *The Great Inversion and the Future of the American City*. New York: Knopf.

Eikelboom, Tessa, and Ron Janssen. 2017. "Collaborative Use of Geodesign Tools to Support Decision-Making on Adaptation to Climate Change." *Mitigation and Adaptation Strategies for Global Change* 22(2): 247–266.

Ellis, Cliff. 2002. "The New Urbanism: Critiques and Rebuttals." *Journal of Urban Design* 7(3): 261–291.

Ewing, Reid H., and Keith Bartholomew. 2019. *Best Practices in Metropolitan Transportation Planning*. New York: Routledge.

Fahmi, Fikri Zul, Muhamad Ihsani Prawira, Delik Hudalah, and Tommy Firman. 2016. "Leadership and Collaborative Planning: The Case of Surakarta, Indonesia." *Planning Theory* 15(3): 294–315.

Faludi, Andreas. 2000. "The Performance of Spatial Planning." *Planning Practice and Research* 15(4): 299–318.

Faranak, Miraftab. 2017. "Insurgent Practices and Decolonization of Future(s)." In *The Routledge Handbook of Planning Theory*, ed. Michael Gunder, Ali Madanipour, and Vanessa Watson, 276–288. Abingdon, UK: Routledge.

FHWA (Federal Highway Administration). 2011. *FHWA Scenario Planning Guidebook*. https://www.fhwa.dot.gov/planning/scenario_and_visualization/scenario_planning/scenario_planning_guidebook/.

Flatow, Nicole. 2018. "The Social Responsibility of Wakanda's Golden City." *Citylab*. November 5. https://www.citylab.com/life/2018/11/black-panther-wakanda-golden-city-hannah-beachler-interview/574420/.

Flaxman, Michael. 2009. "Fundamentals of Geodesign." Paper presented at the Geodesign Summit, Redlands, CA.

Forester, John. 1989. *Planning in the Face of Power*. Berkeley: University of California Press.

Forrester, Jay Wright. 1969. *Urban Dynamics*. Cambridge, MA: MIT Press.

Fregonese Associates. 2012a. *Envision Tomorrow Prototype Builder User Guide Version 3.1 Beta*. http://vibrantneo.org/wp-content/uploads/2014/02/ROI-user-manual-june8.pdf.

———. 2012b. "Envision Tomorrow Scenario Builder User Guide." http://vibrantneo.org/wp-content/uploads/2014/02/ScenarioBuilder-user-guide-june8.pdf.

Frick, Walter. 2015. "What Research Tells Us About Making Accurate Predictions." *Harvard Business Review.* https://hbr.org/2015/02/what-research-tells-us-about -making-accurate-predictions.

Fullilove, Mindy Thompson. 2004. *Root Shock: How Tearing Up City Neighborhoods Hurts America, and What We Can Do About It.* New York: One World/Ballantine Books.

Fung, Archon. 2006. "Varieties of Participation in Complex Governance." *Public Administration Review* 66(S1): 66–75.

Gaber, John. 2007. "Simulating Planning SimCity as a Pedagogical Tool." *Journal of Planning Education and Research* 27(2): 113–121.

Gateway 1 Steering Committee. 2009. "Gateway 1 Corridor Action Plan: Brunswick to Stockton Springs." www.midcoastplanning.org/PDFs/G1-US1-ActionPlan-LR.pdf.

Geertman, Stan. 2006. "Potentials for Planning Support: A Planning-Conceptual Approach." *Environment and Planning B* 33(6): 863.

Geurs, Karst, and Bert van Wee. 2004. "Backcasting as a Tool for Sustainable Transport Policy Making: The Environmentally Sustainable Transport Study in the Netherlands." *European Journal of Transport Infrastructure Research* 4(1): 47–69.

Glick, Margaret B., Thomas J. Chermack, Henry Luckel, and Brian Q. Gauck. 2012. "Effects of Scenario Planning on Participant Mental Models." *European Journal of Training and Development* 36(5): 488–507.

Goldstein, Bruce Evan. 2010. "Epistemic Mediation: Aligning Expertise Across Boundaries Within an Endangered Species Habitat Conservation Plan." *Planning Theory and Practice* 11(4): 523–547.

Goodier, Chris, Simon Austin, Robby Soetanto, and Andrew Dainty. 2010. "Causal Mapping and Scenario Building with Multiple Organisations." *Futures* 42(3): 219–229.

Goodspeed, Robert. 2004. "Urban Renewal in Postwar Detroit." B.A. thesis, University of Michigan.

———. 2013. "Planning Support Systems for Spatial Planning Through Social Learning." Ph.D. diss., Massachusetts Institute of Technology.

———. 2015. "Sketching and Learning: A Planning Support System Field Study." *Environment and Planning B: Planning and Design* 43(3): 444–463.

———. 2016a. "The Death and Life of Collaborative Planning Theory." *Urban Planning* 1(4): 1–5.

———. 2016b. "Digital Knowledge Technologies in Planning Practice: From Black Boxes to Media for Collaborative Inquiry." *Planning Theory and Practice* 17(4): 577–600.

———. 2017. "An Evaluation Framework for the Use of Scenarios in Urban Planning." Working paper. Cambridge, MA: Lincoln Institute of Land Policy.

Goodspeed, Robert, and Cassie Hackel. 2017. "Lessons for Developing a Planning Support System Infrastructure: The Case of Southern California's Scenario Planning Model." *Environment and Planning B: Urban Analytics and City Science* 46(4): 777–796.

Goodspeed, Robert, and Peter Pelzer. 2020. "Organizing, Facilitating, and Evaluating Planning Support System Workshops." In *Handbook of Planning Support Science*, ed. Stan Geertman and John Stillwell. Cheltenham, UK: Edward Elgar.

Goodspeed, Robert, Peter Pelzer, and Christopher Pettit. 2017. "Planning Our Future Cities: The Role Computer Technologies Can Play." In *Planning Knowledge and Research*, ed. Thomas W. Sanchez, 210–225. New York: Routledge.

Greason, Walter. 2013. *Suburban Erasure: How the Suburbs Ended the Civil Rights Movement in New Jersey*. Lanham, MD: Farleigh Dickinson University Press.

Greason, Walter D., and Julian C. Chambliss. 2018. *Cities Imagined: The African Diaspora in Media and History*. Dubuque, IA: Kendall Hunt.

Great Valley Center. 2006. "Valley Futures Project." https://web.archive.org/web/20060622193817/http://www.greatvalley.org:80/valley_futures/stories/sjv/deeper_look.aspx.

Groves, David G., Debra Knopman, Robert J. Lempert, Sandra H. Berry, and Lynne Wainfan. 2008. *Presenting Uncertainty About Climate Change to Water-Resource Managers*. Santa Monica, CA: RAND Corporation.

Gudmundsson, Henrik. 2011. "Analysing Models as a Knowledge Technology in Transport Planning." *Transport Reviews* 31(2): 145–159.

Guerra, Erick. 2015. "Planning for Cars That Drive Themselves: Metropolitan Planning Organizations, Regional Transportation Plans, and Autonomous Vehicles." *Journal of Planning Education and Research* 36(2): 210–224.

Gwinnett County. 2009. *2030 Unified Plan*. https://www.gwinnettcounty.com/web/gwinnett/departments/planninganddevelopment/gwinnett2030unifiedplan.

Haas Lyons, Susanna, Mike Walsh, Erin Aleman, and John Robinson. 2013. "Exploring Regional Futures: Lessons from Metropolitan Chicago's Online MetroQuest." *Technological Forecasting and Social Change* 82(supplement C): 23–33.

Haasnoot, Marjolijn, Jan H. Kwakkel, Warren E. Walker, and Judith ter Maat. 2013. "Dynamic Adaptive Policy Pathways: A Method for Crafting Robust Decisions for a Deeply Uncertain World." *Global Environmental Change* 23(2): 485–498.

Habermas, Jürgen. 1984. *The Theory of Communicative Action. Volume 1: Reason and Rationalization of Society*. Boston, MA: Beacon Press.

———. 1987. *The Theory of Communicative Action. Volume 2: Lifeworld and System: A Critique of Functionalist Reason*. Boston, MA: Beacon Press.

———. 1990. "Discourse Ethics: Notes on a Program of Philosophical Justification." In *Moral Consciousness and Communicative Action*, 43–115. Cambridge, MA: MIT Press.

Harries, Clare. 2003. "Correspondence to What? Coherence to What? What Is Good Scenario-Based Decision Making?" *Technological Forecasting and Social Change* 70(8): 797–817.

Hassan, Rashid M., Robert J. Scholes, Neville Ash, and Millennium Ecosystem Assessment. 2005. *Ecosystems and Human Well-Being: Current State and Trends: Findings of the Condition and Trends Working Group, The Millennium Ecosystem Assessment Series*. Washington, DC: Island Press.

Haug, Constanze, Dave Huitema, and Ivo Wenzler. 2011. "Learning Through Games? Evaluating the Learning Effect of a Policy Exercise on European Climate Policy." *Technological Forecasting and Social Change* 78(6): 968–981.

Healey, Patsy. 1997. *Collaborative Planning: Shaping Places in Fragmented Societies.* Vancouver, CA: UBC Press.

———. 1998. "Building Institutional Capacity Through Collaborative Approaches to Urban Planning." *Environment and Planning A* 30: 1531–1546.

Heijden, Kees van der. 2005. *Scenarios: The Art of Strategic Conversation.* 2nd ed. Chichester, UK: John Wiley.

Helling, Amy. 1998. "Collaborative Visioning: Proceed with Caution! Results from Evaluating Atlanta's Vision 2020 Project." *Journal of the American Planning Association* 64(3): 335–349.

Hendrick, Rebecca. 2010. "What Is Wrong with Advice on Strategic Planning?" *Public Administration Review* 70(S1): S222–S223.

Herzele, Ann van, and Cees M. J. van Woerkum. 2008. "Local Knowledge in Visually Mediated Practice." *Journal of Planning Education and Research* 27(4): 444–455.

Hickman, Robin, and David Banister. 2014. *Transport, Climate Change and the City.* Abingdon, UK: Routledge.

Hirsch, Arnold R. 1983. *Making the Second Ghetto: Race and Housing in Chicago, 1940–1960, Interdisciplinary Perspectives on Modern History.* Cambridge: Cambridge University Press.

Holden, Meg. 2008. "Social Learning in Planning: Seattle's Sustainable Development Codebooks." *Progress in Planning* 69(1): 1–40.

Holway, Jim, C. J. Gabbe, Frank Hebbert, Jason Lally, Robert Matthews, and Ray Quay. 2012. *Opening Access to Scenario Planning Tools.* Policy Focus Report. Cambridge, MA: Lincoln Institute of Land Policy.

Hopkins, Lewis D., and Marisa Zapata. 2007. *Engaging the Future: Forecasts, Scenarios, Plans, and Projects.* Cambridge, MA: Lincoln Institute of Land Policy.

Hulme, Mike, and Suraje Dessai. 2008. "Predicting, Deciding, Learning: Can One Evaluate the 'Success' of National Climate Scenarios?" *Environmental Research Letters* 3(4): 045013.

Hunt, John D., David S. Kriger, and Eric J. Miller. 2005. "Current Operational Urban Land Use–Transport Modelling Frameworks: A Review." *Transport Reviews* 25(3): 329–376.

Huss, William R., and Edward J. Honton. 1987. "Scenario Planning—What Style Should You Use?" *Long Range Planning* 20(4): 21–29.

Huxley, Margo, and Oren Yiftachel. 2000. "New Paradigm or Old Myopia? Unsettling the Communicative Turn in Planning Theory." *Journal of Planning Education and Research* 19(4): 333–342.

IAP2. n.d. "Core Values, Ethics, Spectrum: The 3 Pillars of Public Participation." https://www.iap2.org/page/pillars.

Ingram, Gregory K. 2009. *Smart Growth Policies: An Evaluation of Programs and Outcomes.* Cambridge, MA: Lincoln Institute of Land Policy.

Innes, Judith Eleanor. 1990. *Knowledge and Public Policy: The Search for Meaningful Indicators*. New Brunswick, NJ: Transaction.

———. 1995. "Planning Theory's Emerging Paradigm: Communicative Action and Interactive Practice." *Journal of Planning Education and Research* 14(3): 183–189.

———. 1996. "Planning Through Consensus Building: A New View of the Comprehensive Planning Ideal." *Journal of the American Planning Association* 62(4): 460–472.

Innes, Judith E., and David E. Booher. 1999a. "Consensus Building and Complex Adaptive Systems: A Framework for Evaluating Collaborative Planning." *Journal of the American Planning Association* 65(4): 412–423.

———. 1999b. "Consensus Building as Role Playing and Bricolage: Toward a Theory of Collaborative Planning." *Journal of the American Planning Association* 65(1): 9–26.

———. 1999c. "Metropolitan Development as a Complex System: A New Approach to Sustainability." *Economic Development Quarterly* 13(2): 141–156.

———. 2000. "Indicators for Sustainable Communities: A Strategy Building on Complexity Theory and Distributed Intelligence." *Planning Theory and Practice* 1(2): 173–186.

———. 2010. *Planning with Complexity: An Introduction to Collaborative Rationality for Public Policy*. London: Routledge.

———. 2018. *Planning with Complexity: An Introduction to Collaborative Rationality for Public Policy*. 2nd ed. London: Routledge, Taylor and Francis Group.

IPCC Core Writing Team, Rajendra K. Pachauri, and Leo A. Meyer. 2014. *Climate Change 2014: Synthesis Report. Contribution of Working Groups I, II and III to the Fifth Assessment Report of the Intergovernmental Panel on Climate Change*. Geneva, Switzerland: IPCC.

Isard, Walter. 1998. *Methods of Interregional and Regional Analysis, Regional Science Studies Series*. Aldershot, UK: Ashgate.

Isserman, Andrew M. 1984. "Projection, Forecast, and Plan on the Future of Population Forecasting." *Journal of the American Planning Association* 50(2): 208–221.

———. 2007. "Forecasting to Learn How the World Can Work." In *Engaging the Future: Forecasts, Scenarios, Plans, and Projects*, ed. Lewis D. Hopkins and Marisa A. Zapata, 175–197. Cambridge, MA: Lincoln Institute of Land Policy.

Jackson, Kenneth T. 1985. *Crabgrass Frontier: The Suburbanization of the United States*. New York: Oxford University Press.

Jacobs, Jane. 1961. *The Death and Life of Great American Cities*. New York: Random House.

Jantz, Claire A., Scott J. Goetz, and Mary K. Shelley. 2004. "Using the SLEUTH Urban Growth Model to Simulate the Impacts of Future Policy Scenarios on Urban Land Use in the Baltimore-Washington Metropolitan Area." *Environment and Planning B* 31(2): 251–272.

Jetter, Antonie, and Willi Schweinfort. 2011. "Building Scenarios with Fuzzy Cognitive Maps: An Exploratory Study of Solar Energy." *Futures* 43(1): 52–66.

Kahane, Adam. 2012. *Transformative Scenario Planning: Working Together to Change the Future*. San Francisco, CA: Berrett-Koehler.

Kahn, Herman. 1962. *Thinking About the Unthinkable*. New York: Horizon Press.

Kaufman, Jerome L., and Harvey M. Jacobs. 1987. "A Public Planning Perspective on Strategic Planning." *Journal of the American Planning Association* 53(1): 23–33.

Kemp, Roger L. 1992. *Strategic Planning in Local Government: A Casebook*. Chicago: American Planning Association/Planners Press.

Kim, Annette Miae. 2008. *Learning to be Capitalists: Entrepreneurs in Vietnam's Transition Economy*. New York: Oxford University Press.

———. 2011. "Unimaginable Change: Future Directions in Planning Practice and Research About Institutional Reform." *Journal of the American Planning Association* 77(4): 328–337.

———. 2012. "The Evolution of the Institutional Approach in Planning." In *The Oxford Handbook of Urban Planning*, ed. Randall Crane and Rachel Weber. New York: Oxford University Press.

Klemek, Christopher. 2011. *The Transatlantic Collapse of Urban Renewal: Postwar Urbanism from New York to Berlin, Historical Studies of Urban America*. Chicago: University of Chicago Press.

Klosterman, Richard E. 1990. *Community Analysis and Planning Techniques*. Lanham, MD: Rowman and Littlefield.

———. 1997. "Planning Support Systems: A New Perspective on Computer-Aided Planning." *Journal of Planning Education and Research* 17(1): 45–54.

Klosterman, Richard E., Kerry Brooks, Joshua Drucker, Edward Feser, and Henry Renski. 2018. *Planning Support Methods: Urban and Regional Analysis and Projection*. Lanham, MD: Rowman and Littlefield.

Knapp, Corrine Noel, Nancy Fresco, and Lena Krutikov. 2017. "Managing Alaska's National Parks in an Era of Uncertainty: An Evaluation of Scenario Planning Workshops." *Regional Environmental Change* 17(5): 1541–1552.

Kosko, Bart. 1986. "Fuzzy Cognitive Maps." *International Journal of Man-Machine Studies* 24(1): 65–75.

Kuhn, Kristine M., and Janet A. Sniezek. 1996. "Confidence and Uncertainty in Judgmental Forecasting: Differential Effects of Scenario Presentation." *Journal of Behavioral Decision Making* 9(4): 231–247.

Kwartler, Michael, and Gianni Longo. 2008. *Visioning and Visualization: People, Pixels, and Plans*. Cambridge, MA: Lincoln Institute of Land Policy.

Landis, John D. 1994. "The California Urban Futures Model: A New Generation of Metropolitan Simulation Models." *Environment and Planning B: Planning and Design* 21(4): 399–420.

———. 1995. "Imagining Land-Use Futures: Applying the California Urban Futures Model." *Journal of the American Planning Association* 61(4): 438–457.

———. 2011. "Urban Growth Models: State of the Art and Prospects." In *Global Urbanization*, ed. Eugenie L. Birch and Susan M. Wachter, 126–150. Philadelphia: University of Pennsylvania Press.

Landis, John, and M. Zhang. 1998a. "The Second Generation of the California Urban Futures Model. Part 1: Model Logic and Theory." *Environment and Planning B: Planning and Design* 25(5): 657–666.

———. 1998b. "The Second Generation of the California Urban Futures Model. Part 2: Specification and Calibration Results of the Land-Use Change Submodel." *Environment and Planning B: Planning and Design* 25(6): 795–824.

Lang, Trudi, and Ramírez, Rafael. 2017. "Building New Social Capital with Scenario Planning." *Technological Forecasting and Social Change* 124(supplement C): 51–65.

Langan-Fox, Janice, Sharon Code, and Kim Langfield-Smith. 2000. "Team Mental Models: Techniques, Methods, and Analytic Approaches." *Human Factors* 42(2): 242–271.

Laurian, Lucie, Maxine Day, Philip Berke, Neil Ericksen, Michael Backhurst, Jan Crawford, and Jenny Dixon. 2004. "Evaluating Plan Implementation: A Conformance-Based Methodology." *Journal of the American Planning Association* 70(4): 471–480.

Lee, Douglass B. 1973. "Requiem for Large-Scale Models." *Journal of the American Planning Association* 39(3): 163.

———. 1994. "Retrospective on Large-Scale Urban Models." *Journal of the American Planning Association* 60(1): 35.

Lee, Stephanie, Mike Tremble, Justine Vaivai, Gregory Rowangould, Mohammad Tayarani, Amir Poorfakhraei, and Ecosystem Management. 2015. *Central New Mexico Climate Change Scenario Planning Project: Final Report*. Albuquerque: University of New Mexico.

Lempert, Robert J., Steven W. Popper, and Steven C. Bankes. 2003. *Shaping the Next One Hundred Years: New Methods for Quantitative, Long-Term Policy Analysis and Bibliography*. Santa Monica, CA: RAND Corporation.

Levine, Jonathan, Joe Grengs, and Louis A. Merlin. 2019. *From Mobility to Accessibility: Transforming Urban Transportation and Land-Use Planning*. Ithaca, NY: Cornell University Press.

Lewis, Paul G. 1998. "Regionalism and Representation: Measuring and Assessing Representation in Metropolitan Planning Organizations." *Urban Affairs Review* 33(6): 839–853.

Li, Xia, and Anthony Gar-On Yeh. 2000. "Modelling Sustainable Urban Development by the Integration of Constrained Cellular Automata and GIS." *International Journal of Geographical Information Science* 14(2): 131–152.

Light, Jennifer. 2008. "Taking Games Seriously." *Technology and Culture* 49(2): 347–375.

Lucas, Patricia J., Janis Baird, Lisa Arai, Catherine Law, and Helen M. Roberts. 2007. "Worked Examples of Alternative Methods for the Synthesis of Qualitative and Quantitative Research in Systematic Reviews." *BMC Medical Research Methodology* 7(1): 4.

Lukes, S. 1974. *Power: A Radical View*. London and New York: Macmillan.

Lydon, Mike, and Anthony Garcia. 2015. *Tactical Urbanism*. Washington, DC: Island Press.

Maier, Holger R., Joseph H. A. Guillaume, Hedwig van Delden, Graeme Angus Riddell, Marjolijn Haasnoot, and Jan H. Kwakkel. 2016. "An Uncertain Future, Deep Uncertainty, Scenarios, Robustness and Adaptation: How Do They Fit Together?" *Environmental Modelling and Software* 81(supplement C): 154–164.

Mantzavinos, Chrysostomos, Douglass C. North, and Syed Shariq. 2004. "Learning, Institutions, and Economic Performance." *Perspectives on Politics* 2(1): 75–84.

Marcantonio, Richard, and Alex Karner. 2014. "Disadvantaged Communities Teach Regional Planners a Lesson in Equitable and Sustainable Development." *Poverty and Race* 23(1): 5–12.

Margerum, Richard D. 2002. "Collaborative Planning: Building Consensus and Building a Distinct Model for Practice." *Journal of Planning Education and Research* 21(3): 237–253.

———. 2011. *Beyond Consensus*. Cambridge, MA: MIT Press.

Marlow, Joe, Hannah Oliver, Ray Quay, and Ralph Marra. 2015. "Integrating Exploratory Scenario Planning into a Municipal General Plan Update." Working paper. Cambridge, MA: Lincoln Institute of Land Policy.

Marshall, Stephen. 2012. "Planning, Design and the Complexity of Cities." In *Complexity Theories of Cities Have Come of Age: An Overview with Implications to Urban Planning and Design*, ed. Juval Portugali, Han Meyer, Egbert Stolk, and Ekim Tan, 191–205. Berlin: Springer Berlin Heidelberg.

Mastop, H., and A. Faludi. 1997. "Evaluation of Strategic Plans: The Performance Principle." *Environment and Planning B: Planning and Design* 24(6): 815–832.

Matheson, Alan, Jr. 2011. "Envision Utah: Building Communities on Values." In *Regional Planning for a Sustainable America*, ed. Carleton K. Montgomery, 154–167. New Brunswick, NJ: Rutgers University Press.

Mattila, Hanna. 2016. "Can Collaborative Planning Go Beyond Locally Focused Notions of the 'Public Interest'? The Potential of Habermas' Concept of 'Generalizable Interest' in Pluralist and Trans-Scalar Planning Discourses." *Planning Theory* 15(4): 344–365.

Maxwell, Joseph Alex. 2013. *Qualitative Research Design: An Interactive Approach*. Applied Social Research Methods, 41. 3rd ed. Thousand Oaks, CA: SAGE.

Mayer, Igor. 2009. "The Gaming of Policy and the Politics of Gaming: A Review." *Simulation and Gaming* 40(6): 825–862.

Mayer, Igor, Geertje Bekebrede, Casper Harteveld, Harald Warmelink, Qiqi Zhou, Theo van Ruijven, Julia Lo, Rens Kortmann, and Ivo Wenzler. 2014. "The Research and Evaluation of Serious Games: Toward a Comprehensive Methodology." *British Journal of Educational Technology* 45(3): 502–527.

McCullum, Christine, David Pelletier, Donald Barr, Jennifer Wilkins, and Jean Pierre Habicht. 2004. "Mechanisms of Power Within a Community-Based Food Security Planning Process." *Health Education and Behavior* 31(2): 206–222.

McEvoy, Sadie, Frans H. M. van de Ven, Michiel W. Blind, and Jill H. Slinger. 2018. "Planning Support Tools and Their Effects in Participatory Urban Adaptation Workshops." *Journal of Environmental Management* 207: 319–333.

Meerow, Sara, Joshua P. Newell, and Melissa Stults. 2016. "Defining Urban Resilience: A Review." *Landscape and Urban Planning* 147: 38–49.

Meissner, Philip, and Torsten Wulf. 2013. "Cognitive Benefits of Scenario Planning: Its Impact on Biases and Decision Quality." *Technological Forecasting and Social Change* 80(4): 801–814.

Mellers, Barbara, Eric Stone, Pavel Atanasov, Nick Rohrbaugh, S. Emlen Metz, Lyle Ungar, Michael Bishop, Michael Horowitz, Ed Merkle, and Philip Tetlock. 2015. "The Psychology of Intelligence Analysis: Drivers of Prediction Accuracy in World Politics." *Journal of Experimental Psychology: Applied* 21(1): 1–14.

Menand, L. 2005. "Fat Man: Herman Kahn and the Nuclear Age." *New Yorker.* https://www.newyorker.com/magazine/2005/06/27/fat-man.

Metrolinx. 2017. "Navigating Uncertainty: Background Paper to the Draft 2041 Regional Transportation Plan." (October). www.metrolinx.com/en/regionalplanning/rtp/technical/NavigatingUncertainty.pdf.

Millard-Ball, Adam. 2012. "The Limits to Planning: Causal Impacts of City Climate Action Plans." *Journal of Planning Education and Research* 33(1): 5–19.

Miller, Barry. 2009. "Plans That Fit the Purpose." In *Local Planning: Contemporary Principles and Practice*, ed. Gary Hack, Eugenie L. Birch, Paul H. Sedway, and Mitchell J. Silver, 213–228. Philadelphia, PA: ICMA Press.

Miller, Ronald E., and Peter D. Blair. 2009. *Input-Output Analysis: Foundations and Extensions.* 2nd ed. Cambridge: Cambridge University Press.

Minner, Jennifer S. 2015. "Recoding Embedded Assumptions: Adaptation of an Open Source Tool to Support Sustainability, Transparency and Participatory Governance." In *Planning Support Systems and Smart Cities*, ed. Stan Geertman, Joseph Ferreira Jr., Robert Goodspeed, and John Stillwell, 409–425. New York: Springer.

Mintzberg, Henry. 1994. *The Rise and Fall of Strategic Planning: Reconceiving Roles for Planning, Plans, Planners.* New York: Free Press.

Mohammed, Susan, Richard Klimoski, and Joan R. Rentsch. 2000. "The Measurement of Team Mental Models: We Have No Shared Schema." *Organizational Research Methods* 3(2): 123–165.

Montgomery, Roger. 1998. "Is There Still Life in *The Death and Life*?" *Journal of the American Planning Association* 64(3): 269–274.

Moore, Terry. 2008. "Planning Support Systems: What Are Practicing Planners Looking For?" In *Planning Support Systems for Cities and Region*, ed. Richard Brail, 231–256. Cambridge, MA: Lincoln Institute of Land Policy.

Moriarty, Patrick, and Damon Honnery. 2015. "Future Cities in a Warming World." *Futures* 66: 45–53.

Moss, Richard H., Jae A. Edmonds, Kathy A. Hibbard, Martin R. Manning, Steven K. Rose, Detlef P. van Vuuren, Timothy R. Carter, Seita Emori, Mikiko Kainuma,

Tom Kram, Gerald A. Meehl, John F. B. Mitchell, Nebojsa Nakicenovic, Keywan Riahi, Steven J. Smith, Ronald J. Stouffer, Allison M. Thomson, John P. Weyant, and Thomas J. Wilbanks. 2010. "The Next Generation of Scenarios for Climate Change Research and Assessment." *Nature* 463(7282): 747–756.

MRMPO. 2015. *Futures 2040: Metropolitan Transportation Plan.* Albuquerque, NM: Mid-Region Metropolitan Planning Organization.

Myers, Dowell, and Alicia Kitsuse. 2000. "Constructing the Future in Planning: A Survey of Theories and Tools." *Journal of Planning Education and Research* 19(3): 221.

Nassauer, Joan Iverson, and Robert C. Corry. 2004. "Using Normative Scenarios in Landscape Ecology." *Landscape Ecology* 19(4): 343–356.

Norton, Richard K., Stephen Buckman, Guy A. Meadows, and Zachary Rable. 2019. "Using Simple, Decision-Centered, Scenario-Based Planning to Improve Local Coastal Management." *Journal of the American Planning Association* 85(4): 405–423.

Nostikasari, Dian. 2015. "Representations of Everyday Travel Experiences: Case Study of the Dallas-Fort Worth Metropolitan Area." *Transport Policy* 44: 96–107.

Notten, Philip W. F. van, Jan Rotmans, Marjolein B. A. van Asselt, and Dale S. Rothman. 2003. "An Updated Scenario Typology." *Futures* 35(5): 423–443.

Ogilvy, Jay, and Erik Smith. 2004. "Mapping Public and Private Scenario Planning: Lessons from Regional Projects." *Development* 47(4): 67–72.

Oliveira, Vitor, and Paulo Pinho. 2010. "Evaluation in Urban Planning: Advances and Prospects." *CPL Bibliography* 24(4): 343–361.

Önkal, Dilek, M. Sinan Gönül, Paul Goodwin, Mary Thomson, and Esra Öz. 2017. "Evaluating Expert Advice in Forecasting: Users' Reactions to Presumed vs. Experienced Credibility." *International Journal of Forecasting* 33(1): 280–297.

Oregon, 1000 Friends of. 2012. "What the Zombie Westside Bypass Tells Us About Regional Transportation." www.friends.org/issues/Westside-Bypass.

Oregon Department of Transportation. 2017a. *Oregon Scenario Planning Guidelines.* (August). https://www.oregon.gov/ODOT/Planning/Documents/Oregon-Scenario -Planning-Guidelines.pdf.

———. 2017b. "Place Types Tool." https://www.oregon.gov/lcd/CL/Pages/Place-Types .aspx.

Ostrom, Elinor. 1990. *Governing the Commons: The Evolution of Institutions for Collective Action.* Cambridge: Cambridge University Press.

Oteros-Rozas, Elisa, Berta Martín-López, Tim M. Daw, Erin L. Bohensky, James R. A. Butler, Rosemary Hill, Julia Martin-Ortega, Allyson Quinlan, Federica Ravera, Isabel Ruiz-Mallén, Matilda Thyresson, Jayalaxshmi Mistry, Ignacio Palomo, Garry D. Peterson, Tobias Plieninger, Kerry A. Waylen, Dylan M. Beach, Iris C. Bohnet, Maike Hamann, Jan Hanspach, Klaus Hubacek, Sandra Lavorel, and Sandra P. Vilardy. 2015. "Participatory Scenario Planning in Place-Based Social-Ecological Research: Insights and Experiences from 23 Case Studies." *Ecology and Society* 20(4): 32.

Otto-Banaszak, Ilona, Piotr Matczak, Justus Wesseler, and Frank Wechsung. 2011. "Different Perceptions of Adaptation to Climate Change: A Mental Model Approach Applied to the Evidence from Expert Interviews." *Regional Environmental Change* 11(2): 217–228.

Page, Max, and Timothy Mennel. 2011. *Reconsidering Jane Jacobs*. Chicago: American Planning Association.

Paul, Evan Thomas. 2010. "Projections, Politics, and Practice in Regional Planning: A Case Study of MetroFuture." Master's thesis, MIT.

Perdicoulis, Anastassios, and John Glasson. 2011. "The Use of Indicators in Planning: Effectiveness and Risks." *Planning Practice and Research* 26(3): 349–367.

Peterson, Garry D., Graeme S. Cumming, and Stephen R. Carpenter. 2003. "Scenario Planning: A Tool for Conservation in an Uncertain World." *Conservation Biology* 17(2): 358–366.

Phadnis, Shardul, Chris Caplice, Yossi Sheffi, and Mahender Singh. 2015. "Effect of Scenario Planning on Field Experts' Judgment of Long-Range Investment Decisions." *Strategic Management Journal* 36(9): 1401–1411.

Phelps, Robert, C. Chan, and S. C. Kapsalis. 2001. "Does Scenario Planning Affect Performance? Two Exploratory Studies." *Journal of Business Research* 51(3): 223–232.

Phillips, Rhonda. 2005. *Community Indicators Measuring Systems*. Burlington, VT: Ashgate.

Plummer, Ryan, and Derek Armitage. 2007. "A Resilience-Based Framework for Evaluating Adaptive Co-management: Linking Ecology, Economics and Society in a Complex World." *Ecological Economics* 61(1): 62–74.

Poplin, Alenka. 2012. "Playful Public Participation in Urban Planning: A Case Study for Online Serious Games." *Computers, Environment and Urban Systems* 36(3): 195–206.

Portland Metro. 2016. "Strategic Plan to Advance Racial Equity, Diversity and Inclusion." (June). https://www.oregonmetro.gov/strategic-plan-advance-racial-equity-diversity-and-inclusion.

Portugali, Juval. 1999. *Self-Organization and the City*. Springer Series in Synergetics. New York: Springer.

———. 2011. *Complexity, Cognition and the City*. Berlin: Springer Berlin Heidelberg.

———. 2016. "What Makes Cities Complex?" In *Complexity, Cognition, Urban Planning and Design*, ed. Juval Portugali and Egbert Stolk. Cham: Springer.

Quay, Ray. 2010. "Anticipatory Governance: A Tool for Climate Change Adaptation." *Journal of the American Planning Association* 76(4): 496–511.

———. 2018. "Exploratory Scenario Analysis in the Context of Anticipatory Governance." Unpublished manuscript.

Ralston, Bill, and Ian Wilson. 2006. *The Scenario-Planning Handbook: A Practitioner's Guide to Developing and Using Scenarios to Direct Strategy in Today's Uncertain Times*. Mason, OH: Thomson South-Western.

Ramirez, Rafael, and Angela Wilkinson. 2014. "Rethinking the 2×2 Scenario Method: Grid or Frames?" *Technological Forecasting and Social Change* 86(supplement C): 254–264.

Rasmussen, Benjamin K., James Andrew, Erica Simmons, Alex Epstein, Paige Colton, and David Daddio. 2015. *Integrating Climate Change in Transportation and Land Use Scenario Planning: An Example from Central New Mexico.* Cambridge, MA: John A. Volpe National Transportation Systems Center.

Rayle, Lisa. 2010. "Telling the Future Together: The Potential of Collaborative Scenario-Building in the Transformation of Urban Governance in Portugal." Ph.D. diss., MIT. https://dspace.mit.edu/handle/1721.1/61570.

Reece, Jason, David Norris, Jillian Olinger, Kip Holley, and Matt Martin. 2013. "Place Matters: Using Mapping to Plan for Opportunity, Equity, and Sustainability." Opportunity Mapping Issue Brief. Kirwan Institute for the Ohio State University. (September). http://kirwaninstitute.osu.edu/my-product/opportunity-mapping-issue-brief/.

Rittel, Horst W. J., and Melvin M. Webber. 1973. "Dilemmas in a General Theory of Planning." *Policy Sciences* 4(2): 155–169.

Roberts, Eric J. 2014. "Exploratory Scenario Planning: Lessons Learned in the Field." Working paper. Cambridge, MA: Lincoln Institute of Land Policy.

Rodrigue, Jean-Paul. 2017. "Spatial Interactions and the Gravity Model." In *The Geography of Transport Systems*, ed. Jean-Paul Rodrigue, Claude Comtois, and Brian Slack, 380–385. New York: Routledge.

Rothstein, Richard. 2017. *The Color of Law: A Forgotten History of How Our Government Segregated America.* New York: Liveright.

Rothwell, Jonathan, and Douglas S. Massey. 2009. "The Effect of Density Zoning on Racial Segregation in U.S. Urban Areas." *Urban Affairs Review* 44(6): 779–806.

Roubelat, Fabrice. 2000. "Scenario Planning as a Networking Process." *Technological Forecasting and Social Change* 65(1): 99–112.

Rummler, Geary A., and Alan P. Brache. 1995. *Improving Performance: How to Manage the White Space on the Organization Chart.* 2nd ed. San Francisco, CA: Jossey-Bass.

Rumore, Danya, Todd Schenk, and Lawrence Susskind. 2016. "Role-Play Simulations for Climate Change Adaptation Education and Engagement." *Nature Climate Change* 6(8): 745–750.

Sadik-Khan, Janette, and Seth Solomonow. 2016. *Streetfight: Handbook for an Urban Revolution.* London: Penguin Books.

Sager, Tore. 2013. *Reviving Critical Planning Theory: Dealing with Pressure, Neoliberalism, and Responsibility in Communicative Planning.* RTPI Library Series. New York: Routledge.

Salewski, Christian. 2012. *Dutch New Worlds: Scenarios in Physical Planning and Design in the Netherlands, 1970–2000.* Rotterdam, Netherlands: Nai010.

Salter, Jonathan D., Cam Campbell, Murray Journeay, and Stephen R. J. Sheppard. 2009. "The Digital Workshop: Exploring the Use of Interactive and Immersive

Visualisation Tools in Participatory Planning." *Journal of Environmental Management* 90(6): 2090–2101.

Samuelson, Robert J. 2017. "Why Economists Can't Forecast." *Washington Post*. https://www.washingtonpost.com/opinions/why-economists-cant-forecast/2017/03/08/4cad0644-041f-11e7-b1e9-a05d3c21f7cf_story.html.

Sanchez, Thomas W., and James F. Wolf. 2005. "Environmental Justice and Transportation Equity: A Review of Metropolitan Planning Organizations." Cambridge, MA: Civil Rights Project at Harvard University.

Sandberg, Åke. 1976. *The Limits to Democratic Planning: Knowledge, Power and Methods in the Struggle for the Future*. Stockholm: LiberFörlag.

Sawicki, David S., and Patrice Flynn. 1996. "Neighborhood Indicators: A Review of the Literature and an Assessment of Conceptual and Methodological Issues." *Journal of the American Planning Association* 62(2): 165–183.

Schaffernicht, Martin, and Stefan N. Groesser. 2011. "A Comprehensive Method for Comparing Mental Models of Dynamic Systems." *European Journal of Operational Research* 210(1): 57–67.

Scheer, Brenda. 2012. *The Utah Model: Lessons for Regional Planning*. (December). Las Vegas, NV: Brookings Mountain West, 1–27.

Schively, Carissa. 2007. "A Quantitative Analysis of Consensus Building in Local Environmental Review." *Journal of Planning Education and Research* 27(1): 82–98.

Schoemaker, Paul J. H. 1993. "Multiple Scenario Development: Its Conceptual and Behavioral Foundation." *Strategic Management Journal* 14(3): 193–213.

Schwartz, Peter. 1991. *The Art of the Long View*. New York: Doubleday.

Schwarz, Nina, Dagmar Haase, and Ralf Seppelt. 2010. "Omnipresent Sprawl? A Review of Urban Simulation Models with Respect to Urban Shrinkage." *Environment and Planning B: Planning and Design* 37(2): 265–283.

Senbel, Maged, and Sarah P. Church. 2011. "Design Empowerment: The Limits of Accessible Visualization Media in Neighborhood Densification." *Journal of Planning Education and Research* 31(4): 423–437.

Senge, Peter M. 1990. *The Fifth Discipline: The Art and Practice of the Learning Organization*. New York: Doubleday/Currency.

Shipley, Robert. 2002. "Visioning in Planning: Is the Practice Based on Sound Theory?" *Environment and Planning A* 34(1): 7–22.

Shipley, Robert, Robert Feick, Brent Hall, and Robert Earley. 2004. "Evaluating Municipal Visioning." *Planning Practice and Research* 19(2): 195–210.

Shipley, Robert, and Ross Newkirk. 1998. "Visioning: Did Anybody See Where It Came From?" *Journal of Planning Literature* 12(4): 407–416.

———. 1999. "Vision and Visioning in Planning: What Do These Terms Really Mean?" *Environment and Planning B: Planning and Design* 26(4): 573–591.

Siddiqui, Faiz. 2019. "Tesla Sued by Family of Apple Engineer Killed in Autopilot Crash." *Washington Post*, May 1. https://www.washingtonpost.com/technology/2019/05/01/tesla-sued-by-family-man-killed-autopilot-crash/.

Silva, Elisabete A., and Keith C. Clarke. 2005. "Complexity, Emergence and Cellular Urban Models: Lessons Learned from Applying SLEUTH to Two Portuguese Metropolitan Areas." *European Planning Studies* 13(1): 93–115.

Silva, Elisabete, and Ning Wu. 2012. "Surveying Models in Urban Land Studies." *Journal of Planning Literature* 27(2): 139–152.

Skrimizea, Eirini, Helene Haniotou, and Constanza Parra. 2018. "On the 'Complexity Turn' in Planning: An Adaptive Rationale to Navigate Spaces and Times of Uncertainty." *Planning Theory* 18(1): 122–142.

Slotterback, Carissa Schively, Bryan Runck, David G. Pitt, Len Kne, Nicholas R. Jordan, David J. Mulla, Cindy Zerger, and Michael Reichenbach. 2016. "Collaborative Geodesign to Advance Multifunctional Landscapes." *Landscape and Urban Planning* 156: 71–80.

Smith, Erik. 2007. "Using a Scenario Approach; From Business to Regional Futures." In *Engaging the Future: Forecasts, Scenarios, Plans, and Projects*, ed. Lewis D. Hopkins and Marisa Zapata, 79–102. Cambridge, MA: Lincoln Institute of Land Policy.

Smith, Stanley K., Jeff Tayman, and David A. Swanson. 2001. *State and Local Population Projections: Methodology and Analysis*. Springer Series on Demographic Methods and Population Analysis. New York: Springer.

———. 2013. *A Practitioner's Guide to State and Local Population Projections*. New York: Springer.

Sorkin, Donna L., Nancy Ferris, James Hudak, and United States Department of Housing and Urban Development, Office of Policy Development and Research, Governmental Capacity Sharing Division. 1984. *Strategies for Cities and Counties: A Strategic Planning Guide*. Washington, DC: Public Technology.

Squires, Gregory D., and Charis E. Kubrin. 2005. "Privileged Places: Race, Uneven Development and the Geography of Opportunity in Urban America." *Urban Studies* 42(1): 47–68.

Stapleton, Jeremy. 2017. "Final Report: XSP Demonstration Project with the City and County of Denver." Western Lands and Communities, Lincoln Institute of Land Policy, Sonoran Institute. In author's possession. (June).

Steinitz, Carl. 2012. *A Framework for Geodesign: Changing Geography by Design*. Redlands, CA: Esri Press.

Sterman, John. 2000. *Business Dynamics: Systems Thinking and Modeling for a Complex World*. Boston, MA: Irwin/McGraw-Hill.

Stone, Clarence N. 2001. "Civic Capacity and Urban Education." *Urban Affairs Review* 36(5): 595–619.

Stone-Jovicich, Samantha S., Timothy Lynam, Anne Leitch, and Natalie A. Jones. 2011. "Using Consensus Analysis to Assess Mental Models About Water Use and Management in the Crocodile River Catchment, South Africa." *Ecology and Society* 16(1): 45.

Straatemeier, Thomas, Luca Bertolini, Marco te Brömmelstroet, and Perry Hoetjes. 2010. "An Experiential Approach to Research in Planning." *Environment and Planning B: Planning and Design* 37(4): 578–591.

Stults, Missy, and Larissa Larsen. 2018. "Tackling Uncertainty in US Local Climate Adaptation Planning." *Journal of Planning Education and Research*. https://journals.sagepub.com/doi/full/10.1177/0739456X18769134.

Sugrue, Thomas J. 2005. *The Origins of the Urban Crisis: Race and Inequality in Postwar Detroit*. Princeton, NJ: Princeton University Press.

Sun, Zhanli, Brian Deal, and Varkki George Pallathucheril. 2009. "The Land-Use Evolution and Impact Assessment Model: A Comprehensive Urban Planning Support System." *URISA Journal* 21(1): 57.

Susskind, Lawrence, and Jeffrey L. Cruikshank. 2006. *Breaking Robert's Rules: The New Way to Run Your Meeting, Build Consensus, and Get Results*. Oxford: Oxford University Press.

Susskind, Lawrence, Sarah McKearnan, and Jennifer Thomas-Larmer. 1999. *The Consensus Building Handbook: A Comprehensive Guide to Reaching Agreement*. Thousand Oaks, CA: SAGE.

Susskind, Lawrence, Danya Rumore, Carri Hulet, and Patrick Field. 2015. *Managing Climate Risks in Coastal Communities: Strategies for Engagement, Readiness and Adaptation*. Anthem Environment and Sustainability. New York: Anthem Press.

Sutton, Sharon E., and Susan P. Kemp. 2011. *The Paradox of Urban Space: Inequality and Transformation in Marginalized Communities*. New York: Palgrave Macmillan.

Swanson, Richard A. 1995. "Human Resource Development: Performance Is the Key." *Human Resource Development Quarterly* 6(2): 207–213.

Taiebat, Morteza, Austin L. Brown, Hannah R. Safford, Shen Qu, and Ming Xu. 2018. "A Review on Energy, Environmental, and Sustainability Implications of Connected and Automated Vehicles." *Environmental Science and Technology* 52(20): 11449–11465.

Taleb, N. N. 2007. *The Black Swan: The Impact of the Highly Improbable*. New York: Random House.

Talen, Emily. 1997. "Success, Failure, and Conformance: An Alternative Approach to Planning Evaluation." *Environment and Planning B: Planning and Design* 24(4): 573–587.

Tetlock, Philip E. 2005. *Expert Political Judgment: How Good Is It? How Can We Know?* Princeton, NJ: Princeton University Press.

Tetlock, Philip E., and Dan Gardner. 2016. *Superforecasting: The Art and Science of Prediction*. New York: Broadway Books.

Thomas, June Manning. 1997. *Redevelopment and Race: Planning a Finer City in Postwar Detroit*. Baltimore: Johns Hopkins University Press.

———. 1998. "Racial Inequality and Empowerment: Necessary Theoretical Constructs for Understanding U.S. Planning History." In *Making the Invisible Visible: A Multicultural Planning History*, ed. Leonie Sandercock, 198. Berkeley: University of California Press.

Thomas, June Manning, and Marsha Ritzdorf. 1997. *Urban Planning and the African American Community: In the Shadows*. Thousand Oaks, CA: SAGE.

Timpe, C., and M. J. J. Scheepers. 2003. "A Look into the Future: Scenarios for Distributed Generation in Europe." In SUSTELNET Project: Energy Research Centre of the Netherlands. https://inis.iaea.org/search/search.aspx?orig_q=RN:35101355.

Townsend, Anthony. 2014. "Re-programming Mobility: The Digital Transformation of Transportation in the United States." NYU Wagner Rudin Center for Transportation Policy and Management. https://www.bitsandatoms.net/wp-content/uploads/2019/01/re-programmingmobility-scenarioreport.pdf.

Transportation Research Board. 2007. *Metropolitan Travel Forecasting: Current Practice and Future Direction—Special Report 288.* Washington, DC: National Academies Press.

Twaddell, Hannah, Alanna McKeeman, Michael Grant, Jessica Klion, Uri Avin, Kate Ange, and Mike Callahan. 2016. *Supporting Performance-Based Planning and Programming Through Scenario Planning.* Washington, DC: Federal Highway Administration.

Ulibarri, Nicola. 2018. "Collaborative Model Development Increases Trust in and Use of Scientific Information in Environmental Decision-Making." *Environmental Science and Policy* 82: 136–142.

Umemoto, Karen. 2001. "Walking in Another's Shoes: Epistemological Challenges in Participatory Planning." *Journal of Planning Education and Research* 21(1): 17–31.

Umemoto, Karen, and Hiroki Igarashi. 2009. "Deliberative Planning in a Multicultural Milieu." *Journal of Planning Education and Research* 29(1): 39–53.

United Nations. 2015. *Transforming Our World: The 2030 Agenda for Sustainable Development.* https://sustainabledevelopment.un.org/content/documents/21252030%20Agenda%20for%20Sustainable%20Development%20web.pdf.

Urban Habitat. 2018. "Equity, Environment, and Jobs in Regional Planning." http://urbanhabitat.org/campaigns/equity-environment-and-jobs-regional-planning.

Urry, John. 2016. *What Is the Future?* Cambridge: Polity.

U.S. Department of Transportation Federal Highway Administration. 2018. "Study on Metropolitan Planning Scenario Development: Costs and Benefits." https://www.fhwa.dot.gov/planning/scenario_and_visualization/scenario_planning/publications/mpo_study/index.cfm.

Veliquette, Abigail J., Laura M. Coons, Stephanie L. Mace, Tabitha Coates, Thomas J. Chermack, and Ji Hoon Song. 2012. "The Effects of Scenario Planning on Perceptions of Conversation Quality and Engagement." *International Journal of Technology Intelligence and Planning* 8(3): 254–277.

Verma, Niraj. 2007. *Institutions and Planning.* Current Research in Urban and Regional Studies. Amsterdam: Elsevier.

Visser, Maarten P., and Thomas J. Chermack. 2009. "Perceptions of the Relationship Between Scenario Planning and Firm Performance: A Qualitative Study." *Futures* 41(9): 581–592.

Vlasic, Bill, and Neal E. Boudette. 2016. "Self-Driving Tesla Was Involved in Fatal Crash, U.S. Says." *New York Times*, June 30, A1.

Vliet, Mathijs van, Kasper Kok, and Tom Veldkamp. 2010. "Linking Stakeholders and Modellers in Scenario Studies: The Use of Fuzzy Cognitive Maps as a Communication and Learning Tool." *Futures* 42(1): 1–14.

Volkery, Axel, and Teresa Ribeiro. 2009. "Scenario Planning in Public Policy: Understanding Use, Impacts and the Role of Institutional Context Factors." *Technological Forecasting and Social Change* 76(9): 1198–1207.

Vonk, Guido, Stan Geertman, and Paul Schot. 2007. "A SWOT Analysis of Planning Support Systems." *Environment and Planning A: Economy and Space* 39(7): 1699–1714.

Vonk, Guido, and Arend Ligtenberg. 2010. "Socio-technical PSS Development to Improve Functionality and Usability—Sketch Planning Using a Maptable." *Landscape and Urban Planning* 94(3–4): 166–174.

Wachs, Martin. 2009. "The Systems of the City." In *Local Planning: Contemporary Principles and Practice*, ed. Gary Hack, Eugenie L. Birch, Paul H. Sedway, and Mitchell J. Silver, 343–349. Washington, DC: ICMA.

Wack, Pierre. 1985a. "Scenarios: Uncharted Waters Ahead." *Harvard Business Review* 63(5): 72–89.

———. 1985b. "Scenarios: Shooting the Rapids: How Medium-Term Analysis Illuminated the Power of Scenarios for Shell Management." *Harvard Business Review* 63(6): 139–150.

Waddell, Paul. 2002. "UrbanSim: Modeling Urban Development for Land Use, Transportation, and Environmental Planning." *Journal of the American Planning Association* 68(3): 297–314.

Wakabayashi, Daisuke. 2018. "Woman's Death in Arizona Casts a Pall on Driverless Car Testing." *New York Times*, March 20, A1.

Walker, Doug, and Thomas L. Daniels. 2011. *The Planners Guide to Communityviz: The Essential Tool for a New Generation of Planning*. Chicago: American Planning Association.

Walker, W. E., P. Harremoës, J. Rotmans, J. P. van der Sluijs, M. B. A. van Asselt, P. Janssen, and M. P. Krayer von Krauss. 2003. "Defining Uncertainty: A Conceptual Basis for Uncertainty Management in Model-Based Decision Support." *Integrated Assessment* 4(1): 5–17.

Walsh, Mike, and Sarah Burch. 2012. "Communities at the Crossroads: Using MetroQuest to Help Communities Create Consensus Around a Vision of the Future." In *The Future of Cities and Regions*, 45–64. New York: Springer.

Walzer, Norman. 1996. *Community Strategic Visioning Programs*. Westport, CT: Praeger.

Walzer, Norman, and Gisele Hamm. 2012. *Community Visioning Programs: Processes and Outcomes*. Community Development Research and Practice Series. Abingdon, UK: Routledge.

Weir, Margaret, Jane Rongerude, and Christopher K. Ansell. 2009. "Collaboration Is Not Enough." *Urban Affairs Review* 44(4): 455.

White, Roger, Guy Engelen, Inge Uljee, and ProQuest. 2015. *Modeling Cities and Regions as Complex Systems: From Theory to Planning Applications*. Cambridge, MA: MIT Press.

Wiechmann, Thorsten. 2008. "Errors Expected—Aligning Urban Strategy with Demographic Uncertainty in Shrinking Cities." *International Planning Studies* 13(4): 431–446.

Wong, Cecilia. 2006. *Indicators for Urban and Regional Planning: The Interplay of Policy and Methods*. RTPI Library Series. London: Routledge.

Woodruff, Sierra C. 2016. "Planning for an Unknowable Future: Uncertainty in Climate Change Adaptation Planning." *Climatic Change* 139(3): 445–459.

Wouters, Pieter, Christof van Nimwegen, Herre van Oostendorp, and Erik D. van der Spek. 2013. "A Meta-analysis of the Cognitive and Motivational Effects of Serious Games." *Journal of Educational Psychology* 105(2): 249–265.

Wu, Fulong, and Jingxiang Zhang. 2007. "Planning the Competitive City-Region: The Emergence of Strategic Development Plan in China." *Urban Affairs Review* 42(5): 714–740.

Xiang, Wei-Ning, and Keith C. Clarke. 2003. "The Use of Scenarios in Land-Use Planning." *Environment and Planning B: Planning and Design* 30(6): 885–909.

Xiao, Yu, and Maria Watson. 2017. "Guidance on Conducting a Systematic Literature Review." *Journal of Planning Education and Research* 39(1): 93–112.

Zapata, Marisa A. 2013. "Five Years Later: How California Community Members Acted on Transformative Learning Achieved in a Participatory Planning Process." *Planning Theory and Practice* 14(3): 373–387.

———. 2007. "Person-Oriented Narratives: Extensions on Scenario Planning for Multicultural and Multivocal Communities." In *Engaging the Future: Forecasts, Scenarios, Plans, and Projects*, ed. Lewis D. Hopkins and Marisa A. Zapata, 261–282. Cambridge, MA: Lincoln Institute of Land Policy.

Zapata, Marisa A., and Nikhil Kaza. 2015. "Radical Uncertainty: Scenario Planning for Futures." *Environment and Planning B: Planning and Design* 42(4): 754–770.

Zegras, Christopher, and Lisa Rayle. 2012. "Testing the Rhetoric: An Approach to Assess Scenario Planning's Role as a Catalyst for Urban Policy Integration." *Futures* 44(4): 303–318.

Zellner, Moira, and Scott D. Campbell. 2015. "Planning for Deep-Rooted Problems: What Can We Learn from Aligning Complex Systems and Wicked Problems?" *Planning Theory and Practice* 16(4): 457–478.

Zitcer, Andrew. 2018. "Making Up Creative Placemaking." *Journal of Planning Education and Research*. https://journals.sagepub.com/doi/full/10.1177/0739456X 18773424.

Zmud, Johanna P., Vincent P. Barabba, Mark Bradley, J. Richard Kuzmyak, Mia Zmud, and David Orrell. 2014. *Strategic Issues Facing Transportation. Volume 6: The Effects of Socio-demographics on Future Travel Demand.* Washington, DC: National Academies Press.

Zmud, Johanna, Melissa Tooley, Trey Baker, and Jason Wagner. 2015. *Paths of Automated and Connected Vehicle Deployment: Strategic Roadmap for State and Local Transportation Agencies.* Texas A&M Transportation Institute. (September).

Index

Page references in italics indicate a figure or a table.

About the Author

ROBERT GOODSPEED is assistant professor of urban and regional planning at the University of Michigan's Taubman College of Architecture and Urban Planning. He teaches and conducts research in collaborative planning, urban informatics, and scenario planning theory and methods. He is a member of the American Institute of Certified Planners, and he is a board member of the biannual conference "Computation in Urban Planning and Urban Management" (CUPUM) and of the Lincoln Institute of Land Policy's Consortium for Scenario Planning.